Oracle Certification Prep

Study Guide for

1Z0-067: Upgrade Oracle9i/10g/11g OCA

to Oracle Database 12c OCP

Matthew Morris

Study Guide for Upgrade Oracle9i/10g/11g OCA to Oracle Database 12c OCP (Exam 1Z0-067) Rev 1.0

ISBN-13: 978-1-941404-03-4
ISBN-10: 1941404034

Table of Contents

What to expect from the test

The test consists of 102 multiple choice or multiple answer questions and you will have 120 minutes to complete it. This works out to about 70 seconds per question which means you are likely to feel a time crunch. The passing score at this time is 60%, but as with all Oracle certification tests, it is subject to change. The questions will be either multiple choice or multiple answer. Answer every question – an unanswered question counts off the same amount as an incorrect one. Take your time reading the question and all of the answers. Sometimes later questions will answer earlier ones and I have found that marking questions I'm not sure of and re-reading them again at the end of the test is valuable.

Oracle University created this test by pulling topics from several existing exams: 1Z0-043, 1Z0-050, 1Z0-052, 1Z0-053, 1Z0-062, 1Z0-063, and 1Z0-060. As a result, it has a huge number of topics. While the topics as a whole are all over the map, the largest single focus is on backup & recovery operations. If you are not familiar with using RMAN, you are extremely unlikely to pass this exam. If you were going to pick just one book to read other than this guide (and I highly suggest you do more than that), it would have to be Oracle's RMAN User Guide.

My experiences with the last several exams from Oracle University have led me to believe that the certification team is working to make exams more challenging for exam takers. The 1Z0-067 exam is a convenient path for Oracle professionals with OCAs in 9i, 10g, or 11g to upgrade with a single exam. However, I would caution you strongly to avoid thinking of it as an easy way to upgrade your certification. This exam is likely to be a bear. You should plan to spend a lot of time preparing before scheduling the exam. Also, be aware that this exam does **not** exempt candidates from the 12c hands-on training requirement. Because this exam is likely to be difficult and the training is required, I highly recommend that you take a course that will cover some of the tested topics before scheduling the exam. This will increase your chances of passing it on your first attempt.

What to Expect from this Study Guide

This book is built around the subject matter topics that Oracle Education has indicated will be tested. I've gathered together material from several Oracle documentation sources along with examples to familiarize you with the types of questions you're likely to see on the exam. The guide covers a significant percentage of the information and operations that you must be familiar with in order to pass.

The guide is intended to present information that will be covered on the exam at the level it will likely be asked. It assumes you have passed the exams to become an OCA in 9i, 10g or 11g. You should therefore have a reasonable level of Oracle knowledge. If you have been working with Oracle since earning your OCA, much of what this guide covers should be familiar. If you earned your OCA years ago and have not been working with Oracle since then, most likely you have a lot of re-learning to do.

No book in and of itself is a substitute for hands-on experience. In preparing for this exam, you should install and configure an Oracle 12c database, create users and tables, and use RMAN to create backups and perform restore operations. Practicing the concepts discussed on this guide on your own database prior to scheduling your exam will increase the probability of success greatly.

The goal of this guide is to present to you the concepts and information most likely to be the subject of test questions, and to do so in a very compact format that will allow you to read through it more than once to reinforce the information. If much of the information presented in this guide is completely new to you, then you need to supplement this guide with other sources of study materials. If you have a reasonable grounding in Oracle administration tasks, then the guide will serve to reinforce those portions that you will likely be questioned about on the exam. If you don't have any experience with Oracle at all, the compressed format of this guide is not likely to be the best method for learning. It might provide you with sufficient information to pass the test, but you're likely to have serious deficiencies as an Oracle database administrator.

Additional Study Resources

The companion website to this series is www.oraclecertificationprep.com.
The site contains many additional resources that can be used to study for
this exam (and others). From the entry page of the website, click on the
'Exams' button, and then select the link for this test. The Exam Details
page contains links to the following information sources:

- Applicable Oracle documentation.
- Third-party books relevant to the exam.
- White papers and articles on Oracle Learning Library on topics
  covered in the exam.
- Articles on the Web that may be useful for the exam.

The website will <u>never</u> link to unauthorized content such as brain dumps
or illegal content such as copyrighted material made available without the
consent of the author. I cannot guarantee the accuracy of the content
links. While I have located the data and scanned it to ensure that it is
relevant to the given exam, I did not write it and have not proofread it
from a technical standpoint. The material on the Oracle Learning Library is
almost certain to be completely accurate and most of the other links
come from highly popular Oracle support websites and are created by
experienced Oracle professionals.

I recommend that you use more than one source of study materials
whenever you are preparing for a certification. Reading information
presented from multiple different viewpoints can help to give you a more
complete picture of any given topic. The links on the website can help you
to do this. Fully understanding the information covered in this
certification is not just valuable so that getting a passing score is more
likely – it will also help you in your career. I guarantee that in the long run,
any knowledge you gain while studying for this certification will provide
more benefit to you than any piece of paper or line on your resume.

Practice Questions

The guides in the Oracle Certification Prep series do not contain example questions. The format that they are designed around is not really compatible. The concise format used for the study guides means that adding a reasonable number of questions would nearly double the size of the guides themselves. However, because practice questions have been a common request from readers of my books, I have created a series of practice tests for the exams. The practice tests are available from the companion website listed in the previous section of this guide. They are not free, but the price is a fraction of that charged by other vendors for Oracle certification practice tests.

Unlike much of the material advertised online, these tests are not brain dumps. All of the tests are original content that I developed. Using these exams will not endanger your certification status with the Oracle certification program. I submit each test to the certification team after I finish developing it so that they can verify that they do not contain illicit material. These tests serve as an inexpensive means for any certification candidate that wants to determine how successful their preparation has been before scheduling the real exam.

As a purchaser of this study guide, you can use the following promotional code to get $2.00 off the purchase price of the practice exam for 1Z0-067: **067_DGTTB.**

The tests are available at the following URL:

http://oraclecertificationprep.com/apex/f?p=OCPSG:Practice_Tests

Backup and Recovery

Oracle Data Protection Solutions

Explain Oracle backup and recovery solutions

One of the primary duties of an Oracle database administrator is to design, implement, and manage a backup and recovery strategy. A well-designed backup strategy should protect the database against data loss and provide the ability to reconstruct the database in the event of a failure that involves damage or destruction to the data.

There are a number of third-party backup solutions available that can be used to back up an Oracle database. However, they are outside the scope of the topic. The three backup and recovery options that can be used with native Oracle capabilities include:

- **Recovery Manager (RMAN)** -- Oracle's Recovery Manager is fully integrated with the Oracle Database. It can perform a wide range of tasks and can automate much of the backup and recovery process. RMAN can be accessed through the command line or through Oracle Enterprise Manager.
- **Enterprise Manager Cloud Control** -- EM Cloud Control provides a web-based front end and scheduling facilities for RMAN. From the web interface, it is possible to enter job parameters and specify a job schedule. From this, Cloud Control will execute RMAN to conduct the backup and recovery operations.
- **User-managed backup and recovery** -- With user-managed backup and recovery, the database administrator will use a mixture of host operating system commands and SQL*Plus recovery commands to back up and recovery the files that make up an Oracle database. The DBA is responsible for determining all aspects of when and how backups and recovery are done.

User-managed recovery is supported by Oracle and is fully documented. However, RMAN is the preferred solution. It provides a common interface for backup tasks across different host operating systems. There are a number of backup techniques that are available through RMAN that cannot be performed when utilizing user-managed methods.

Describe types of database failures

There are a number of different problems that can affect the normal operation of an Oracle database or impair database I/O operations. However, the failures that require DBA intervention and data repair generally fall into one of three categories: user errors, application errors, and media failures.

- **User Errors** – These occur when data in your database is changed or deleted incorrectly through the actions of users. The root cause might be an error in application logic or a manual mistake. An example would be when a user drops a database table by mistake.
- **Application Errors** – It is possible for a software malfunction to corrupt data blocks. If this takes the form of a physical corruption (also known as a media corruption), the database does not recognize the block.
- **Media Failures** – In a media failure, a problem external to the database prevents it from reading from or writing to a database file while the instance is running. Common media failures include disk failures and the deletion of database files.

There are other failure classes. However, these do not typically result in the need for DBA intervention or media recovery:

- **Statement Failure** – If a SQL statement fails, all changes made by it will be automatically rolled back. The failure of a single SQL statement will not impact other statements in the transaction.
- **User Process Failure** – If a user session or process fails, PMON will automatically detect this and clean up after it. Any transactions that were active at the time of the failure will be rolled back and all locks held will be released.

- **Instance Failure** – If the database instance fails or is shut down with the ABORT clause, the database will perform instance recovery on the next startup.

Describe the tools available for backup and recovery tasks

The tool provided by Oracle to handle backup and recovery tasks is Recovery Manager (RMAN). RMAN is an Oracle Database client application that provides a command-line interface. It automates the administration of the backup strategy for an Oracle database and can be used to perform backup and recovery tasks. The elements of the RMAN environment include:

- **Target database** -- This is an Oracle Database to which RMAN is connected with the TARGET keyword. This is the database for which RMAN is performing backup and recovery operations.
- **RMAN client** -- The RMAN executable is installed along with an Oracle database, generally in the same directory as the other database executables. This database interprets commands from RMAN and directs server sessions to execute those commands.
- **Fast recovery area** -- Optionally, this disk location can be used to store and manage files related to backup and recovery.
- **Media management** -- Software is required if RMAN must interact with sequential media devices such as tape libraries.
- **Recovery catalog** -- When used, this is a database schema used to record RMAN activity against one or more target databases. It will preserve RMAN repository metadata if the control file of the target database is lost

If RMAN is not used for backup and recovery, it is possible to make use of third-party tools to perform this task. There are a number of such applications on the market. Generally when using third-party tools to make backups, it is necessary to use SQL or SQL*Plus commands to perform database recovery.

Describe RMAN and maximum availability architecture

Maximum Availability Architecture (MAA) is essentially the process of reducing or avoiding unplanned downtime, enabling rapid recovery from failures, and minimizing planned downtimes. RMAN plays a huge role in the second portion of that goal. When there is a database failure due to a media failure, minutes count in getting the database back online. There are several new features in RMAN with 12c designed to reduce the impact that backup and recovery operations have on availability:

- **Fine grained recovery** -- It is now possible to use a RECOVER TABLE command to perform a point-in-time recovery of a table or partition. Previously, recovering a table often required a manual point-in-time recovery process. The RECOVER TABLE command automatically performs several steps to generate an export of the table to be recovered and import it back into the production database.

- **Multitenant** -- When using the Oracle Multitenant capability, it is possible to use RMAN to perform backup and recovery at the CDB level, which includes and protects all the associated PDBs. Alternately, it is possible to perform backup and recovery for an individual PDB or a selected group of PDBs.

- **Improved RMAN duplication performance** -- Prior to 12c, the ACTIVE DUPLICATE command used production database processes to send image copies across the network. When performing ACTIVE DUPLICATE in 12c, backup sets are used instead of image copies. Because backup sets are smaller than the equivalent image copies, the information being transferred across the network is reduced. Compression and multi-section options can also be used for even faster duplication.

- **Faster Data Guard recovery** -- If there is either primary or standby datafile corruption, the recovery process prior to 12c would have been to copy the backup over the network and perform a restore/recovery. With 12c, the new RMAN keyword "FROM

SERVICE" restores directly from the standby or primary depending on which site has been corrupted. The "FROM SERVICE" command creates a backup set and streams it over the network, dramatically reducing the overall recovery time.

Use the SYSBACKUP privilege

The SYSBACKUP administrative privilege has been added in Oracle 12c. This privilege is intended to allow system administrators to enable a user to perform backup and recovery of the Oracle database without providing the complete set of privileges provided by SYSDBA. SYSBACKUP provides all of the permissions required for backup and recovery including the ability to connect to a closed database. Unlike SYSDBA, someone with the SYSBACKUP privilege does not receive DBA-level data access privileges such as SELECT ANY TABLE.

In order for users to connect to a target or auxiliary database via RMAN, they must have either the SYSDBA or SYSBACKUP system privilege. Users who have been assigned to the OSBACKUPDBA operating system group can connect with the SYSBACKUP privilege via OS authentication. The following example demonstrates explicit OS Authentication using the SYSBACKUP Privilege:

```
% rman target '"/ as sysbackup"'
```

For databases that use a password file, the database creates an entry in the password file when you grant the SYSBACKUP privilege to a user. It is then possible for that user to connect to the target or auxiliary database even if the database is not open. The password file must be in the 12c format in order to support the SYSBACKUP privilege. The following example demonstrates explicit password file authentication as SYSBACKUP. The backup_admin user has been granted the SYSBACKUP privilege in the target database:

```
% rman target '"backup_admin@ocp1 as sysbackup"'
target database Password: [password]
connected to target database: OCP1 (DBID=25947551)
```

Use RMAN stand-alone and job commands

Job Commands

Job commands can only be used within the brackets of a RUN command. Some examples of job commands are:

- **ALLOCATE CHANNEL** -- Manually allocates a connection between RMAN and a database instance.
- **SWITCH** -- This is equivalent to the SQL statement ALTER DATABASE RENAME FILE. The names of the files in the RMAN repository are updated, but the database does not rename the files at the operating system level.

The RUN command is used to group a series RMAN commands into a block to be executed sequentially. RMAN will compile the list of job commands into one or more job steps and then execute the steps.

```
RUN
{
ALLOCATE CHANNEL c1 DEVICE TYPE DISK FORMAT "/u02/%U";
BACKUP DATABASE PLUS ARCHIVELOG;
}
```

Standalone Commands

Standalone commands cannot appear as subcommands within a RUN block. These commands are used directly from the RMAN prompt. Some examples include:

- **CONNECT** -- Establishes a connection between RMAN and a target, auxiliary, or recovery catalog database.
- **CONFIGURE** -- Used to create or change a persistent configuration affecting RMAN backup, restore, duplication, and maintenance jobs on a particular database.
- **CREATE CATALOG** -- Creates a recovery catalog.
- **CREATE SCRIPT** -- Creates a stored script in the recovery catalog.
- **LIST** -- Displays backups and information about other objects recorded in the RMAN repository.
- **REPORT** -- Performs detailed analyses of the RMAN repository and writes the report to standard output or the message log file.

Exceptions

A number of commands can be issued either at the prompt or within a RUN block. The following examples can function as both standalone and job commands:

- **BACKUP** -- Used to back up a primary or standby database, tablespace, data file (current or copy), control file (current or copy), server parameter file, archived redo log file, or backup set.
- **RESTORE** -- Used to restore, validate, or preview RMAN backups.
- **RECOVER** -- Used to perform complete recovery of the whole database, point-in-time recovery of a database (DBPITR) or tablespace (TSPITR), apply incremental backups to a data file image copy, or recover a corrupt data block or set of data blocks within a data file.
- **VALIDATE** -- Used to check for corrupt blocks and missing files, or to determine whether a backup set can be restored.

Performing Basic Backup and Recovery

Back up and recover a NOARCHIVELOG database

Perform backup and recovery in NOARCHIVELOG mode

When a database is run in NOARCHIVELOG mode, archiving of the redo logs is disabled. The database control file indicates that filled groups are not required to be archived. When a filled group becomes inactive after a log switch, the group is immediately available for reuse by the LGWR process. A database running in NOARCHIVELOG mode is protected from instance failure but not from media failure. Only the changes made to the database stored in the online redo log groups are available for instance recovery. If a media failure occurs to a database that is in NOARCHIVELOG mode, it is only possible to restore the database to the point of the most recent full database backup.

A full database backup can be either consistent or inconsistent. When a backup is consistent, all read/write data files and control files have the same checkpoint SCN. This ensures that these files contain all changes up to this SCN. A consistent backup does not require recovery after it is restored and one can only be created after a consistent shutdown of the database. A database operating in NOARCHIVELOG mode can only create a valid backup of a consistent database.

If the database has been shut down with the NORMAL, IMMEDIATE, or TRANSACTIONAL options, then it is in a consistent state and you can create a usable backup by copying all of the data files with operating system commands. If the database is open, has just had an instance failure or been shut down with the ABORT option, the database is in an inconsistent state. Copying the files at this time will create a backup that is inconsistent with the database SCN. The backup will be unusable. When a database is in ARCHIVELOG mode, it is possible to take inconsistent backups because the archived redo logs can be used to apply recovery to the datafiles to bring them to a consistent state.

28

Creating a user-managed consistent whole database backup:

1. Shut down the database with the NORMAL, IMMEDIATE, or TRANSACTIONAL options.

   ```
   SQL> SHUTDOWN IMMEDIATE
   SQL> STARTUP FORCE DBA
   SQL> SHUTDOWN IMMEDIATE
   ```

2. Use an operating system utility to make backups of all data files, all control files, and the initialization parameter file.
3. Restart the database with the STARTUP command.

   ```
   SQL> STARTUP
   ```

Restoring the database:

When performing a user-managed restore, the DBA is responsible for locating all of the required backup files and placing them in the correct locations. The basic steps to perform a user-managed complete database recovery are:

1. Shut down the database with the NORMAL, IMMEDIATE, or TRANSACTIONAL options.

   ```
   SQL> SHUTDOWN IMMEDIATE
   SQL> STARTUP FORCE DBA
   SQL> SHUTDOWN IMMEDIATE
   ```

2. Use an operating system utility to restore backups of all data files, control files, and the initialization parameter file.
3. Restart the database with the STARTUP command.

   ```
   SQL> STARTUP
   ```

Use SQL in RMAN

It has been possible to execute SQL statement from the RMAN prompt in previous releases by making use of the RMAN 'SQL' command and enclosing the SQL text in double-quotes. For example, the following command archives all unarchived online redo logs:

```
RMAN> SQL "ALTER SYSTEM ARCHIVE LOG CURRENT";
```

In 12c, the SQL command still exists in RMAN, so the above command would work. However, it is now possible to issue most SQL commands from the RMAN prompt without using the SQL keyword. The SQL text also does not need to be enclosed in quotes. The previous example can be executed as follows in 12c:

```
RMAN> ALTER SYSTEM ARCHIVE LOG CURRENT;
```

There are a few commands that exist in both RMAN and SQL but which have very different uses. In these cases, it may be advisable to specify the SQL keyword to eliminate ambiguity. Finally, a DESCRIBE command has been added to RMAN which provides the same functionality as the SQL*Plus DESCRIBE command.

Configuring for Recoverability

Configure and manage RMAN settings

Configure database parameters that affect RMAN operations

The database initialization parameters which have RMAN implications include the following:

- **CONTROL_FILE_RECORD_KEEP_TIME** -- This specifies the minimum number of days before a reusable record in the control file can be reused. The control file contains information used by RMAN for backups and recovery operations. When all available record slots are full, Oracle either expands the control file to make room for a new record or overwrites the oldest record. The CONTROL_FILE_RECORD_KEEP_TIME value should be set to slightly longer than the oldest file that must be kept. For example, if you the whole database is backed up once a week, then the record keep time must be at least 7 days.
- **DB_RECOVERY_FILE_DEST** -- Specifies the default location for the fast recovery area. The fast recovery area contains multiplexed copies of current control files and online redo logs, as well as archived redo logs, flashback logs, and RMAN backups.
- **DB_RECOVERY_FILE_DEST_SIZE** -- Specifies (in bytes) the hard limit on the total space to be used by target database recovery files created in the fast recovery area.
- **LOG_ARCHIVE_DEST_n** -- Defines up to 31 (where n = 1, 2, 3, ...31) destinations, each of which must specify either the LOCATION or the SERVICE attribute to specify where to archive the redo data.
- **DB_CREATE_ONLINE_LOG_DEST_n** -- Specifies the default location for Oracle-managed control files and online redo logs.
- **DB_CREATE_FILE_DEST** -- Specifies the default location for Oracle-managed datafiles. This location is also used as the default location for Oracle-managed control files and online redo logs if none of the DB_CREATE_ONLINE_LOG_DEST_n initialization parameters are specified.

- **DB_UNIQUE_NAME** -- Specifies a globally unique name for the database. For RMAN to work correctly in a Data Guard environment, the DB_UNIQUE_NAME must be unique across all the databases with the same DBID.
- **NLS_DATE_FORMAT** -- Specifies the default date format for the database. It also determines the format used for the time parameters in RMAN commands such as RESTORE, RECOVER, and REPORT.
- **COMPATIBLE** -- Enables you to use a new release of Oracle, while at the same time guaranteeing backward compatibility with an earlier release. In order to make use of unused block compression, the COMPATIBLE initialization parameter must be set to 10.2 or higher.

Configure persistent settings for RMAN

RMAN has a number of different settings to control the specific actions taken during backups. The default settings for most of these parameters make sense for performing standard backup and recovery operations. Understanding what these parameters are will allow you to optimize the behavior for a given database. Persistent settings can be set for each target database, such as backup destinations, device type, and retention policy. The CONFIGURE command allows you to change RMAN current behavior for your backup and recovery environment. If used with the keyword CLEAR, this command will reset the parameter to the default RMAN value. Some examples of the options that can be set follow:

Set the backup retention policy

The following command sets the backup retention policy to maintain three full or level 0 backups of each data file and control file. Any backups older than the third file are considered obsolete. The default value is 1.

```
CONFIGURE RETENTION POLICY TO REDUNDANCY 3;
```

Alternately, the retention policy can be given a recovery window that ensures sufficient backups are kept to recover the database to any point in time back to the supplied value:

```
CONFIGURE RETENTION POLICY TO RECOVERY WINDOW OF 7 DAYS;
```

Set the default device type

When a destination device type is not specific for a backup, RMAN sends it to whatever device type is configured as the default. RMAN is preset to use disk as the default device type. The following command allows you to change the default device type to tape:

```
CONFIGURE DEFAULT DEVICE TYPE TO sbt;
```

Regardless of the default device type, you can specifically direct a backup to a specific device type using the DEVICE TYPE clause of the BACKUP command, as shown in the following examples:

```
BACKUP DEVICE TYPE SBT DATABASE;
BACKUP DEVICE TYPE DISK DATABASE;
```

Configuring Channels

An RMAN channel is a connection to a database server session. The CONFIGURE CHANNEL command is used to configure options for disk or SBT channels. When the CONFIGURE CHANNEL command is used to specify default channel settings for a device, any previous settings are lost. Any settings not specified in the CONFIGURE CHANNEL command will be returned to their default value.

```
CONFIGURE CHANNEL DEVICE TYPE DISK MAXPIECESIZE 1G;
CONFIGURE CHANNEL DEVICE TYPE DISK FORMAT /tmp/%U;
```

Configuring Channels for Disk

RMAN allocates a single disk channel for all operations by default. You can change the default location and format for the file name for that channel. Be aware that when an explicit format is configured for disk channels, RMAN does not create backups by default in the fast recovery area.

```
CONFIGURE CHANNEL DEVICE TYPE DISK FORMAT '/u01/ora_df%t_s%s_s%p';
CONFIGURE CHANNEL DEVICE TYPE DISK FORMAT '+dgroup1';
```

Set the parallelism for a device

When multiple channels are available, RMAN can read or write in parallel. The number of channels should normally match the number of devices available (i.e. three tape drives = three channels). Allocating multiple channels for a single device can negatively affect performance unless your disk subsystem is optimized for multiple channels. The channel parallelism can be set for each device type as follows.

```
CONFIGURE DEVICE TYPE SBT PARALLELISM 2;
```

The command above only affects the parallelism for tape devices and does not alter the values of other device settings not specified.

Configure Control File and Server Parameter File Autobackups

RMAN can be set to automatically back up the control file and server parameter file whenever a backup record is added. In addition, if the database structure metadata in the control file changes and the database is in ARCHIVELOG mode, an autobackup will be taken. Control file autobackup adds additional redundancy to the recovery strategy, allowing RMAN to recover the database even after the loss of the current control file, recovery catalog, and server parameter file. The autobackup feature is enabled and disabled as follows:

```
CONFIGURE CONTROLFILE AUTOBACKUP ON;
CONFIGURE CONTROLFILE AUTOBACKUP OFF;
```

Resetting default values

The RMAN configuration settings can be returned to their default values by using the CLEAR keyword:

```
CONFIGURE DEFAULT DEVICE TYPE CLEAR;
CONFIGURE RETENTION POLICY CLEAR;
CONFIGURE CONTROLFILE AUTOBACKUP CLEAR;
```

View persistent settings

The CONFIGURE command is used to create or change persistent configuration settings that affect RMAN backup, restore, duplication, and maintenance jobs on a particular database. Once created, these settings will be in effect for any RMAN session on this database until explicitly cleared or changed. The SHOW command can be used to display the configurations for one or more databases. The SHOW command can be executed only at the RMAN prompt. In order to perform the SHOW command, one of the following conditions must be met:

- RMAN is connected to a target database, which must be mounted or open.
- RMAN is connected to a recovery catalog and SET DBID must have been run.

Executing SHOW ALL from the RMAN prompt will display all of the RMAN persistent settings. When the settings are at the default value, the results will indicate that by listing '# default' to the right of the configuration setting. For example:

```
RMAN> SHOW ALL;
RMAN configuration parameters for database with db_unique_name OCP1
are:
CONFIGURE RETENTION POLICY TO REDUNDANCY 2;
CONFIGURE BACKUP OPTIMIZATION OFF; # default
CONFIGURE DEFAULT DEVICE TYPE TO DISK; # default
CONFIGURE CONTROLFILE AUTOBACKUP ON;
CONFIGURE CONTROLFILE AUTOBACKUP FORMAT FOR DEVICE TYPE DISK TO
'/u01/oracle/dbs/%F';
CONFIGURE CONTROLFILE AUTOBACKUP FORMAT FOR DEVICE TYPE SBT_TAPE TO
'%F'; # default
CONFIGURE DEVICE TYPE DISK PARALLELISM 1 BACKUP TYPE TO BACKUPSET; #
default
CONFIGURE DEVICE TYPE SBT_TAPE PARALLELISM 1 BACKUP TYPE TO
BACKUPSET; # default
CONFIGURE DATAFILE BACKUP COPIES FOR DEVICE TYPE DISK TO 1; # default
CONFIGURE DATAFILE BACKUP COPIES FOR DEVICE TYPE SBT_TAPE TO 1; #
default
CONFIGURE ARCHIVELOG BACKUP COPIES FOR DEVICE TYPE DISK TO 1; #
default
CONFIGURE ARCHIVELOG BACKUP COPIES FOR DEVICE TYPE SBT_TAPE TO 1; #
default
CONFIGURE CHANNEL DEVICE TYPE 'SBT_TAPE'
PARMS "SBT_LIBRARY=/usr/local/oracle/backup/lib/libobk.so";
CONFIGURE MAXSETSIZE TO UNLIMITED; # default
CONFIGURE ENCRYPTION FOR DATABASE ON;
CONFIGURE ENCRYPTION ALGORITHM 'AES128'; # default
CONFIGURE ARCHIVELOG DELETION POLICY TO NONE; # default
CONFIGURE SNAPSHOT CONTROLFILE NAME TO '/u01/oracle/dbs/cf_snap .f'
```

It is also possible to display the settings individually using the SHOW command. The following example displays only the default device type and channel settings respectively:

```
RMAN> SHOW DEFAULT DEVICE TYPE;
RMAN configuration parameters for database with db_unique_name OCP1
are:
CONFIGURE DEFAULT DEVICE TYPE TO DISK;

RMAN> SHOW CHANNEL;
RMAN configuration parameters for database with db_unique_name OCP1
are:
CONFIGURE CHANNEL DEVICE TYPE 'SBT_TAPE'
PARMS "SBT_LIBRARY=/usr/local/oracle/backup/lib/libobk.so";
```

Information about the RMAN persistent configuration settings can also be found in the view V$RMAN_CONFIGURATION.

- **CONF#** -- A unique key identifying this configuration record within the target database that owns it.
- **NAME** -- The type of configuration.
- **VALUE** -- The CONFIGURE command setting. Example: RETENTION POLICY TO RECOVERY WINDOW OF 10 DAYS
- **CON_ID** -- The ID of the container to which the data pertains.

When a recovery catalog exists, the view RC_RMAN_CONFIGURATION contains information about RMAN persistent configuration settings. It is equivalent to the V$RMAN_CONFIGURATION view.

Specify a retention policy

RMAN retention policies are intended to insure that you have sufficient redundancy in the number of database backups to prevent a catastrophic data loss while keeping you from storing so many that you run out of disk space. The RMAN command CONFIGURE RETENTION POLICY is used to define an automatic backup retention policy. The backup retention policy provides RMAN with the information required to decide if a given backup of datafiles or control files is obsolete. Obsolete backups are no longer needed for recovery. These files can be viewed using the REPORT OBSOLETE command or removed using the DELETE OBSOLETE command.

Even when a retention policy is in place, RMAN will never automatically delete backup files simply because they have become obsolete. The files will remain until removed via the DELETE OBSOLETE command. However, if a database has been configured with a fast recovery area, it is possible that obsolete files can be deleted to satisfy the fast recovery area disk quota rules. If additional space is needed for new files then the database will delete files in the fast recovery area that are either obsolete or have already been backed up to tape. However, the database will <u>not</u> violate the retention policy in order to free up space in the fast recovery area.

Obsolete recovery files should not be confused with expired files. The two have different definitions:

- **Obsolete** -- Backup files are obsolete when according to the current retention policy, they are no longer required for recovery.
- **Expired** -- Backup files are set to expired when an RMAN CROSSCHECK operation is performed and the file cannot be located.

Only control file backups and full or level 0 datafile backups are directly subject to retention policies. If datafiles are part of a backup set, RMAN cannot delete the set until <u>all</u> of the datafile backups within it are obsolete. For individual datafile copies or proxy copies, RMAN can delete them as soon as it is no longer needed according to the policy.

Incremental level 1 backups and archived redo logs become obsolete when no full backups exist that require them. RMAN initially determines which datafile and control file backups are obsolete. All incremental level 1 backups and archived logs that are not required to recover the remaining (non-obsolete) datafile or control file backup are tagged as obsolete. When using a retention policy, backup files should not be removed via non-RMAN utilities. If disk or tape files are removed via OS or media manager commands then this invalidates the ability of RMAN to intelligently control the retention of files.

There are two different types of retention policy. It is only possible to use <u>one</u> of them -- they are mutually exclusive.

- **Recovery Window** -- This is a rolling window of time starting with the present and extending backward in time for a set length. A recovery window defines a point of recoverability, which will be the earliest time from which it is possible to recover following a media failure. If the defined recovery window is two weeks, then RMAN retains full backups and required incremental backups and archived logs that will allow the database to be recovered up to 14 days in the past. A recovery window policy is implemented as follows:

```
CONFIGURE RETENTION POLICY TO RECOVERY WINDOW OF 14 DAYS;
```

- **Backup Redundancy** -- The redundancy retention policy specifies the number backups of each datafile to be retained. When there are more available than the number required, the oldest backups beyond the defined number are obsolete. The default retention policy is configured to REDUNDANCY 1. A backup redundancy of 3 is implemented as follows:

```
CONFIGURE RETENTION POLICY TO REDUNDANCY 3;
```

Configure the Fast Recovery Area

Explain the Fast Recovery Area

The Fast Recovery Area is a location in which the database can store and manage files related to backup and recovery. The location is separate from the database area, where the current database files are located. The fast recovery area can contain control files, online redo logs, archived redo logs, flashback logs, and RMAN backups. A fast recovery area minimizes the need to manually manage disk space for backup related files and balance the use of space among the different types of files. Files in the recovery area are labeled as permanent or transient.

- **Permanent files** -- These are active files used by the database instance. Permanent files that can be in the recovery area include multiplexed copies of the current control file and online redo log files.
- **Transient files** -- These files are not accessed by the database instance and are needed only during recovery operations. Transient files include: archived redo log files, foreign archived redo log files, image copies of datafiles and control files, backup pieces, and flashback logs.

Transient files are generally deleted after they become obsolete or have been backed up to tape. Files placed in the fast recovery area are maintained by Oracle Database and the generated file names use the Oracle Managed Files (OMF) format. When files are no longer needed for recovery, they become eligible for deletion when space for new files is required.

Oracle recommends that archive logs be written to the fast recovery area so that they are automatically managed by the database. Because the fast recovery area is managed by OMF, the generated file names for the archived logs are not determined by the parameter LOG_ARCHIVE_FORMAT. Whether the fast recovery area is used or not, it is always best practice to create multiple copies of archived redo logs.

The following basic options for archiving redo logs are possible, listed in descending order of what Oracle considers to be best practice:

- Enable archiving to the fast recovery area only and use disk mirroring for redundancy. If DB_RECOVERY_FILE_DEST is specified and no LOG_ARCHIVE_DEST_n is specified, then LOG_ARCHIVE_DEST_1 is implicitly set to the recovery area.
- Enable archiving to the fast recovery area and set one or more LOG_ARCHIVE_DEST_n initialization parameters to locations outside the fast recovery area. The fast recovery area can be set as an archiving destination by setting any LOG_ARCHIVE_DEST_n parameter to LOCATION=USE_DB_RECOVERY_FILE_DEST.
- Set LOG_ARCHIVE_DEST_n initialization parameters to archive only to non-fast recovery area locations.

There are several RMAN commands or implicit actions that can create files in the fast recovery area:

- **BACKUP** -- If the FORMAT clause is not specified for disk backups, then RMAN creates backup pieces and image copies in the fast recovery area, with names in Oracle Managed Files (OMF) format.
- **Control File Autobackup** -- RMAN will create control file autobackups in the fast recovery area when no other destination is configured.

- **RESTORE ARCHIVELOG** -- RMAN will restore archived redo log files to the fast recovery area unless the SET ARCHIVELOG DESTINATION is specifically set elsewhere.
- **RECOVER...** -- The RECOVER DATABASE, RECOVER TABLESPACE, and RECOVER ... BLOCK options restore archived redo log files from backup to the recovery area for use during media recovery. RMAN will automatically delete the files after they are applied.
- **FLASHBACK DATABASE** -- As with the RECOVER... options, RMAN will pull any required archived log files to the recovery area and delete them after they have been applied.

Configure the Fast Recovery Area

The following initialization parameters are used to enable the Fast Recovery Area. Only the first two are required, and the database does not require a restart after they have been set.

- **DB_RECOVERY_FILE_DEST_SIZE** -- Specifies the maximum total bytes to be used by the Fast Recovery Area. The basic (minimum) recovery area size should be the sum of all the database files, plus sufficient size for incremental backups and all archive logs that have not been copied to tape. The required size varies widely depending on the backup strategy and whether flashback retention is enabled. This initialization parameter must be specified before DB_RECOVERY_FILE_DEST is enabled.
- **DB_RECOVERY_FILE_DEST** -- Location of the Fast Recovery Area. This can be a directory, file system, or Automatic Storage Management (Oracle ASM) disk group. It cannot be a raw file system.
- **DB_FLASHBACK_RETENTION_TARGET** -- Specifies the upper limit (in minutes) on how far back in time the database may be flashed back. This parameter is required only for Flashback Database.

These parameters cannot be enabled if you have set values for the parameters LOG_ARCHIVE_DEST and LOG_ARCHIVE_DUPLEX_DEST. You must disable those parameters before setting up the Fast Recovery Area. In order to use the Fast Recovery Area, you must instead set values for the LOG_ARCHIVE_DEST_n parameters. Oracle recommends that DB_RECOVERY_FILE_DEST be set to a different value from DB_CREATE_FILE_DEST or any of the DB_CREATE_ONLINE_LOG_DEST_n initialization parameters. A warning will be written to the alert log if DB_RECOVERY_FILE_DEST equals these parameters.

Managing Space in the Fast Recovery Area

The database issues a warning alert when reclaimable space is less than 15% and a critical alert when reclaimable space is less than 3%. An entry is added to the alert log and to the **DBA_OUTSTANDING_ALERTS** table to warn the DBA of this condition. If not resolved, the database will consume space in the fast recovery area until there is no space left.

You can resolve low space issues in the Fast Recovery Area in several ways:

- Make more disk space available and increase DB_RECOVERY_FILE_DEST_SIZE.
- Move backups from the fast recovery area to tertiary storage such as tape. The BACKUP RECOVERY AREA command will back up all of your recovery area files to tape.
- Run DELETE for any files that have been removed with an operating system utility. The database is not aware of file removed by OS commands.
- Run the RMAN CROSSCHECK command to have RMAN recheck the contents of the fast recovery area and identify expired files, and then use the DELETE EXPIRED command to delete every expired backup from the RMAN repository.
- Delete any unnecessary guaranteed restore points.
- Review your backup retention policy and make it less restrictive.

Information about the Fast Recovery Area is stored in the V$RECOVERY_FILE_DEST dynamic view. In addition, the column IS_RECOVERY_DET_FILE has been added to the following views: V$CONTROLFILE, V$LOGFILE, V$ARCHIVED_LOG, V$DATAFILE_COPY, V$DATAFILE, V$BACKUP_PIECE and the RMAN tables. This column has a value of YES if a file of the corresponding kind has been created in the fast recovery area.

Configure control files and redo log files for recoverability

Multiplex control files

Every Oracle database should have a minimum of two control files whether it is in production or just a development database. Control files are critical to the functioning of the database; the file size is small in comparison to data files; and maintaining multiple copies has a negligible performance impact on the database. Each copy should be stored on a different physical disk. If a control file is damaged or lost due to a disk failure, the associated instance must be shut down. If the control file has been multiplexed, the problem file can be restored using an undamaged copy from another disk and the instance restarted.

When a database has multiplexed control files, the following actions occur:

- Oracle writes to all files listed in the CONTROL_FILES parameter of the database initialization parameter file.
- Oracle reads only the first file listed in the CONTROL_FILES parameter during database operation.
- If any of the control files become unavailable, the instance becomes inoperable and should be aborted.

It is possible to create an additional control file for multiplexing by copying an existing control file to a new location while the database is shut down. The complete process of adding a new multiplexed copy of the current control file is:

1. Shut down the database.
2. Copy an existing control file to a new location, using operating system commands.
3. Edit the CONTROL_FILES parameter in the database initialization parameter file to add the new control file name.
4. Restart the database.

Multiplex redo log files

It is arguably even more important to multiplex redo log groups than the database control file. While both are required for an instance to operate, redo logs are critical to database consistency and the loss of a redo log group is more likely to result in a need for media recovery. As with the control file, multiplexing redo log groups involves creating two or more copies of the redo log files in different locations. The location should ideally be on separate physical disks to eliminate the possibility of a single drive failure destroying all of the copies. When redo log files are multiplexed, LGWR concurrently writes redo log information to each of the multiplexed redo log files.

An Oracle database always has at least two redo log groups. One group is always 'current' and is what the database is currently writing redo log entries to. All other groups are inactive. LGWR never writes concurrently to members of different groups. Each group can be multiplexed with two or more identical copies. These copies provide redundancy that can prevent an unplanned instance shutdown. If LGWR cannot write to the current logfile group, then the instance will shut down immediately. However, if the group is multiplexed and LGWR can write to at least one of the files, then LGWR will ignore the unavailable members and the instance will continue uninterrupted.

As a general rule, multiplexed redo logs should be symmetrical. Each redo log group should have the same number of members, but this is not required. One group could have three multiplexed copies while a second group had only two, and a third only a single file. The only firm requirement is that the database has at least two log groups. Nevertheless, the best practice is to multiplex all groups to the same level.

It is possible to create new redo log members for an existing group with the SQL statement ALTER DATABASE with the ADD LOGFILE MEMBER clause. The following example adds a new member to redo log group number 2:

```
ALTER DATABASE ADD LOGFILE MEMBER '/oracle/dbs/log2b.rdo' TO GROUP 2;
```

The size of the new redo log file is determined from the size of the existing members of the group. An alternate syntax to perform the same task is to identify the target group by specifying all of the other group members of the group in the TO clause:

```
ALTER DATABASE ADD LOGFILE MEMBER '/oracle/dbs/log2c.rdo'
TO ('/oracle/dbs/log2a.rdo', '/oracle/dbs/log2b.rdo');
```

Using the RMAN Recovery Catalog

Create and use an RMAN recovery catalog

Configure a recovery catalog

The RMAN recovery catalog is a database schema in an Oracle database that is used to store metadata about one or more Oracle databases. The data from this schema is used by RMAN when performing recovery operations. While the catalog can be stored in a database used for other purposes, it is generally stored in a dedicated database. The catalog stores information about RMAN operations for all of the target databases that have been registered in it. Any time that RMAN is connected to a recovery catalog, all metadata will be pulled exclusively from the catalog instead of the control file. By centralizing the metadata for multiple target databases, the recovery catalog makes reporting and administration easier. A recovery catalog includes the following information:

- Datafile and archived redo log backup sets and backup pieces
- Datafile copies
- Archived redo logs and their copies
- Database structure (tablespaces and datafiles)
- Stored scripts, which are named user-created sequences of RMAN commands
- Persistent RMAN configuration settings

Recovery catalogs are required in the following cases:

- **Loss of control files** -- If the current control file and all backups are lost for a given database, a recovery catalog is required. Recovery catalogs contain the same metadata as the RMAN repository stored in the control file of each target database.

- **Recovery from very old backup** -- The control file contains a more limited amount of history than a recovery catalog. If you need to perform a recovery from a backup that goes back further in time than is stored in the control file, then a recovery catalog is required.
- **RMAN Scripts** -- RMAN scripts can be stored in a recovery catalog. The scripts are then available to every RMAN client that can connect to the target database and recovery catalog. By contrast, command files are only available if the RMAN client has access to the file system on which they are stored.
- **Data Guard** -- If you want to use RMAN in a Data Guard environment, a recovery catalog is required. The recovery catalog stores RMAN metadata for all primary and standby databases.

Before creating a recovery catalog, you must determine what database to put it in and what schema to use. You should not put the catalog in a database that will itself be a target of the catalog. Using a dedicated catalog database is the normal and suggested option. In addition, the catalog database should not be on the same hard drive as any of its target databases or a single hard drive failure can take out both the target database and the catalog required to recover the target. The greater the independence between the catalog and target databases, the more robust the recovery scenario becomes. Once a database is selected, the catalog will be stored in a schema on that database (which cannot be SYS).

The space required by the catalog schema depends primarily on the number of databases that will be targets of the catalog. The size will also increase as the number of backups and archived log files for each individual database grows. RMAN scripts stored in the catalog will use space as well. The Oracle Database Backup and Recovery User's Guide contains more information and formulas on estimating size requirements.

Once a catalog database and schema have been determined and sufficient space exists in the catalog tablespace, you can create the schema owner and grant the schema all of the privileges required. In the example below, a dedicated database (catdb) with a tablespace called RMANCAT_TS exists. The SYS user has connected to catdb with SYSDBA privileges.

To create the recovery catalog schema and set up the default and temporary tablespaces:

```
SQL>  CREATE USER recodude IDENTIFIED BY [password]
      TEMPORARY TABLESPACE temp
      DEFAULT TABLESPACE rmancat_ts
      QUOTA UNLIMITED ON rmancat_ts;
```

Grant the RECOVERY_CATALOG_OWNER role to the rman schema.

```
SQL> GRANT RECOVERY_CATALOG_OWNER TO recodude;
```

Once the catalog schema exists, the RMAN CREATE CATALOG command is used to create the catalog tables in the default tablespace of the catalog owner. To create the recovery catalog you must start RMAN and connect to the catalog database as the recovery catalog owner. Once connected, run the CREATE CATALOG command to create the catalog. This can take several minutes.

```
RMAN> CREATE CATALOG;
```

You can specify the tablespace name for the catalog in the CREATE CATALOG command to store it in a tablespace other than the default for the schema:

```
RMAN> CREATE CATALOG TABLESPACE users;
```

Register target databases in a recovery catalog

Once a catalog exists, you must register the target databases in the catalog. Until a database has been registered, RMAN cannot store any metadata about backup operations in the catalog. Unregistered databases will continue to use the control file as their sole source of RMAN metadata during backup and recovery operations. To register a new target database, you must:

Start RMAN and connect to both the target database and to the recovery catalog. The database containing the recovery catalog must be open and the target database must be mounted.

```
% rman TARGET / CATALOG recodude@catdb
```

Register the target database in the connected recovery catalog via the REGISTER DATABASE command:

```
REGISTER DATABASE;
```

RMAN will add information about the target database to the appropriate catalog tables. It then copies information from the control file of the target database into the catalog to synchronize the catalog with the control file. Once the command has completed, you can verify that the registration was successful by running the REPORT SCHEMA command:

```
REPORT SCHEMA;

Report of database schema
File Size(MB)    Tablespace       RB segs  Datafile Name
---- ---------- ---------------- -------  ------------------
1       327680 SYSTEM            NO       /u01/oradata/system01.dbf
2        30720 UNDOTBS           YES      /u01/oradata/undotbs01.dbf
3        20480 INDEX_TS          NO       /u01/oradata/index_ts01.dbf
4        10240 TOOLS_TS          NO       /u01/oradata/tools_ts01.dbf
5        20480 USER_TS           NO       /u01/oradata/user_ts01.dbf
```

Catalog additional backup files

When you first create the recovery catalog, it is possible that you have datafile copies, backup pieces, or archived logs on disk that have aged out of the control file. It is possible to add them to the recovery catalog with the CATALOG command. Doing this allows RMAN to make use of the older backups during restore operations. The following commands can be used to add files to the catalog:

- **CATALOG DATAFILECOPY** -- Allows you to add a data file backup to the catalog.
- **CATALOG ARCHIVELOG** -- Allows you to add one or more archived log files to the catalog.
- **CATALOG BACKUPPIECE** -- Allows you to add a backup piece to the catalog.
- **CATALOG START WITH** -- Allows you to add multiple files from a given directory to the catalog. RMAN will list the files to be added to the RMAN repository and prompts for confirmation before adding the backups.

When using the CATALOG START WITH command, you should be aware that if multiple directory paths contain the text supplied, you may catalog files that you did not intend to. Consider a file system that has one directory called **/u01/backups** and another called **/u01/backups/old** that contain backup files. Issuing the following command catalogs all files in both directories:

```
CATALOG START WITH '/u01/backups';
```

To catalog only backups in the /u01/backups directory, the correct command should be:

```
CATALOG START WITH '/u01/backups/';
```

Resynchronize a recovery catalog

Synchronizing the recovery catalog is the process of comparing the recovery catalog to the control file (either the current file or a backup) and updating the catalog with any metadata that has been changed or is not present on the catalog. RMAN automatically resynchronizes the catalog when most commands are issued, so long as the target control file is mounted and the catalog is available. It is possible to perform a full or a partial resynchronization of the catalog.

- **Partial** -- During a partial resynchronization, RMAN will update changed metadata about new backups, new archived redo logs, and so on from the target control file. Metadata in the catalog about the database physical schema will not be updated.
- **Full** -- In a full resynchronization, RMAN will locate and update all changed metadata records, including those for the database schema. A full resynchronization is performed only after structural changes have been made to the database (such as changes to database files) or if the RMAN persistent configuration has been altered.

During a full resynchronization, RMAN will create a temporary backup called a snapshot control file. This file is used to ensure that RMAN has a consistent view of the control file. It is intended only to be used for a short period of time and is not registered in the catalog. The control file checkpoint is maintained in the recovery catalog to verify the catalog currency.

If RMAN is connected to the target database and the recovery catalog, it will automatically resynchronize the recovery catalog whenever commands are executed. You should seldom need to manually resynchronize the catalog. However, there are times when it is required:

- **Catalog Unavailability** -- If you issue RMAN commands at a time when the recovery catalog is unavailable, you should open the catalog database later and use the RESYNC CATALOG command to resynchronize it manually. This might be the case if your target database and catalog database are in different locations and the availability of both at the same time cannot be guaranteed.
- **Infrequent Backups** -- If a target database running in ARCHIVELOG mode is backed up infrequently, it possible that a significant number of redo logs are archived between database backups. The recovery catalog is not updated automatically when a redo log switch occurs or when a redo log is archived. Metadata about redo log switches and archived redo logs is stored only in the control file. When RMAN backup operations are infrequent, you should regularly issue a RESYNC CATALOG to ensure this information is stored in the recovery catalog.
- **Standby Database** -- It is possible to create or alter the RMAN configuration for a standby database while not connected to the database as TARGET. After doing so, to update the control file of the standby database you can resynchronize the standby database manually.
- **Prevent Loss of Metadata** -- The data in the recovery catalog originates from the control file and the data in the control file is only kept for a limited time before being overwritten. You must ensure that the catalog is synchronized with the control file before uncataloged metadata gets overwritten. The initialization parameter CONTROL_FILE_RECORD_KEEP_TIME sets the minimum number of days that records are guaranteed to be kept in the control file. The catalog must be resynchronized at intervals less than that value by either performing backup operations that implicitly resynchronize the catalog or performing manual resynchronizations.

The RESYNC CATALOG command forces a full resynchronization of the recovery catalog. The steps to perform this are:

- Start RMAN and connect to a target database and recovery catalog.
- Mount or open the target database if it is not already mounted or open via the STARTUP MOUNT command.

- Resynchronize the recovery catalog using the RESYNC CATALOG command at the RMAN prompt.

Use and maintain RMAN stored scripts

RMAN recovery catalogs allow for the creation of stored scripts. Stored scripts act much like RMAN command files. However, command files require access to the file system where they are saved, whereas stored scripts require only a connection to the catalog. The CREATE SCRIPT command is used to create a stored script in the recovery catalog. It allows you to create a named sequence of RMAN commands in the recovery catalog for later execution. The CREATE SCRIPT command can only be executed from the RMAN prompt while connected to a target database and an open recovery catalog. Stored scripts can be either Global or Local:

- **GLOBAL** -- A global script is available for use with any database registered in the recovery catalog. Global scripts are available to virtual private catalogs with read-only access. It is only possible to create or update global scripts while connected to the base recovery catalog.
- **LOCAL** -- Local scripts created for the current target database only. They are not available to virtual private catalogs.

Local and Global scripts have different namespaces. It is possible to have a local and a global script of the same name. It is not possible to have two global scripts of the same name or two local scripts of the same name for a given target database.

Stored scripts can make use of substitution variables. &1 indicates where to place the first value, &2 indicate where to place the second value, and so on. If any special characters are included, they must be quoted. The syntax for substitution variables is &integer followed by an optional period. When the substitution variable is parsed, the optional period is replaced with the value. This allows the substitution text to be followed by another integer. In the following three cases, the value **orcl_backup** is passed:

- &1 -> orcl_backup
- &1.1 -> orcl_backup1
- &1..1 -> orcl_backup.1

Stored scripts with substitution variables must be provided with example values at create time. These values can be provided explicitly with the USING clause when starting RMAN or they can be entered when prompted.

Create a Local Stored Script

After starting RMAN, connect to the target database as TARGET, and connect to a recovery catalog. The following steps create a stored script called full_backup and then run it:

```
RMAN> CONNECT TARGET SYS@oraprod

target database Password: [password]
connected to target database: PROD (DBID=38752058)

RMAN> CONNECT CATALOG recodude@catdb

recovery catalog database Password: [password]
connected to recovery catalog database

RMAN> CREATE SCRIPT full_backup
COMMENT "Perform full backup of database and archive logs"
{
    BACKUP
      INCREMENTAL LEVEL 0 TAG full_backup
      FORMAT "/u02/backup/%U"
      DATABASE PLUS ARCHIVELOG;
}

RMAN> RUN { EXECUTE SCRIPT full_backup; }
```

Create a Global Stored Script

This example creates a global script that backs up the database and archived redo log files:

```
RMAN> CONNECT TARGET SYS@oraprod

target database Password: [password]
connected to target database: ORAPROD (DBID=38752058)

RMAN> CONNECT CATALOG recoman@catdb

recovery catalog database Password: [password]
connected to recovery catalog database

RMAN> CREATE GLOBAL SCRIPT global_full_backup
        { BACKUP DATABASE PLUS ARCHIVELOG; }
```

This script can now be accessed while connected to a different database:

```
RMAN> CONNECT TARGET SYS@oradev

target database Password: [password]
connected to target database: ORADEV (DBID=39823641)

RMAN> CONNECT CATALOG recoman@catdb

recovery catalog database Password: [password]
connected to recovery catalog database

RMAN> RUN { EXECUTE SCRIPT global_full_backup; }
```

Create a Stored Script with Substitution Variables

The following example creates a backup script that includes three substitution variables. As the last step in creating the script, RMAN prompts for initial values for the substitution variables.

```
RMAN> CONNECT TARGET /
RMAN> CONNECT CATALOG recoman@catdb

recovery catalog database Password: [password]
connected to recovery catalog database
```

```
RMAN> CREATE SCRIPT datafile_backup
2> { BACKUP DATAFILE &1 TAG &2 FORMAT '/u01/&3_%U'; }
Enter value for 1: 1

Enter value for 2: dfile1_bkup

Enter value for 3: dfile1

created script datafile_backup
```

When the script is executed, it is possible to pass different values to it:

```
RMAN> RUN { EXECUTE SCRIPT backup_df USING 2 dfile2_bkup dfile2; }
```

After the values are substituted, the script executes as follows:

```
BACKUP DATAFILE 2 TAG dfile2_bkup FORMAT '/u01/dfile2_%U';
```

Deleting a stored script

You can delete stored scripts with the DELETE SCRIPT command. The following example deletes the global script named global_full_backup:

```
RMAN> DELETE GLOBAL SCRIPT global_full_backup;

deleted global script: global_full_backup
```

Replacing an Existing Script

You can overwrite an existing stored script using the REPLACE SCRIPT command. The following example shows how to replace an existing script:

```
RMAN> CONNECT TARGET SYS@oraprod

target database Password: [password]
connected to target database: ORAPROD (DBID=38752058)

RMAN> CONNECT CATALOG recoman@catdb

recovery catalog database Password: [password]
connected to recovery catalog database
```

↗ replace ?

```
RMAN> CREATE SCRIPT full_backup
COMMENT "Perform full backup of database and archive logs"
{
    BACKUP
      INCREMENTAL LEVEL 0 TAG full_backup
      FORMAT "/u02/backup/%U"
      DATABASE;
}
```

The LIST SCRIPT NAMES command will list all scripts known to the recovery catalog:

```
RMAN> LIST SCRIPT NAMES;

List of Stored Scripts in Recovery Catalog


    Scripts of Target Database ORAPROD


      Script Name
      Description
      -------------------------------------------------
      full_backup
      Perform full backup of database and archive logs

      datafile_backup
```

However -- the script description is incorrect. As created, it does not back up the archive logs. You can replace the script with the following command:

```
RMAN> REPLACE SCRIPT full_backup
COMMENT "Perform full backup of database and archive logs"
{
    BACKUP
      INCREMENTAL LEVEL 0 TAG full_backup
      FORMAT "/u02/backup/%U"
      DATABASE PLUS ARCHIVELOG;
}
replaced script full_backup
```

Note that if you are replacing a Global script, you must use the REPLACE GLOBAL SCRIPT command.

Viewing stored scripts

The PRINT SCRIPT command allows you to see what actions are performed by a stored script:

```
RMAN> PRINT SCRIPT full_backup;

printing stored script: full_backup
 { BACKUP
       INCREMENTAL LEVEL 0 TAG full_backup
       FORMAT "/u02/backup/%U"
       DATABASE PLUS ARCHIVELOG;
 }
```

Upgrade and drop a recovery catalog
Upgrading a Recovery Catalog

If your RMAN client requires a version of the recovery catalog schema that is newer than what you currently have installed, then you must upgrade the catalog. It is possible to use the compatibility matrix in the Oracle Database Backup and Recovery Reference to determine which schema versions are compatible with which versions of RMAN. If the recovery catalog is at a version greater than what is required by the RMAN client and you issue the UPGRADE CATALOG command, an error will be generated. However, even if the recovery catalog is current and does not require upgrading, it is possible to issue the UPGRADE CATALOG command. This allows you to re-create the catalog packages at any time.

Before attempting to upgrade the catalog, you should determine what the current version is. The schema version of the recovery catalog is stored in the recovery catalog itself. To determine the version of the recovery catalog, query the RCVER view:

1. Start SQL*Plus and connect to the recovery catalog database as the catalog owner.
2. Query the RCVER table to obtain the schema version:

```
SELECT *
FROM   rcver;

VERSION
------------
09.00.01
```

If the query returns multiple rows, it means that the catalog has been upgrade since it was first installed. The highest version in the RCVER table is the current catalog schema version. The steps to upgrade the recovery catalog are:

1. If you created the recovery catalog owner in a release before 10gR1, and if the RECOVERY_CATALOG_OWNER role did not include the CREATE TYPE privilege, then grant it.

```
SQL> GRANT CREATE TYPE TO rman;
SQL> EXIT;
```

2. Start RMAN and connect RMAN to the recovery catalog database.
3. Run the UPGRADE CATALOG command:

```
RMAN> UPGRADE CATALOG;
recovery catalog owner is rman
enter UPGRADE CATALOG command again to confirm catalog
upgrade
```

4. Run the UPDATE CATALOG command again to confirm:

```
RMAN> UPGRADE CATALOG;
recovery catalog upgraded to version 12.01.00
DBMS_RCVMAN package upgraded to version 12.01.00
DBMS_RCVCAT package upgraded to version 12.01.00
```

Dropping a Recovery Catalog

The RMAN DROP CATALOG command will remove the objects that were created by the CREATE CATALOG command. If any objects in the schema exist that were <u>not</u> created by CREATE CATALOG, these will not be removed by the DROP CATALOG command. When a recovery catalog is dropped and there are no backups of the recovery catalog schema, backups of all target databases registered in the dropped catalog may become unusable. The DROP CATALOG command cannot be used to unregister a single database from a recovery catalog that has multiple target databases registered. The command will delete the recovery catalog record of backups for all target databases registered in the catalog. The steps to drop a recovery catalog schema are:

1. Start RMAN and connect to a target database and recovery catalog. Connect to the recovery catalog as the owner of the catalog schema to be dropped.

    ```
    % rman TARGET / CATALOG rmandude@catdb
    ```

2. Run the DROP CATALOG command:

    ```
    DROP CATALOG;
    recovery catalog owner is rmandude
    enter DROP CATALOG command again to confirm catalog removal
    ```

3. Run the DROP CATALOG command again to confirm:

    ```
    DROP CATALOG;
    ```

Protect the RMAN recovery catalog

Back up the recovery catalog

When creating a backup strategy, you must be sure that it includes backing up the recovery catalog database. If a hardware failure destroys the database holding your recovery catalog, this will lose the metadata for all of your target databases. Losing the metadata will make any recovery of those databases considerably more difficult. The recovery catalog database should be backed up as often as the target databases. As a general rule, the recovery catalog should be backed up on the same schedule as your target databases and after the last has completed. For example, if you have three databases being backed up each week, one each Thursday, Friday, and Saturday, then back up the recovery catalog database on Sunday. Having a backup of the recovery catalog will be useful in a disaster recovery scenario. In a situation where you have to restore the recovery catalog database, the record of backups in the restored recovery catalog database will allow you to restore any of the three target databases.

RMAN can be used to make the backups for the recovery catalog database. However, since you will be backing up the catalog itself, start RMAN with the NOCATALOG option so that RMAN will use the control file of the catalog database for the metadata repository. The following guidelines should be used for a recovery catalog backup strategy:

- The recovery catalog database should always be run in ARCHIVELOG mode.
- The retention policy should be set to a REDUNDANCY value greater than 1.
- Use two separate media to back up the database (i.e. disk and tape).
- Execute BACKUP DATABASE PLUS ARCHIVELOG at regular intervals.
- Use the control file rather than another recovery catalog as the metadata repository.
- Configure the control file autobackup feature to ON.

Re-create an unrecoverable recovery catalog

A recovery catalog is composed of data in an Oracle database like any other schema. If it has been backed up, then it should be possible to restore and recover it as you would any other database with RMAN. However, if it is not possible to restore the recovery catalog database through standard Oracle recovery procedures, the catalog must be recreated. This might happen if the recovery catalog database has never been backed up or it has been backed up but the data file backups or archived logs are not available.

It is possible to partially re-creating the contents of the missing recovery catalog using the following two options:

- **RESYNC CATALOG** -- This command can be used to update the recovery catalog with any RMAN repository information from the control file of the target database or a control file copy. This will not be able to restore any metadata from records that have been aged out of the control file.
- **CATALOG START WITH** -- This command can be used to recatalog any available backups.

Export and import the recovery catalog

It is possible to export a recovery catalog from one database and import it back into a second database. An export can also serve as a logical backup to help prevent the loss of data in the event of a media failure. The following steps can be used to export a recovery catalog from one database and import it into another.

1. Use one of the Oracle Export utilities to export the catalog data from the database.
2. Create a recovery catalog user on the database you are exporting to and grant the user necessary privileges.
3. Use the corresponding Import utility to import the catalog data into the recovery catalog user schema.

The CREATE CATALOG command should not be issued against the new database either before or after importing the catalog into the database. The import operation will create the catalog in the second database.

Create and use Virtual Private Catalogs

A virtual private catalog is a set of synonyms and views that enable user access to a subset of the base recovery catalog. Prior to Oracle 11g, access to the RMAN recovery catalog was an all-or-nothing proposition. Now it is possible to grant catalog access for a specific subset of databases to a given user. The owner of the base recovery catalog can GRANT or REVOKE restricted access to the catalog. Each VPC user has full read/write access to the metadata in the virtual private catalog granted to them. The RMAN metadata is stored in the schema of the virtual private catalog owner. Virtual catalog users cannot modify global RMAN scripts, although they can execute them.

Creating a virtual private catalog for a database user involves four steps from three locations. The first two steps are from the SQL*Plus as a user with admin privileges. The third step is executed from RMAN as the base catalog owner. The fourth step is executed from RMAN as the virtual private catalog user. The four steps are:

1. Create the VPC User.
2. Grant recovery_catalog_owner to the VPC user.
3. Grant the catalog to the new VPC user.
4. Create the virtual catalog.

From SQL*Plus, connected to the base recovery catalog database with administrator privileges:

```
SQL> CREATE USER vpc1 IDENTIFIED BY password
2 DEFAULT TABLESPACE vpcusers
3 QUOTA UNLIMITED ON vpcusers;
SQL> GRANT recovery_catalog_owner TO vpc1;
SQL> EXIT
```

From RMAN, connected to the recovery catalog database as the catalog owner catowner:

```
RMAN> CONNECT CATALOG catowner@catdb
recovery catalog database Password: password
connected to recovery catalog database
RMAN> GRANT CATALOG FOR DATABASE prod1 TO vpc1;
RMAN> EXIT;
```

From RMAN connected to the recovery catalog database as the virtual private catalog owner:

```
RMAN> CONNECT CATALOG vpc1@catdb
recovery catalog database Password: password
connected to recovery catalog database
RMAN> CREATE VIRTUAL CATALOG;
RMAN> EXIT;
```

Implementing Backup Strategies

Use various RMAN backup types and strategies

Enable ARCHIVELOG mode

In order to toggle the archiving mode of the database, use the ALTER DATABASE statement with the ARCHIVELOG or NOARCHIVELOG clause. You must be logged in to the database with administrator privileges in order to alter the archiving mode. The following steps will enable ARCHIVELOG on a database:

1. Shut down the database instance. The database must be closed and all associated instances shut down in order to switch the database archiving mode. It is also not possible to change the mode from ARCHIVELOG to NOARCHIVELOG if any datafiles need media recovery.
2. Edit the initialization parameter file. Add required parameters to specify the destinations for the archived redo log files.
3. Perform a STARTUP MOUNT on the database.
4. Change the database archiving mode by issuing ALTER DATABASE ARCHIVELOG.
5. Open the database for normal operations by issuing ALTER DATABASE OPEN.
6. Shut down the database.
7. Back up the database. Because changing the archiving mode updates the control file, you must back up all of your database files and control file. Previous backups are no longer usable.

Create tape and disk based backups

When a backup command is issued but no destination device type is specified, it will be directed to the configured default device. RMAN is preconfigured to use disk as the default device type. It may be necessary to alter the default device type from disk to tape, or change it back from tape to disk. The commands to change the default device types are:

- **CONFIGURE DEFAULT DEVICE TYPE TO DISK** -- This specifies that backups go to disk by default. When a recovery area is enabled, then the backup location defaults to the fast recovery area. Otherwise, the backup location defaults to an operating system-specific directory on disk.
- **CONFIGURE DEFAULT DEVICE TYPE TO sbt** -- Specifies that backups go to tape by default. For this to work, RMAN must be set up for use with a media manager. Once this has been done, it is possible to configure RMAN to make backups to tape and specify SBT as the default device type.

The default device type can be overridden by using the DEVICE TYPE clause of the BACKUP command:

```
BACKUP DEVICE TYPE sbt DATABASE;
BACKUP DEVICE TYPE DISK DATABASE;
```

To change the configured default device type:

1. Start RMAN and connect to a target database and a recovery catalog (if used).
2. Run the SHOW ALL command to show the currently configured default device.
3. Run the CONFIGURE DEFAULT DEVICE TYPE command, specifying either TO DISK or TO sbt.

Create whole database backups

A whole database backup includes a backup of the control file and all data files that belong to a database. When a database has archiving enabled, a whole database backup can be made with the database mounted or open. The RMAN command BACKUP DATABASE can be used to perform a whole database backup.

```
BACKUP DATABASE;
```

Adding the PLUS ARCHIVELOGS clause will back up the database, switch the online redo logs, and include archived logs in the backup. This guarantees that you have the full set of archived logs through the time of the backup and guarantees that you can perform media recovery after restoring this backup.

```
BACKUP DATABASE PLUS ARCHIVELOG;
```

It is also possible to create a whole database backup using OS commands or a third party backup utility. When using OS commands, tablespaces being backed up must be placed into backup mode.

Create consistent and inconsistent backups

To make a consistent database backup using RMAN, the database must have been shut down cleanly. The following steps will make a consistent backup:

1. Start RMAN and connect to a target database.
2. Shut down the database consistently and then mount it. The following commands will guarantee that the database is in a consistent state for a backup:

   ```
   RMAN> SHUTDOWN IMMEDIATE;
   RMAN> STARTUP FORCE DBA;
   RMAN> SHUTDOWN IMMEDIATE;
   RMAN> STARTUP MOUNT;
   ```

3. Run the BACKUP DATABASE command. The following command will back up the database to the default backup device:

   ```
   RMAN> BACKUP DATABASE;
   ```

4. Open the database and resume normal operations. The following command opens the database:

   ```
   RMAN> ALTER DATABASE OPEN;
   ```

Inconsistent database backups are created while the database is running. Technically they could also be made when the database has not been shut down cleanly, but it is difficult to imagine why anyone would do that. The database must be running in ARCHIVELOG mode for an inconsistent backup to be usable for recovery. The following steps will make an inconsistent backup of a running database:

1. Start RMAN and connect to a target database.
2. Run the BACKUP DATABASE command. The following command will back up the database to the default backup device:

```
RMAN> BACKUP DATABASE;
```

The RESTORE DATABASE and RECOVER DATABASE commands are used to recover the whole database. In order for the recovery to work, backups of all needed files must exist. The steps below assume that it is possible to restore all data files to their original locations. If the original locations are inaccessible, the SET NEWNAME command must be used to restore them to a different location.

To recover the whole database using RMAN:

1. Place the database in a mounted state. The following command terminates the database instance if it is started and mounts the database.

```
RMAN> STARTUP FORCE MOUNT;
```

2. Restore the database. The following command uses the preconfigured disk channel to restore the database.

```
RMAN> RESTORE DATABASE;
```

3. Recover the database.

```
RMAN> RECOVER DATABASE;
```

4. Open the database.

```
RMAN> ALTER DATABASE OPEN;
```

Create backup sets and image copies

When backing up to disk, RMAN can be configured to create either backup sets or image copies by default. Backups to tape devices can <u>only</u> be a backup set. Backup sets contain one or more data files, control files, server parameter files, and archived redo log files. Each binary file in a backup set is referred to as a backup piece. The contents of a backup set are divided among multiple backup pieces only if the backup piece size is limited using MAXPIECESIZE. This keyword is an option of the ALLOCATE CHANNEL or CONFIGURE CHANNEL command. Backup sets are written in a proprietary format that can only be created or restored using RMAN. The default RMAN backup type for disk is an uncompressed backup set. This is the equivalent of performing the following configure command:

```
CONFIGURE DEVICE TYPE DISK BACKUP TYPE TO BACKUPSET;
```

Unless the configure command has been used to set the default backup type to COPY, all RMAN backups will use backup sets unless explicitly set otherwise. On a database where the default has been set to COPY, the following command overrides the default with the AS BACKUPSET clause of the BACKUP command:

```
BACKUP AS BACKUPSET
   DEVICE TYPE DISK
   DATABASE;
```

When RMAN creates image copies, the result is bit-for-bit copies of each data file, archived redo log file, or control file. Images copies can be used as-is to perform recovery. They are generated with the RMAN BACKUP AS COPY command, an operating system command such as the UNIX cp, or by the Oracle archiver process. The default RMAN backup type can be set to image using the CONFIGURE DEVICE TYPE COMMAND:

```
CONFIGURE DEVICE TYPE DISK BACKUP TYPE TO COPY;
```

It is also possible to override the default with the AS COPY clause of the BACKUP command:

```
BACKUP AS COPY
  DEVICE TYPE DISK
  DATABASE;
```

Create backups of read-only tablespaces

When a tablespace has been marked as read-only, it is possible to simply back up the online data files. There is no requirement to place the tablespace in backup mode because the database does not permit changes to the data files. To back up online read-only tablespaces in an open database:

1. Query the DBA_TABLESPACES view to determine which tablespaces are read-only.

    ```
    SELECT tablespace_name
    FROM   dba_tablespaces
    WHERE  status = 'READ ONLY';
    ```

2. Identify all of the tablespace's data files by querying the DBA_DATA_FILES data dictionary view.

    ```
    SELECT file_name
    FROM   sys.dba_data_files
    WHERE  tablespace_name = 'ARCHIVE_RO';

    FILE_NAME
    -----------------------------------------
    /u01/oradata/ocp1/archive01.dbf
    /u01/oradata/ocp1/archive02.dbf
    ```

3. Back up the online data files of the read-only tablespace with operating system commands. There is no need to take the tablespace offline or put the tablespace in backup mode:

    ```
    % cp $ORACLE_HOME/oradata/ocp1/archive*.dbf /u02/backup/
    ```

4. Optionally, export the metadata in the read-only tablespace. By using the transportable tablespace feature, you can quickly restore the data files and import the metadata in case of media failure or user error.

```
% expdp DIRECTORY=dpump_dir1 DUMPFILE=archive.dmp
TRANSPORT_TABLESPACES=archive_ro LOGFILE=tts.log
```

Employ best practices for data warehouse backups

By their nature, data warehouses can consist of enormous amounts of data -- potentially hundreds of terabytes. Creating a feasible backup and recovery strategy for them is critical to avoid the potential for losing data. Oracle has suggested several best practices for implementing a backup and recovery strategy for a data warehouse.

- **Use ARCHIVELOG Mode** -- It is difficult to imagine any production database not being run in archivelog mode. Archived redo logs are crucial for recovery when no data can be lost, because they constitute a record of changes to the database. Archivelog mode provides considerably more recovery options that are possible with noarchivelog mode.
- **Use RMAN** -- RMAN has numerous advantages over user-managed backups. Some of the reasons for integrating RMAN into the backup and recovery strategy for a data warehouse include: extensive reporting, incremental backups, downtime free backups, backup and restore validation, backup and restore optimization, easily integrates with media managers, block media recovery, archive log validation and management, and corrupt block detection.
- **Use Read-Only Tablespaces** -- The size of a typical data warehouse can mean that backups take several hours. Minimizing the amount of data to be backed up can significantly improve the overall backup performance. Read-only tablespaces are an easy way to reduce the amount of data to be backed up in a data warehouse. A read-only tablespace only need to be backed up once (possibly more than once for redundancy).

- **Plan for NOLOGGING Operations** -- Data warehouses often execute bulk-data operations using the NOLOGGING mode. When an operation runs in NOLOGGING mode, no data is written to the redo log. However, since the data to support recovery is written to the log file during NOLOGGING operations, this has implications for the backup strategy. Database backup operations should never take place when a NOLOGGING operation is occurring. Oracle does not enforce this, so the DBA is responsible for scheduling the backup jobs so that they do not overlap NOLOGGING operations.

- **Not All Tablespaces are Equally Important** -- DBAs can create more efficient backup and recovery strategies that take into account how important tablespaces are in their warehouse. For example, there may be tablespaces that are dedicated to scratch space for end-users to store temporary tables and incremental results. It is possible that these tablespaces may not need to be backed up and restored. In the event that these tablespaces are lost, end users would need to re-create their own data objects. Whether this type of optimization can be made depends entirely upon the use of the data warehouse in question.

Performing Backups

Perform full and incremental backups

Create full and incremental backups

The RMAN BACKUP INCREMENTAL command creates an incremental backup of a database. Incremental backups capture block-level changes to a database made after a previous incremental backup. Recovery with incremental backups is faster than using redo logs alone. There are three types of incremental backups:

- **Level 0** -- This is the starting point for an incremental backup. It backs up all blocks in the database and is identical in content to a full backup.
- **Level 1 Differential** -- This backup contains only blocks changed since the most recent incremental backup. This is the default Level 1 backup.
- **Level 1 Cumulative** -- This backup contains only blocks changed since the most recent level 0 backup.

When restoring incremental backups, RMAN uses the level 0 backup as the starting point. It then uses the level 1 backups to update changed blocks where possible to avoid reapplying changes from redo one at a time. If incremental backups are available, then RMAN uses them during recovery.

The following example creates a level 0 incremental backup to serve as a base for an incremental backup strategy:

```
BACKUP INCREMENTAL LEVEL 0 DATABASE;
```

The following example creates a level 1 cumulative incremental backup:

```
BACKUP INCREMENTAL LEVEL 1 CUMULATIVE DATABASE;
```

The following example creates a level 1 differential incremental backup:

```
BACKUP INCREMENTAL LEVEL 1 DATABASE;
```

Use the Oracle-suggested backup strategy

Oracle's suggested backup strategy is a scheduled disk backup that provides efficient recoverability to any point in a specified recovery window. It makes use of incrementally updated backups to provide improved performance over full-database backups. This strategy requires an initial image copy of each data file. It then rolls forward the image copies daily by applying an incremental level 1 backup.

In order to use the Oracle suggested backup strategy, the following requirements must be met:

- The database must be in ARCHIVELOG mode.
- A fast recovery area must exist, or a default device for storing backups be configured.
- A database host user must be added to the OSBACKUPDBA operating system group.

For each data file, the strategy calls for the following:

- On day 1 of the strategy, RMAN creates an incremental level 0 image copy. This contains the data file contents at the beginning of day 1.
- On day 2, RMAN creates a differential incremental level 1 backup that contains the blocks changed during day 1.
- On day n for day 3 and onward, RMAN applies the level 1 backup from the beginning of day n-1 to the level 0 backup. This action brings the data file copy to its state at the beginning of day n-1. RMAN then creates a new level 1 backup that contains the blocks changed during day n-1.

In the event that recovery is required, RMAN can apply this incremental level 1 backup to the data file rolled forward on day n-1 to the beginning of day n. RMAN can use archived redo log files to recover the database to any point during day n.

The following script implements the Oracle suggested backup strategy in a Linux environment. The script can be used to back up a non-CDB or a whole multitenant container database (CDB). Once the script exists, a crontab file should be created to run it every day well before business hours (for example 2 A.M.).

```
#!/bin/sh
export ORACLE_HOME=/u01/app/oracle/product/11.2.0/dbhome_1
export ORACLE_SID=orcl
PATH=$ORACLE_HOME/bin:$PATH
rman <<EOF
connect target /
RUN {
  ALLOCATE CHANNEL disk_iub DEVICE TYPE DISK;
  RECOVER COPY OF DATABASE WITH TAG daily_iub;
  BACKUP INCREMENTAL LEVEL 1 FOR RECOVER OF COPY WITH TAG daily_iub
  DATABASE;
}
exit
EOF
```

Manage backups

Configure and monitor block change tracking

The block change tracking feature improves backup performance for incremental backups by recording changed blocks for each data file. If block change tracking is enabled, RMAN uses a block change tracking file to identify changed blocks during incremental backups. This file keeps RMAN from having to scan every block in the data file that it is backing up. Block change tracking is disabled by default. A single block change tracking file is created for the whole database. By default, the change tracking file is created as an Oracle managed file in the destination specified by the DB_CREATE_FILE_DEST initialization parameter.

To enable block change tracking, execute the following ALTER DATABASE statement:

```
ALTER DATABASE ENABLE BLOCK CHANGE TRACKING;
```

You can also create the change tracking file in a specific location:

```
ALTER DATABASE ENABLE BLOCK CHANGE TRACKING
USING FILE '/ocpdir/rman_change_track.f' REUSE;
```

You can disable block change tracking by executing the following command:

```
ALTER DATABASE DISABLE BLOCK CHANGE TRACKING;
```

The V$BLOCK_CHANGE_TRACKING view can be used to determine whether change tracking is enabled, and the file name of the block change tracking file.

```
SELECT status, filename
FROM   v$block_change_tracking;

STATUS    FILENAME
--------  -------------------------------------------------------
ENABLED   /u01/ocp/RDBMS/changetracking/e1_cs_2e61nr6j_.chg
```

Report on backups using LIST, REPORT commands

A repository of RMAN metadata is always stored in the control file of each database on which it performs backup operations. In addition, a recovery catalog can be used to store metadata. When utilized, RMAN can store metadata for multiple target databases in a set of tables in a separate recovery catalog database. The LIST and REPORT commands provide a number of reports to aid in determining backup actions that have been (or should be) performed..

RMAN LIST Command

The LIST command uses the information in the RMAN repository to provide lists of backups and other objects relating to backup and recovery.

- **LIST BACKUP** -- Allows you to list all backup sets, copies, and proxy copies of a database, tablespace, datafile, archived redo log, control file, or server parameter file.
- **LIST COPY** -- Allows you to list datafile copies and archived redo log files. By default, LIST COPY displays copies of all database files and archived redo logs.
- **LIST ARCHIVELOG** -- Allows you to list archive redo log files. You can list all archive log redo log files or you specify individual archive log files through SCN, time, or sequence number ranges.
- **LIST INCARNATION** -- Allows you to list all incarnations of a database. A new database incarnation is created when you open with the RESETLOGS option.
- **LIST DB_UNIQUE_NAME** -- In a Data Guard environment, each database is distinguished by its DB_UNIQUE_NAME initialization parameter setting. You can list all databases that have the same DBID.
- **LIST ... FOR DB_UNIQUE_NAME** -- Allows you to list all backups and copies for a specified database in a Data Guard environment or for all databases in the environment.
- **LIST RESTORE POINT** -- Allows you to list restore points known to the RMAN repository.
- **LIST SCRIPT NAMES** -- Allows you to list the names of recovery catalog scripts created with the CREATE SCRIPT or REPLACE SCRIPT command.
- **LIST FAILURE** -- A failure is a persistent data corruption mapped to a repair option.

List has a number of options that enable you to control how output is displayed. Some of the most common LIST options are:

- **LIST EXPIRED** -- Lists backups or copies that are recorded in the RMAN repository but that were not present at the expected location on disk or tape during the most recent crosscheck.
- **LIST ... BY FILE** -- Lists backups of each datafile, archived redo log file, control file, and server parameter file. Each row describes a backup of a file.
- **LIST ... SUMMARY** -- Provides a one-line summary of each backup.

RMAN REPORT Command

The RMAN REPORT command performs an analysis of the available backups for your database. The results of this can be used to determine actions that should be taken, such as backing up specific files or removing obsolete backups to free up disk space. Some of the common uses of the REPORT command are:

- **REPORT NEED BACKUP** -- Reports which database files need to be backed up to meet a configured or specified retention policy.
- **REPORT UNRECOVERABLE** -- Reports which database files require backup because they have been affected by some NOLOGGING operation such as a direct-path INSERT.
- **REPORT OBSOLETE** -- Returns full backups, datafile copies, and archived redo logs recorded in the RMAN repository that can be deleted because they are no longer required.
- **REPORT SCHEMA** -- Returns the names of all datafiles and tablespaces for the target database at the specified point in time.

Manage backups using CROSSCHECK, DELETE commands

The CROSSCHECK command is used to ensure that the information regarding backups in the recovery catalog or control file is synchronized with corresponding data on disk or in the media management catalog. The CROSSCHECK command will only operate on files that are recorded in the recovery catalog or the control file. If archived logs are deleted from the physical disk using an operating system command, the RMAN repository will still indicate that the logs exist. The CROSSCHECK command will update outdated RMAN repository information about backups whose repository records do not match their physical status. When the backup is on disk, CROSSCHECK will determine whether the header of the file is valid. For backups that are on tape, the command only checks that the backup exists. The possible status values for backups are AVAILABLE, UNAVAILABLE, and EXPIRED.

The status of backups can be determined using the RMAN LIST command, or by querying V$BACKUP_FILES. If a recovery catalog exists, the status can be found in catalog views such as RC_DATAFILE_COPY and RC_ARCHIVED_LOG. For all backups in the RMAN repository, they will be marked as EXPIRED if the backup is no longer available. For backups that are marked as EXPIRED but are now available, RMAN will change the status to AVAILABLE.

Executing CROSSCHECK command does not delete operating system files. It also does not remove the RMAN repository records of backups that are not available. The only action taken is to update the repository records with the current status of the backups.

The DELETE EXPIRED command can be used to remove records of expired backups from the RMAN repository. If the expired files still exist, then the DELETE EXPIRED command will terminate with an error. The following example will delete expired repository records:

1. Issue a CROSSCHECK command.

    ```
    CROSSCHECK BACKUP;
    ```

2. Delete the expired backups.

    ```
    DELETE EXPIRED BACKUP;
    ```

Configuring RMAN Backup Options and Creating Backup of Non-Database Files

Use techniques to improve backups

Create compressed backups

For any use of the BACKUP command that creates backup sets, you can enable binary compression of backup sets by adding the AS COMPRESSED BACKUPSET option to the BACKUP command. RMAN will compress the backup set contents before writing to disk. Information regarding the binary compression level used is automatically recorded in the backup set. When recovering, there is no need to explicitly mention the type of compression used or how to decompress. Note that binary compression imposes a performance overhead during backup and restore operations. It consumes CPU resources, so compressed backups should not be scheduled when CPU usage is high.

Specifying the COMPRESSED option in the BACKUP TYPE TO ... BACKUPSET clause configures RMAN to use compressed backup sets by default for a given device type. Omitting the COMPRESSED keyword disables compression. The preconfigured backup type for disk is an uncompressed backup set (the equivalent of the following CONFIGURE command):

```
CONFIGURE DEVICE TYPE DISK BACKUP TYPE TO BACKUPSET;
```

To enable compression on backup sets by default, you can add the COMPRESSED keyword to the above command:

```
CONFIGURE DEVICE TYPE DISK BACKUP TYPE TO COMPRESSED BACKUPSET;
```

If the CONFIGURE command has been used to set the default backup type to compressed backup set, backups will use compression by default. It is also possible to enable compression explicitly for a single backup. An example of a command to make a compressed backup is:

```
BACKUP
AS COMPRESSED BACKUPSET
DATABASE PLUS ARCHIVELOG;
```

Create multi-section backups of very large files

Multisection backups enable RMAN channels to back up a single large file in parallel. The work is divided among multiple channels, with each channel backing up one file section in a file. This can improve the performance of backups of large datafiles. Multisection backups are enabled by specifying the SECTION SIZE parameter on the BACKUP command. Each file section is a contiguous range of blocks in a file. The SECTION SIZE parameter cannot be used in conjunction with MAXPIECESIZE. If the value of SECTION SIZE is larger than the file size, then RMAN will not use multisection backup for the file. If the section size would result in more than 256 file sections, then RMAN will increase the section size so that the result is exactly 256 sections. In the following example, the TOOLS tablespace contains a single datafile of 1 GB. The environment has two tape drives with channels allocated and the parallelism for SBT is set to two. The following command will break the tablespace datafile into two file 500MB file sections:

```
BACKUP
  SECTION SIZE 500M
  TABLESPACE tools;
```

Create proxy copies

When performing a proxy copy, RMAN turns over control of the data transfer to a media manager that supports this feature. Proxy copy cannot be used with channels of type DISK. The feature can only be used with media managers that support it. By giving the media manager more control over the data movement, CPU resources on the target node are reduced.

For each file that being backed up using the BACKUP PROXY command, RMAN will query the media manager to determine whether it can perform a proxy copy. If the media manager is unable to proxy copy the file, RMAN will back up the file as if the PROXY option had not been used. If the PROXY ONLY option is used, RMAN will fail if a proxy copy cannot be performed. Control files are never backed up with proxy copy. Backups with the PROXY option that include control files will ignore the option when backing up the control file.

Create duplexed backup sets

RMAN has the ability to create up to four duplexed copies when creating a backup set. Duplexing is not possible when making image copies. Duplexing is enabled using the COPIES parameter in the CONFIGURE, SET, or BACKUP commands. When duplexing, RMAN produces a single backup set with a unique key, and generates the requested number of identical copies of each backup piece in the set. It is possible to duplex backups to either disk or tape, but not to tape and disk simultaneously. The FORMAT parameter of the BACKUP command sets the destinations for the backup sets. The number of copies should never exceed the number of available tape devices when backup up to tape. Duplexing backup sets to the fast recovery area is not possible. The following command creates two backup set copies of data file 3:

```
BACKUP DEVICE TYPE DISK COPIES 2 DATAFILE 3
   FORMAT '/u01/%U','/u02/%U';
```

It is also possible to use CONFIGURE BACKUP COPIES to enable duplexing by default. The default setting will apply to all backup sets except control file autobackups and backupsets that are backed up using the BACKUP BACKUPSET command. By default, CONFIGURE ... BACKUP COPIES is set to 1 for disk and tape. The following example sets duplexing for datafiles and archivelog files on disk to two.

```
CONFIGURE CHANNEL DEVICE TYPE DISK FORMAT '/u01/%U', '/u02/%U';
CONFIGURE DATAFILE BACKUP COPIES FOR DEVICE TYPE DISK TO 2;
CONFIGURE ARCHIVELOG BACKUP COPIES FOR DEVICE TYPE DISK TO 2;
```

Given the above configuration, the following command backs up the database and archived logs to disk, making two copies of each data file and archived log, placing one copy of the backup sets produced in the /u01 directory and the other in the /u02 directory:

```
BACKUP DEVICE TYPE DISK AS BACKUPSET DATABASE PLUS ARCHIVELOG;
```

Create backups of backup sets

You can use RMAN to make copies of existing previously created backup sets with the BACKUP BACKUPSET command. This will back up backup sets that were created on disk and can be used to spread backups among multiple media. If RMAN determines that a backup set is corrupted or missing, it will search for other copies of the same backup set. The following example backs up existing backup sets to tape to ensure that all your backups exist on both media types.

```
BACKUP DEVICE TYPE DISK AS BACKUPSET
   DATABASE PLUS ARCHIVELOG;
BACKUP
   DEVICE TYPE sbt
   BACKUPSET ALL;
```

The BACKUP BACKUPSET can also be used to manage backup space allocation. The following backs up backup sets that were created more than 14 days ago from disk to tape, and then deletes the backup sets from disk. If a backup was duplexed to multiple locations on disk, RMAN will delete all copies of the pieces in the backup set.

```
BACKUP
   DEVICE TYPE SBT
   BACKUPSET COMPLETED BEFORE 'SYSDATE-14'
   DELETE INPUT;
```

Create archival backups

The RMAN KEEP option specifies that a backup be created as an archival backup. An archival backup is a self-contained backup that is exempt from the configured retention policy. Archival backups contain all of the files necessary to restore the backup and recover it to a consistent state. If the database is open at the time an archival backup is created, RMAN automatically generates and backs up the redo logs needed to make the backup consistent. When available, RMAN will use archival backups for disaster recovery restore operations. However, their intended purpose is to produce a snapshot of the database that can be restored on another system for testing or historical usage.

KEEP

When computing the retention policy RMAN does not consider backup pieces with the KEEP option. The KEEP option cannot be used to override the retention policy for files stored in the fast recovery area. When KEEP is specified, RMAN backs up datafiles, archived redo logs, the control file, and the server parameter file. A recovery catalog is required when KEEP FOREVER is specified because the backup records will eventually age out of the control file.

UNTIL TIME 'date_string'

This clause specifies an end date for retaining the RMAN backup or copy. After this date the backup is obsolete, regardless of the backup retention policy settings. It's possible to provide a specific date/time by using the current NLS_DATE_FORMAT, or a SQL date expression such as 'SYSDATE+90'. If a KEEP TIME is provided with a date only, then the backup becomes obsolete one second after midnight on that date.

RESTORE POINT restore_point_name

Creates a restore point matching the SCN to which RMAN must recover the backup to a consistent state. The name provided must not already exist. RMAN captures the SCN immediately after the datafile backups complete. The restore point acts as a label for the SCN to which this archival backup can be restored.

NOKEEP

This option indicates that any KEEP attributes no longer apply to the backup. After specifying NOKEEP, the backup is subject to the configured backup retention

Perform backup of non-database files

Back up a control file to trace
It is possible to back up the control file to a text file that contains a CREATE CONTROLFILE statement. This trace file can then be edited to generate a script to create a new control file based on the one that was current when the trace was created. The trace file will be created in a subdirectory determined by the DIAGNOSTIC_DEST initialization parameter. The database alert log will also contain the name and location of the newly created trace file. The steps to back up the control file to a trace file are:

1. Mount or open the database.
2. Execute the following SQL statement:

```
ALTER DATABASE BACKUP CONTROLFILE TO TRACE;
```

Back up archived redo log files

The BACKUP ARCHIVELOG command is used to back up archived logs. If backup optimization has been enabled, RMAN will skip backups of archived logs that have already been backed up to the specified device. The steps to back up archived redo log files are:

1. Start RMAN and connect to a target database and a recovery catalog (if used).
2. Ensure that the target database is mounted or open.
3. Execute the BACKUP ARCHIVELOG or BACKUP ... PLUS ARCHIVELOG command.
   The following example backs up the database and all archived redo logs:

   ```
   BACKUP DATABASE PLUS ARCHIVELOG;
   ```

   The following example backs up one copy of each log sequence number for all archived redo logs:

   ```
   BACKUP ARCHIVELOG ALL;
   ```

Back up ASM diskgroup metadata

The ASM command-line utility (ASMCMD) allows ASM disk identification, disk bad block repair, and backup and restore operations of your ASM environment for faster recovery, among other capabilities. ASMCMD allows ASM diskgroup data to be backed up using the md_backup command. The MD_BACKUP command creates a file containing the metadata for one or more disk groups. The backup file can be used to restore disk groups rapidly in the event of a catastrophic failure of the ASM instance. By default all the mounted disk groups are included in the backup file which is saved in the current working directory. If the name of the backup file is not specified, ASM names the file AMBR_BACKUP_INTERMEDIATE_FILE.

The syntax of the md_backup command is:

```
md_backup [-b location_of_backup] [-g dgname [-g dgname …]]
```

Where:

-b   Specifies the location in which you want to store the backup file

-g   Specifies the disk group name to be backed up. Multiple diskgroups can be specified by repeating the –g option

Using RMAN-Encrypted Backups

Create RMAN-encrypted backups

Use transparent-mode encryption

RMAN allows backup sets to be created using encryption. If files of the backup sets are obtained by unauthorized users, they cannot be read or used to restore a database. Encryption can be transparent, which is based on an encryption key stored in Oracle Wallet. Alternately it can be password-based, which makes use of a user-supplied password. Dual-mode encryption combines both wallet and password-based encryption. The following commands are used to activate and modify the default encryption behavior of RMAN:

- **CONFIGURE ENCRYPTION** -- This command can be used to configure RMAN to perform transparent encryption of backup sets by default. It is not possible to persistently configure dual mode or password mode encryption.
- **SET ENCRYPTION** -- This command is used to configure dual mode or password mode encryption at the RMAN session level.

The default algorithm used for encrypting backups is AES 128-bit. However, it is possible to use any of the values listed in V$RMAN_ENCRYPTION_ALGORITHMS. The CONFIGURE command can be used to persistently configure the default algorithm to another value:

1. Start RMAN and connect to a target database and a recovery catalog (if used).
2. Ensure that the target database is mounted or open.
3. Execute the CONFIGURE ENCRYPTION ALGORITHM command. The following example set RMAN to use AES 256-bit encryption:

```
CONFIGURE ENCRYPTION ALGORITHM TO 'AES256';
```

If the CONFIGURE command is used to enable transparent encryption, no additional action is required to make encrypted backups. RMAN backups will be encrypted by default. To make transparent-mode encrypted backups, the default encryption mode must have been set:

```
CONFIGURE ENCRYPTION FOR DATABASE ON;
```

Once the mode has been set, backups will require no additional syntax to be encrypted:

1. Start RMAN and connect to a target database and recovery catalog (if used).
2. Back up the database.

```
BACKUP DATABASE PLUS ARCHIVELOG;
```

Use password-mode encryption

It is not possible to configure password-mode encryption to occur by default. Creating a password-encrypted backup set requires the session to be specifically configured. To make password-mode encrypted backups:

1. Start RMAN and connect to a target database and recovery catalog (if used).
2. Execute the SET ENCRYPTION ON IDENTIFIED BY password ONLY command.

```
SET ENCRYPTION ON IDENTIFIED BY password ONLY FOR ALL
TABLESPACES;
```

3. Back up the database.

```
BACKUP DATABASE PLUS ARCHIVELOG;
```

Use dual-mode encryption

The value of dual-mode encrypted backups is that it is possible to restore them either transparently or by specifying the encryption password. This might be used when backups are normally restored on-site using the Oracle keystore, but might have a requirement to be restored at another site that does not have access to the Oracle keystore. To create a dual-mode encrypted backup set:

1. Start RMAN and connect to a target database and recovery catalog (if used).
2. Execute the SET ENCRYPTION ON IDENTIFIED BY password command.

```
SET ENCRYPTION ON IDENTIFIED BY password FOR ALL TABLESPACES;
```

3. Back up the database.

Restore encrypted backups

A single restore operation can process backups encrypted in different modes. When restoring each backup piece, RMAN will determine whether or not it is encrypted. If the Oracle keystore is open and available, backups created using transparent encryption need no intervention. If RMAN detects a backup piece that has used password encryption, it searches for a matching key in the list of passwords provided in the SET DECRYPTION command. If it locates a usable key, the restore operation will proceed. If no usable key is found in the SET DECRYPTION command, RMAN searches for a key in the Oracle keystore. If it locates a usable key, then the restore operation proceeds. If no key is found in the keystore, RMAN signals an error that the backup piece cannot be decrypted.

Diagnosing Failures

Describe the Automatic Diagnostic Workflow

Use the Automatic Diagnostic Repository

The Automatic Diagnostic Repository (ADR) is a directory structure for diagnostic files such as traces, dumps, the alert log, health monitor reports, and more. The directory structure supports multiple instances and multiple Oracle products. Each instance of each product will store diagnostic data underneath its own home directory within the ADR. It provides a unified directory structure along with consistent diagnostic data formats across products and instances. This plus a unified set of tools enables diagnostic data to be correlated and analyzed across multiple Oracle products.

Because all diagnostic data, including the alert log, is stored in the ADR, the initialization parameters BACKGROUND_DUMP_DEST and USER_DUMP_DEST have been deprecated. They have been replaced by the initialization parameter DIAGNOSTIC_DEST. The DIAGNOSTIC_DEST parameter identifies the directory which serves as the ADR Base location.

The V$DIAG_INFO view lists all the important ADR locations for the current Oracle database instance. It also provides the number of active problems and incidents and the tracefiles for the current instance.

- **ADR Base** -- Path of ADR base
- **ADR Home** -- Path of ADR home for the current database instance
- **Diag Trace** -- Location of background process trace files, server process trace files, SQL trace files, and the text-formatted version of the alert log
- **Diag Alert** -- Location of the XML-formatted version of the alert log
- **Default Trace** -- File Path to the trace file for the current session
- **Diag Incident** -- File path for incident packages
- **Diag Cdump** -- Equivalent to cdump. Location for core dump files.
- **Health Monitor** -- Location for health monitor output.

```
SELECT name, value
FROM    v$diag_info;

NAME VALUE
------------------- ----------------------------------------------------
Diag Enabled        TRUE
ADR Base            /u01/oracle
ADR Home            /u01/oracle/diag/rdbms/orcl/orcl
Diag Trace          /u01/oracle/diag/rdbms/orcl/orcl/trace
Diag Alert          /u01/oracle/diag/rdbms/orcl/orcl/alert
Diag Incident       /u01/oracle/diag/rdbms/orcl/orcl/incident
Diag Cdump          /u01/oracle/diag/rdbms/orcl/orcl/cdump
Health Monitor      /u01/oracle/diag/rdbms/orcl/orcl/hm
Default Trace File  /u01/oracle/diag/rdbms/orcl/orcl/trace/
                    orcl_ora_2259.trc
Active Problem Count  8
Active Incident Count 20
```

Use ADRCI

The Automatic Diagnostic Repository Command Interpreter (ADRCI) is a command-line utility that is part of the fault diagnosability infrastructure. ADRCI's primary functions include:

- Viewing diagnostic data in the Automatic Diagnostic Repository.
- Viewing Health Monitor reports.
- Packaging incident and problem information for Oracle Support.

Diagnostic data viewable from within ADRCI includes incident and problem descriptions, trace files, dumps, health monitor reports, alert log entries, and more. ADRCI can be used in interactive mode or within scripts. ADRCI can also execute scripts of ADRCI commands just as SQL*Plus can execute scripts of SQL and PL/SQL commands. There is no login to ADRCI -- it is secured by OS-level file permissions only.

An ADR home is the root directory for all diagnostic data for a particular instance of a given Oracle product or component. All ADR homes share the same hierarchical directory structure that starts at the ADR_BASE directory. Some ADRCI commands can work with multiple ADR homes simultaneously while others require that a single ADR home be set within ADRCI before issuing the command. The current ADRCI homepath determines the ADR homes that are searched for diagnostic data when an ADRCI command is issued. It does so by pointing to a specific directory within the ADR base hierarchy. When pointed to a single ADR home directory, that ADR home is the only current ADR home. If the homepath points to a higher directory, all ADR homes that are below the directory that is pointed to become current. The ADR homepath is null by default when ADRCI starts, which means that all the ADR homes beneath the ADR_BASE are current. The SHOW HOME and SHOW HOMEPATH commands display the current ADR homes. The SET HOMEPATH command sets the homepath to a specific directory.

The alert log is written as both an XML-formatted file and as a plain text file. You can view either format with any text editor. Alternately, you can use ADRCI to view the XML-formatted alert log with the XML tags stripped. By default, ADRCI displays the alert log in your default editor. You can use the SET EDITOR command to change the editor used by ADRCI.

You can use ADRCI to view the names of trace files that are currently in the ADR. You can view the names of all trace files, or a filtered subset of names. ADRCI has commands to obtain a list of trace files whose file name matches a search string, exist in a particular directory, pertain to a particular incident, or a combination of these. The SHOW TRACEFILE command displays a list of the files in the trace directory and in all incident directories under the current ADR home.

The ADRCI SHOW INCIDENT command can be used to display information about open incidents. For each incident, the incident ID, problem key, and incident creation time are shown. If the ADRCI homepath includes multiple current ADR homes, the report displays incidents from all of them.

```
SHOW INCIDENT
ADR Home =
/u03/app/oracle/product/11.1.0/db_2/log/diag/rdbms/orcl12c/orcl12c:
********************************************************************
INCIDENT_ID        PROBLEM_KEY                 CREATE_TIME
---------------    --------------    ---------------------------------
4218               ORA 603           2011-03-18 21:35:49.322161 -07:00
4219               ORA 600 [4134]    2011-03-20 21:35:47.862114 -07:00
4224               ORA 600 [4138]    2011-04-01 21:35:25.012579 -07:00
3 rows fetched
```

The following are variations on the SHOW INCIDENT command:

```
SHOW INCIDENT -MODE BRIEF
SHOW INCIDENT -MODE DETAIL
SHOW INCIDENT -MODE DETAIL -P "INCIDENT_ID=1681"
```

Find and interpret message output and error stacks

RMAN generates several different types of output that can be useful in diagnosing problems. These include:

- **RMAN messages** -- RMAN stores completed job information in V$RMAN_STATUS and RC_RMAN_STATUS. Information for current jobs is stored in V$RMAN_OUTPUT. When RMAN is run from the command line, it is also possible to direct output to standard output, a log file, or a file created by redirecting RMAN output.
- **alert_SID.log** -- The Oracle server will write output to the alert log, in the alert subdirectory of the Automatic Diagnostic Repository (ADR) home. It contains a chronological log of errors, initialization parameter settings, and administration operations.
- **Oracle trace file** -- The Oracle server will create trace files in the trace subdirectory of the ADR home. Trace files contain detailed output generated by Oracle Database processes. A trace file is created when an ORA-600 or ORA-3113 error message occurs, whenever RMAN cannot allocate a channel, and when the database fails to load the media management library.

- **sbtio.log** -- Third-party media management software can create this file in the trace subdirectory of the ADR home. It contains vendor-specific information written by the media management software.

RMAN error stacks are covered in a later chapter devoted specifically to them. Why Oracle certification has two chapters for this exam that reference RMAN error stacks is one of the world's great mysteries.

Use the Data Recovery Advisor

Oracle's Data Recovery Advisor is a data corruption repair function integrated with Support Workbench, database health checks and RMAN. It can display data corruption problems, assess their extent and impact, recommend repair options, and automate the repair process. In the context of Data Recovery Advisor, a health check is a diagnostic procedure run by the Health Monitor to assess the state of the database or its components. Health checks are invoked reactively when an error occurs and can also be invoked manually. Data Recovery Advisor can diagnose failures such as the following:

- Components such as data files and control files that are not accessible by the database.
- Physical corruptions such as block checksum failures and invalid block header field values.
- Inconsistencies such as a data file that is older than other database files.
- I/O failures such as hardware errors, operating system driver failures, and exceeding operating system resource limits.

In some cases, the Data Recovery Advisor may be able to detect or handle logical corruptions. As a general rule, detecting and repairing logical corruptions will require assistance from Oracle Support Services.

Failures

A failure is a persistent data corruption detected by a health check. They are usually detected reactively when a database operation encounters corrupted data and generates an error. This will automatically invoke a health check in the database. The check will search the database for failures related to the error and record any findings in the Automatic Diagnostic Repository. Data Recovery Advisor can generate repair advice and repair failures only after failures have been detected by the database and stored in the ADR. Data Recovery Advisor can report on and repair failures such as inaccessible files, physical and logical block corruptions, and I/O failures. All failures are assigned a priority: CRITICAL, HIGH, or LOW, and a status of OPEN or CLOSED.

- **CRITICAL** priority failures require immediate attention because they make the whole database unavailable. Typically, critical failures bring down the instance and are diagnosed during the subsequent startup.
- **HIGH** priority failures make a database partially unavailable or unrecoverable, and usually have to be repaired in a reasonably short time.
- **LOW** priority indicates that failures can be ignored until more important failures are fixed.

DRA Repairs

Data Recovery Advisor allows you to view repair options. Repairs might involve the use of block media recovery, datafile media recovery, or Oracle Flashback Database. In general, Data Recovery Advisor presents both automated and manual repair options. If appropriate, you can choose an automated repair option in order to perform a repair. In an automated repair, Data Recovery Advisor performs the repair, verifies the repair success, and closes the relevant failures.

The recommended workflow for repairing data failures from RMAN is to run the following commands in sequence during an RMAN session: LIST FAILURE to display failures, ADVISE FAILURE to display repair options, and REPAIR FAILURE to fix the failures.

LIST FAILURE

The LIST FAILURE command displays failures against which you can run the ADVISE FAILURE and REPAIR FAILURE commands.

```
RMAN> LIST FAILURE;
List of Database Failures
=========================
Failure ID Priority Status  Time Detected Summary
---------- -------- ------- ------------- ----------------------
274        HIGH     OPEN    21-FEB-14     One or more non-system
                                          datafiles are missing
329        HIGH     OPEN    21-FEB-14     Datafile 1:
                                          '/u01/oradata/prod/
                                          system01.dbf'
                                          contains one or more
                                          corrupt blocks
```

ADVISE FAILURE

Use the ADVISE FAILURE command to display repair options for the specified failures. This command prints a summary of the failures identified by the Data Recovery Advisor and implicitly closes all open failures that are already fixed. The ADVISE FAILURE command indicates the repair strategy that Data Recovery Advisor considers optimal for a given set of failures. Data Recovery Advisor verifies repair feasibility before proposing a repair strategy. For example, it will check that all backups and archived redo log files needed for media recovery are available. It can generate both manual and automated repair options.

The ADVISE command maps a set of failures to the set of repair steps that Data Recovery Advisor considers to be optimal. When possible, Data Recovery Advisor consolidates multiple repair steps into a single repair. For example, if the database has corrupted datafile, missing control file, and lost current redo log group, then Data Recovery Advisor would recommend a single, consolidated repair plan to restore the database and perform point-in-time recovery.

```
RMAN> ADVISE FAILURE;
List of Database Failures
===========================

Failure ID Priority Status  Time Detected Summary
---------- -------- ------- ------------- ----------------------
274        HIGH     OPEN    21-FEB-14     One or more non-system
                                          datafiles are missing
329        HIGH     OPEN    21-FEB-14     Datafile 1:
                                          '/u01/oradata/prod/
                                           system01.dbf'
                                          contains one or more
                                          corrupt blocks

analyzing automatic repair options; this may take some time
using channel ORA_DISK_1
analyzing automatic repair options complete

Mandatory Manual Actions
========================
no manual actions available

Optional Manual Actions
========================
1. If file /u01/oradata/prod/data01.dbf was unintentionally renamed
or moved, restore it

Automated Repair Options
========================
Option Repair Description
--- ---------
Restore and recover datafile 31; Perform block
    media recovery of block 43481 in file 1

Strategy: The repair includes complete media recovery with no data
loss
Repair script:
/u01/oracle/log/diag/rdbms/prod/prod/hm/reco_740113269.hm
```

CHANGE FAILURE

The CHANGE FAILURE command allows you to change the failure priority from HIGH to LOW or the reverse, or to close it. You cannot change to or from CRITICAL priority.

```
RMAN> CHANGE FAILURE 3 PRIORITY LOW;
```

REPAIR FAILURE

The REPAIR FAILURE command is used to repair database failures identified by the Data Recovery Advisor. The target database instance must be started, it must be a single-instance database and cannot be a physical standby database. It is important that at most one RMAN session is running the REPAIR FAILURE command. The only exception is REPAIR FAILURE ... PREVIEW, which is permitted in concurrent RMAN sessions. To perform an automated repair, the Data Recovery Advisor may require specific backups and archived redo logs. If the files are not available, then the recovery will not be possible. Data Recovery Advisor consolidates repairs whenever possible so that a single repair can fix multiple failures. If one has not yet been issued in the current RMAN session, REPAIR FAILURE performs an implicit ADVISE FAILURE. RMAN always verifies that failures are still relevant and automatically closes failures that have already been repaired. After executing a repair, RMAN reevaluates all open failures on the chance that some of them may also have been fixed.

Handle block corruption

Detect block corruption using RMAN

The VALIDATE command of RMAN can be used to manually check for physical and logical corruptions in database files. The command performs the same types of checks as BACKUP VALIDATE, but VALIDATE has the ability to check a larger selection of objects. When validating files, RMAN will check every block of the input file. If a previously unmarked corrupt block is discovered, RMAN will update the V$DATABASE_BLOCK_CORRUPTION view with rows describing the corruptions. Some of the possible targets for the VALIDATE command include:

- **VALIDATE BACKUPSET** -- This command checks every block in a backup set to ensure that the backup can be restored. If RMAN finds block corruption, then it issues an error and terminates the validation.
- **VALIDATE DATABASE** -- This command will validate all data files, control files and the server parameter file if one is in use.
- **VALIDATE DATAFILE 1** -- This command will validate the specified datafile.
- **VALIDATE DATAFILE 1 BLOCK 10** -- This command will validate a single block within the specified datafile.

If a large data file must be validated, it is possible for RMAN to perform the work in parallel by dividing the file into sections and processing each file section simultaneously. Multiple channels must be allocated and the SECTION SIZE parameter specified in the VALIDATE command. The following example performs parallel validation of a data file:

1. Start RMAN and connect to a target database. The target database must be mounted or open.
2. Run VALIDATE with the SECTION SIZE parameter.

```
RUN
{
ALLOCATE CHANNEL c1 DEVICE TYPE DISK;
ALLOCATE CHANNEL c2 DEVICE TYPE DISK;
VALIDATE DATAFILE 1 SECTION SIZE 600M;
}
```

The BACKUP VALIDATE command can also be used to detect block corruption. It can be used to perform the following functions:

- Check data files for physical and logical block corruption
- Confirm that all database files exist and are in the correct locations

During the BACKUP VALIDATE operation, RMAN reads the files to be backed up in their entirety. The operation does not produce any backup sets or image copies. It is not possible to use the BACKUPSET, MAXCORRUPT, or PROXY parameters with the BACKUP VALIDATE command. The following example validate that all database files and archived logs contain no physical corruptions and can be backed up:

1. Start RMAN and connect to a target database and recovery catalog (if used).
2. Run the BACKUP VALIDATE command.

```
BACKUP VALIDATE
DATABASE
ARCHIVELOG ALL;
```

In order to check for logical corruptions in addition to physical corruptions, the CHECK LOGICAL option must be added to the preceding command:

```
BACKUP VALIDATE
CHECK LOGICAL
DATABASE
ARCHIVELOG ALL;
```

The RESTORE ... VALIDATE command is used to test whether RMAN can restore a specific file or set of files from a backup. The database must be mounted or open for this command, but there is no need to take data files offline. Validating backups of the data files only reads the backups and does not affect the production data files. The following example shows how to validate backups with the RESTORE command:

1. Run the RESTORE command with the VALIDATE option.

```
RESTORE DATABASE VALIDATE;
RESTORE ARCHIVELOG ALL VALIDATE;
```

If no error stack is generated, then RMAN can use these backups successfully during a real restore and recovery.

It is possible to validate a CDB in much the same fashion as a non-CDB. The primary difference is that you must connect to the root as a common user with the common SYSBACKUP or SYSDBA privilege.

The following command, when connected to the root, validates the whole CDB:

```
VALIDATE DATABASE;
```

The following command validates the root:

```
VALIDATE DATABASE ROOT;
```

The following command, when connected to the root, validates the PDBs ocp_pdb and dev_pdb.

```
VALIDATE PLUGGABLE DATABASE ocp_pdb, dev_pdb;
```

The following command, when connected to a PDB, validates only the current PDB.

```
VALIDATE DATABASE;
```

The following command, when connected to a PDB, validates the restore of the database.

```
RESTORE DATABASE VALIDATE;
```

Perform block recovery using RMAN

Block media recovery allows you to recover individual corrupt data blocks within a data file. It is faster than data file media recovery because only blocks that need recovery are restored and recovered. Also, unlike data file media recovery, the affected data files remain online during the recovery process. Prior to the block media recovery capability, a single corrupt block in a datafile required taking the data file offline and restoring from backup.

When the database encounters a corrupt block, it marks the block as media corrupt and then writes it to disk. After being marked corrupt, no subsequent read of the block will be successful until the block is recovered. If block corruption has been detected, block media recovery can be performed manually using the RECOVER ... BLOCK command. By default, RMAN first searches for good blocks in the real-time query physical standby database (if one exists), then flashback logs and then blocks in full or level 0 incremental backups.

All known corrupted block in the database can be located by querying the V$DATABASE_BLOCK_CORRUPTION view. It contains blocks marked corrupt by database components such as RMAN, ANALYZE, dbv, and SQL queries. The following types of corruption result in the addition of rows to this view:

- **Physical corruption** -- Physical corruption, also known as media corruption, means that the database does not recognize the block: the checksum is invalid, the block contains all zeros, or the block header is corrupt. Physical corruption checking is enabled by default. Checksum checking can be disabled by specifying the NOCHECKSUM option of the BACKUP command, but other physical consistency checks cannot be disabled.
- **Logical corruption** -- Logical corruption occurs when the block has a valid checksum, the header and footer match, and so on, but the contents are logically inconsistent. Logical corruption cannot always be corrected by block media recovery. It may be necessary to use alternate recovery methods, such as tablespace point-in-time recovery, or dropping and re-creating the affected objects.

Logical corruption checking is disabled by default. It can be enabled by specifying the CHECK LOGICAL option of the BACKUP, RESTORE, RECOVER, and VALIDATE commands.

The following prerequisites apply to the RECOVER ... BLOCK command:

- The target database must run in ARCHIVELOG mode and be open or mounted with a current control file.
- If the target database is a standby database, then it must be in a consistent state, recovery cannot be in session, and the backup must be older than the corrupted file.
- The backups of the data files containing the corrupt blocks must be full or level 0 backups and not proxy copies.
- RMAN can use only archived redo logs for the recovery.
- Flashback Database must be enabled on the target database for RMAN to search the flashback logs for good copies of corrupt blocks.
- The target database must be associated with a real-time query physical standby database for RMAN to search a standby database for good copies of corrupt blocks.

Recovering Individual Blocks

To recover specific data blocks, you must obtain the data file numbers and block numbers of the corrupted blocks. When Oracle encounters a corrupted block, you may get an error in a trace file like the following:

```
ORA-01578: ORACLE data block corrupted (file # 4, block # 213)
ORA-01110: data file 4: '/oracle/oradata/trgt/users01.dbf'
```

To recover this block, perform the following steps:

1. Start RMAN and connect to the target database, which must be mounted or open.
2. Run the SHOW ALL command to confirm that the appropriate channels are preconfigured.

3. Run the RECOVER ... BLOCK command at the RMAN prompt, specifying the file and block numbers for the corrupted blocks.

```
RECOVER
DATAFILE 4 BLOCK 213;
```

Recovering All Blocks in V$DATABASE_BLOCK_CORRUPTION

Rather than recovering blocks individually, you can have RMAN automatically recover all blocks listed in the V$DATABASE_BLOCK_CORRUPTION view. The steps to do this are:

1. Start SQL*Plus and connect to the target database.
2. Query V$DATABASE_BLOCK_CORRUPTION to determine whether corrupt blocks exist.

```
SELECT * FROM V$DATABASE_BLOCK_CORRUPTION;
```

3. Start RMAN and connect to the target database.
4. Recover all blocks marked corrupt in V$DATABASE_BLOCK_CORRUPTION.

```
RMAN> RECOVER CORRUPTION LIST;
```

Once recovered, the blocks will automatically be removed from the view.

Detect database corruptions using the ANALYZE and DBVERIFY utility

Data corruption can occur in two broad forms:

*   **Intrablock** -- With this type of corruption, the problem exists within a single data block. Intrablock corruption can be either physical (i.e. the data has been physically altered on the storage media), or logical (the block is readable, but the information contained in it is logically invalid).

- **Interblock** -- Interblock corruption occurs between two or more data blocks. This type of corruption can only be logical.

Intrablock corruption is recorded in the V$DATABASE_BLOCK_CORRUPTION view. The Automatic Diagnostic Repository (ADR) tracks all types of corruptions. Many Oracle database utilities, including RMAN, can detect intrablock corruption. Interblock corruption can only be detected by the DBVERIFY utility or the ANALYZE command.

DBVERIFY

This is command-line utility that is external to the Oracle database. It is used to perform a physical data structure integrity check on database files and backup files. When run against a database file, the database can be either open or closed. DBVERIFY can only be used with data files, and is not applicable for control files or redo logs. DBVERIFY can check the disk blocks of a single data file or a specific segment.

To perform an integrity check on data file index01.dbf on Linux, run the dbv command as follows:

```
% dbv file=index01.dbf
```

To perform an integrity check on a segment, you must determine the segment id. The segment ID is composed of the tablespace ID number (tsn), segment header file number (segfile), and segment header block number (segblock). This information can be obtained from SYS_USER_SEGS. The relevant columns are TABLESPACE_ID, HEADER_FILE, and HEADER_BLOCK. To scan a segment 3.1.14, run the dbv command as follows:

```
% dbv segment_id=3.1.14
```

Reference the Oracle 12c Utilities manual for more information on the DBVERIFY utility.

ANALYZE

The SQL statement ANALYZE can be used to validate the structure of an index or index partition, table or table partition, index-organized table, cluster, or object reference. To enable this capability, the VALIDATE STRUCTURE clause must be specified. ANALYZE will check the integrity of each of the data blocks in a table or index. If corruption is detected in the structure of the object, then an error message is returned.

Detect database corruptions using the DBMS_REPAIR package

The DBMS_REPAIR package contains a number of procedures designed to detect and repair corrupt blocks in tables and indexes. The package enables administrators to address corruptions where possible. DBMS_REPAIR requires two administration tables that will be used to store a list of corrupt blocks and any index keys pointing to those blocks. The tables are created via the ADMIN_TABLES procedure:

```
BEGIN
  DBMS_REPAIR.ADMIN_TABLES (
      table_name => 'DR_REPAIR_TABLE',
      table_type => DBMS_REPAIR.repair_table,
      action     => DBMS_REPAIR.create_action,
      tablespace => 'USERS');

  DBMS_REPAIR.ADMIN_TABLES (
      table_name => 'DR_ORPHAN_TABLE',
      table_type => DBMS_REPAIR.orphan_table,
      action     => DBMS_REPAIR.create_action,
      tablespace => 'USERS');
END;
```

Once the administration tables exist, the CHECK_OBJECT procedure can be used to diagnose the suspect table for corrupt blocks:

```
DECLARE
  v_corr_blocks    NUMBER   := 0;
BEGIN
  DBMS_REPAIR.check_object (
      schema_name        => 'OCGURU',
      object_name        => 'EMPLOYEES',
      repair_table_name => 'DR_REPAIR_TABLE',
      corrupt_count      => v_corr_blocks);
  DBMS_OUTPUT.PUT_LINE('Corrupt block count: ' ||
TO_CHAR(v_corr_blocks));
END;
```

Implement the DB_BLOCK_CHECKING parameter to detect corruptions

The initialization parameter DB_BLOCK_CHECKING is used to specify whether or not Oracle will perform block checking for database blocks. When enabled, Oracle will go through the data in a block, ensuring that it is logically self-consistent. This check can often prevent memory and data corruption. However, performing the check can incur a 1% to 10% overhead in reading the block. The specific overhead depends on the database workload and the parameter value used. Oracle recommends setting the DB_BLOCK_CHECKING parameter to FULL if the performance overhead is acceptable. The valid values for the parameter are:

- **OFF** -- No block checking is performed for blocks in user tablespaces. However, semantic block checking for SYSTEM tablespace blocks is always turned on. For backward compatibility, a value of FALSE will be treated as OFF.
- **LOW** -- Basic block header checks are performed after block contents change in memory (for example, after UPDATE or INSERT statements, on-disk reads, or inter-instance block transfers in Oracle RAC).

- **MEDIUM** -- All LOW checks and full semantic checks are performed for all objects except indexes (whose contents can be reconstructed by a drop and rebuild on encountering a corruption).
- **FULL** -- All LOW and MEDIUM checks and full semantic checks are performed for all objects. For backward compatibility, a value of TRUE will be treated as FULL.

Performing Restore and Recovery Operations

Describe and tune instance recovery

Instance and crash recovery is the automatic application of redo log records to data blocks after a crash or system failure. Any time an instance is shut down cleanly, changes that are in memory but have not been written to the data files are written to disk during the shutdown checkpoint. However, if a database is shut down with the abort option, or a single instance database crashes or if all instances of an Oracle RAC configuration crash, then this checkpoint does not occur. In these cases, the Oracle Database will perform a crash recovery on the next startup. There are two steps to instance and crash recovery: cache recovery followed by transaction recovery. Because the database can be opened once cache recovery completes, improving the performance of this step increases availability of the database.

- **Cache Recovery** – In the cache recovery step (also known as rolling forward), the Database applies all committed and uncommitted changes in the redo log files to the affected data blocks. The amount of work required for cache recovery is proportional to the rate of change for the database and the time between checkpoints.
- **Transaction Recovery** – Once all changes from the redo log are applied to the data files, any changes that were not committed at the time of the crash must be rolled back. In the transaction recovery step, the database uses rollback information to back out the uncommitted changes.

Periodically, Oracle Database records the highest system change number (SCN) for which all data blocks less than or equal to that SCN are known to be written out to the data files. This is called a checkpoint. If there is an instance failure, only redo records with changes above the last checkpoint SCN must be applied during recovery. The duration of cache recovery processing is determined by two factors: the number of data blocks that have changes at SCNs higher than the SCN of the checkpoint, and the number of log blocks that need to be read to find those changes. A database that checkpoints frequently will write dirty buffers to the data files more often. This will reduce cache recovery time in the event of an instance failure because fewer redo blocks will have to be applied to the datafiles. However, frequent checkpointing in a high-update system can reduce database performance.

Oracle's Fast-Start Fault Recovery feature is intended to reduce cache recovery time and make it more predictable. It does this by limiting the number of dirty buffers and the number of redo records generated between the most recent redo record and the last checkpoint. This feature uses the Fast-Start checkpointing architecture instead of conventional event-driven checkpointing. Instead of the bulk writes used by conventional checkpointing, fast-start checkpointing occurs incrementally. Each DBWn process periodically writes buffers to disk to advance the checkpoint position. This eliminates the I/O spikes that occur with conventional checkpointing. The FAST_START_MTTR_TARGET initialization parameter enables Fast-Start Fault Recovery and simplifies the configuration of recovery time from instance or system failure. The parameter sets a target for the expected mean time to recover (MTTR). The value of parameter is the time (in seconds) that it should take to start up the instance and perform cache recovery. Once set, the database manages incremental checkpoints in an attempt to meet that target.

Perform complete and incomplete recovery

Use RMAN RESTORE and RECOVER commands

The RESTORE and RECOVER commands are used for the restoration and recovery of physical database files. The RESTORE command retrieves files from backups as needed for a recovery operation. The RECOVER command performs media recovery. Media recovery is the application of changes from redo logs and incremental backups to a restored data file in order to bring the data file forward to a desired SCN or point in time

In order to use the RESTORE DATABASE and RECOVER DATABASE commands to recover the database, backups of all needed files must have been taken and be accessible. This example below assumes that it is possible restore all data files to their original locations. The following example uses the RESTORE AND RECOVER commands to recover the whole database:

1. Start RMAN and connect to the target database.
2. Optionally, list the current tablespaces and data files, as shown in the following command:

   ```
   RMAN> REPORT SCHEMA;
   ```

3. Run the RESTORE DATABASE command with the PREVIEW option.

   ```
   RMAN> RESTORE DATABASE PREVIEW SUMMARY;
   ```

4. Place the database in a mounted state.

   ```
   RMAN> STARTUP FORCE MOUNT;
   ```

5. Restore the database.

   ```
   RMAN> RESTORE DATABASE;
   ```

6. Recover the database, as shown in the following example:

   ```
   RMAN> RECOVER DATABASE;
   ```

7. Open the database, as shown in the following example:

   ```
   RMAN> ALTER DATABASE OPEN;
   ```

Restore ASM disk groups

The ASM command-line utility (ASMCMD) provides the ability to backup and restore the metadata for ASM disk groups. Earlier in this guide, the ASMCMD command **md_backup** was introduced. This command is used to create a backup of disk group metadata. The **md_restore** command is the complement to the **md_backup** command. It uses a previously created ASM metadata backup file to recreate diskgroups in an ASM instance.

The syntax of the md_restore command is:

```
md_restore -b backup_file
```

- **-b** -- Specifies the backup_file.
- **-I** -- Ignore errors. Normally, if md_restore encounters an error, it will stop.
- **-t** -- Specifies the type of disk group to be created:
- **full** -- Create disk group and restore metadata
- **nodg** -- Restore metadata only.
- **newdg** -- Create disk group with a different name and restore metadata; -o is required.
- **-f** -- Write SQL commands to <sql_script_file> instead of executing them.
- **-g** -- Select the disk groups to be restored. If left off, all disk groups will be restored.
- **-o** -- Rename disk group old_diskgroup_name to new_diskgroup_name.

Recover from media failures

A media failure occurs when there is a physical problem with a drive that stores one or more files used by the Oracle database. The physical problem causes a failure of a read from or write to a disk file that is required to run the database. The elements affected can be any of the files used by Oracle, including the data files, archived redo log files, or control file. Any time that a media failure is detected by Oracle, it takes the affected files offline. The appropriate recovery technique following a media failure depends on the files affected and the types of backup available.

113

The most common form of recovery following a media failure is data file media recovery. This involves restoring data file backups and applying archived redo logs or incremental backups to recover lost changes. When using data file media recovery, it is possible to either recover a whole database or a subset of the database. Data file media recovery is the most general-purpose form of recovery and can protect against both physical and logical failures. A number of the following chapters deal with specific subsets of data file media recovery.

Perform complete and incomplete or "point-in-time" recoveries using RMAN

Incomplete recovery of a database, also known as Database Point-In-Time recovery (DBPITR) restores a database to a time earlier than the one that is the target time. It then uses incremental backups and/or redo to roll the database forward until the target point is reached. It is possible to recover to a specific time, SCN, log sequence number, or restore point. Creating restore points at important times is recommended to make PITR easier if it is required. If it is possible to perform a Flashback Database operation to the desired point, then this is a considerably easier option than performing DBPITR through media recovery. In order to perform DBPITR, the following pre-requisites must be met:

- The database must be running in ARCHIVELOG mode.
- There must be backups of all data files from before the target SCN and archived logs for the period between the SCN of the backups and the target SCN.

When performing DBPITR, setting the target time using the SET UNTIL command at the beginning of the procedure reduces the potential for problems. Specifying the UNTIL clause on the RESTORE and RECOVER commands individually has the potential to restore backups that are not early enough to be used in the RECOVER operation. The DBPITR example below makes the following assumptions:

- The DBPITR is being performed within the current database incarnation.
- The control file is current.
- The database is using the current server parameter file.

1. Determine the time, SCN, restore point, or log sequence that ends recovery.
2. When using a target time expression instead of a target SCN, verify the time format environment variables before invoking RMAN.
3. Connect RMAN to the target database and, if applicable, the recovery catalog database. The database should be set to MOUNT status:

```
SHUTDOWN IMMEDIATE;
STARTUP MOUNT;
```

4. Perform the following operations within a RUN block:
   o Use SET UNTIL to specify the target time, SCN, or log sequence number, or SET TO when specifying a restore point.
   o If automatic channels are not configured, then manually allocate disk and tape channels as needed.
   o Restore and recover the database.

```
RUN
{
SET UNTIL SCN 123456;
RESTORE DATABASE;
RECOVER DATABASE;
}
```

Alternately, the SET line can use time expressions, restore points, or log sequence numbers:

```
SET UNTIL TIME '12-JAN-2014 12:00:00';
SET UNTIL SEQUENCE 4397;
SET TO RESTORE POINT fy2015_end;
```

5. If the operation completes with no errors, open the database read-only in SQL*Plus. Perform queries as needed to ensure that the database contains the desired information.

```
ALTER DATABASE OPEN READ ONLY;
```

6. If you are satisfied with the results, then open the database for read/write, abandoning all changes after the target SCN. The database must be shut down, remounted, and then opened with RESETLOGS:

```
SHUTDOWN IMMEDIATE;
STARTUP MOUNT;
ALTER DATABASE OPEN RESETLOGS;
```

Performing a complete recovery is less complex than an incomplete recovery. There is no requirement to pick a point to end the recovery at and there is no need to use the RESETLOGS command when opening the database after the recovery operation is complete.

1. Connect RMAN to the target database and, if applicable, the recovery catalog database. The database should be set to MOUNT status:

```
SHUTDOWN IMMEDIATE;
STARTUP MOUNT;
```

2. Perform the following operations within a RUN block:
    o If automatic channels are not configured, then manually allocate disk and tape channels as needed.
    o Restore and recover the database.

```
RUN
{
RESTORE DATABASE;
RECOVER DATABASE;
}
```

3. If the operation completes with no errors, open the database in SQL*Plus

```
ALTER DATABASE OPEN;
```

Perform automated TSPITR

TSPITR stands for Tablespace Point-In-Time Recovery. Recovery Manager TSPITR enables you to recover one or more tablespaces in a database to an earlier time. Unlike incomplete recovery TSPITR can be performed without affecting the rest of the tablespaces and objects in the database. TSPITR is useful in several situations:

- Recovering a logical database to a point different from the rest of the physical database, when multiple logical databases exist in separate tablespaces of one physical database.
- Recovering data lost after data definition language (DDL) operations that change the structure of tables.
- Recovering a table after it has been dropped with the PURGE option.
- Recovering from the logical corruption of a table.
- Recovering dropped tablespaces.

RMAN TSPITR is complex enough that I highly recommend reading the "Performing RMAN Tablespace Point-in-Time Recovery (TSPITR)" chapter in the Oracle Database Backup and Recovery User's Guide. While this section of the study guide will cover the test topic as listed on the Oracle Education site, if you don't really understand TSPITR, you will not have the background to really perform this function. Also, depending on how the questions are worded in the test, you may not have sufficient context to answer them.

To perform fully automated RMAN TSPITR, the user performing the operation should be able to connect as SYSDBA using operating system authentication. The AUXILIARY DESTINATION parameter is used to set a location for RMAN to use for the auxiliary set data files. The auxiliary destination must be a location on disk with enough space to hold auxiliary set data files.

1. Start an RMAN session on the target database and, if applicable, connect to a recovery catalog.
2. Configure any channels required for TSPITR on the target instance.
3. Run the RECOVER TABLESPACE command, specifying both the UNTIL clause and the AUXILIARY DESTINATION parameter.

```
RECOVER TABLESPACE users, tools
UNTIL LOGSEQ 1700 THREAD 1
AUXILIARY DESTINATION '/u01/auxdest';
```

4. If TSPITR completes successfully, then back up the recovered tablespace before bringing it online. After you perform TSPITR on a tablespace, you can no longer use previous backups of that tablespace.
5. Bring the tablespace back online.

```
RMAN> SQL "ALTER TABLESPACE users, tools ONLINE";
```

Recovering Files Using RMAN

Perform recovery for spfile, control file, redo log files

When the server parameter file of a database is lost, RMAN can restore the file to its default location or to a specified location. Losing the server parameter file does not cause the instance to immediately stop. However, the instance must be shut down and restarted after restoring the file. There are several considerations when restoring the server parameter file:

- If an instance is started with a given server parameter file, then the existing file cannot be overwritten.
- When the instance has been started with a client-side initialization parameter file, RMAN will restores the server parameter file to the default location unless the TO clause is used in the restore command.
- Restoring an SPFILE is simplified when a recovery catalog is used because it contains the DBID.

The steps to restore the server parameter file from autobackup are:

1. Start RMAN.
2. If the database instance is started, then connect to the target database. If the instance is not started and a recovery catalog is not being used, run the SET DBID command to set the DBID of the target database.
3. Shut down the database instance and restart it to NOMOUNT status.

   ```
   STARTUP FORCE NOMOUNT;
   ```

4. Execute a RUN command to restore the server parameter file. The following example restores a server parameter file from an autobackup on tape:

```
RUN
{
ALLOCATE CHANNEL c1 DEVICE TYPE sbt PARMS ...;
SET UNTIL TIME 'SYSDATE-4';
SET CONTROLFILE AUTOBACKUP FORMAT
FOR DEVICE TYPE sbt TO '/u01/control_files/autobackup_%F';
SET DBID 348745982;
RESTORE SPFILE
TO '/tmp/spfileOCP.ora'
FROM AUTOBACKUP MAXDAYS 8;
}
```

5. Restart the database instance with the restored file.

If control file autobackups have been configured, the server parameter file will be backed up with the control file whenever an autobackup is taken. When restoring the server parameter file from a control file autobackup, the DBID for your database must be set before executing the RESTORE SPFILE FROM AUTOBACKUP command. If the autobackup is in a non-default format, the SET CONTROLFILE AUTOBACKUP FORMAT command must be executed to specify the format. The following example sets the DBID and restores the server parameter file using a control file autobackup in a non-default location.

```
SET DBID 348745982;
RUN
{
SET CONTROLFILE AUTOBACKUP FORMAT
FOR DEVICE TYPE DISK TO 'autobackup_format';
RESTORE SPFILE FROM AUTOBACKUP;
}
```

Recovering from the loss of a control file

The control file is critical to recovery of an Oracle database and so backing it up is of paramount importance. There are numerous ways to back up the control file. If you are using RMAN as your backup tool, the easiest of these is simply to configure RMAN to automatically back up the control file and server parameter file whenever a backup record is added. The autobackup feature is enabled and disabled as follows:

```
CONFIGURE CONTROLFILE AUTOBACKUP ON;
```

Even if CONTROLFILE AUTOBACKUP is not enabled, performing a whole database backup in RMAN will include a copy of the control file. The RMAN command BACKUP DATABASE is used to perform a whole database backup.

```
BACKUP DATABASE;
```

Outside of RMAN, there are two ALTER DATABASE commands that can be used to back up a control file. You can back up the control file to a binary file using the following statement:

```
ALTER DATABASE BACKUP CONTROLFILE TO '/oracle/backup/control.bkp';
```

Alternately, the following command writes a SQL script to a trace file that can be used to reproduce the control file. The alert log will contain the name and location of the trace file.

```
ALTER DATABASE BACKUP CONTROLFILE TO TRACE;
```

Finally, for a user managed backup while the database is shut down, you can use operating system commands to copy the control file.

In a recovery scenario where all copies of the current control file are lost or damaged, you must restore and mount a backup control file. Copy the backup control file to all of the locations listed in the CONTROL_FILES initialization parameter. After the files are in place, the RECOVER command must be issued, even if no datafiles have been restored.

```
RECOVER DATABASE USING BACKUP CONTROLFILE UNTIL CANCEL;
```

Once the restore operation has been completed, open the database with the RESETLOGS option.

Recovering from the loss of Redo Log files

If all members of an online redo log group are damaged, the recovery process depends on the type of online redo log group affected and the whether or not the database is in archivelog mode. If the damaged online redo log group is current and active, then it is needed for crash recovery; otherwise, it is not. You can determine the status of the group associated with the damage files from V$LOGFILE:

```
SELECT group#, status, member
FROM   v$logfile;

GROUP#     STATUS        MEMBER
-------    -----------   --------------------
0001                     /oracle/dbs/log1a.f
0001                     /oracle/dbs/log1b.f
0002       INVALID       /oracle/dbs/log2a.f
0002       INVALID       /oracle/dbs/log2b.f
0003                     /oracle/dbs/log3a.f
0003                     /oracle/dbs/log3b.f
```

You can determine which groups are active from the V$LOG view:

```
SELECT group#, status, archived
FROM   v$log;

GROUP#   STATUS      ARCHIVED
------   ---------   -----------
 0001    INACTIVE    YES
 0002    ACTIVE      NO
 0003    CURRENT     NO
```

If all members of an inactive online redo log group are damaged, then the procedure depends on whether it is possible to repair the media problem that damaged the group. If the failure is transient, then fix the problem. The log writer will reuse the redo log group when required. For permanent failures, the damaged redo log group will halt normal database operation when the database tries to use it. The damaged group must be reinitialized manually by issuing the ALTER DATABASE CLEAR LOGFILE statement.

If all members of an active (but not current) log group are damaged and the database is still running, issue the ALTER SYSTEM CHECKPOINT statement. If the checkpoint is successful, then the redo log group will become inactive. At this point you can follow the steps for an inactive online redo log group. If the checkpoint is unsuccessful, or the database has halted, then depending on the archiving mode you must follow the recovery procedures corresponding to the current log group.

The current log group is the one LGWR is currently writing to. If a LGWR I/O operation fails, then LGWR terminates and the instance is terminated. In this case, you must restore a backup, perform incomplete recovery, and open the database with the RESETLOGS option.

Recovering from the Loss of Active Logs in NOARCHIVELOG Mode

If the media failure is temporary, then correct the problem so that the database can reuse the group when required.

- Restore the database from a consistent, whole database backup (data files and control files).
- Mount the database:
- To allow the database to reset the online redo logs, you must first mimic incomplete recovery:

```
RECOVER DATABASE UNTIL CANCEL
CANCEL
```

- Open the database using the RESETLOGS option:

```
ALTER DATABASE OPEN RESETLOGS;
```

- Shut down the database consistently.

  `SHUTDOWN IMMEDIATE`

- Make a whole database backup.

Recovering from Loss of Active Logs in ARCHIVELOG Mode

- Begin incomplete media recovery, recovering up through the log before the damaged log.
- Ensure that the current name of the lost redo log can be used for a newly created file. If not, then rename the members of the damaged online redo log group to a new location.
- Open the database using the RESETLOGS option:

  `ALTER DATABASE OPEN RESETLOGS;`

Perform table recovery from backups

It is now possible to use RMAN backups to recover a single table or table partition without affecting the remaining data in the database. In order for this to be possible, you must have a full backup of the SYSTEM, SYSAUX, and UNDO tablespaces, the SYSEXT tablespace if one exists plus the tablespace containing the table or table partition to be recovered. This can be very useful when a small number of tables need to recovered without affecting the entire database and Flashback table is not possible for one of the following reasons:

- The desired point-in-time is older than available undo.
- Data was lost after a TRUNCATE or a DDL operation that modified the structure of tables.

When recovering tables and table partitions using an RMAN backup, the following information must be provided:

- The name(s) of the table or table partition that must be recovered.
- The point in time the data should be recovered to.
- Whether the recovered tables or table partitions must be imported into the target database.

This information allows RMAN to automate the process of recovering the specified objects. When performing a table recovery, RMAN creates an auxiliary database. This database is then used as a temporary container to recover the supplied tables to the specified point in time. The steps performed by RMAN during a table recovery are:

1. It determines which backup contains the tables or table partitions that need to be recovered.
2. An auxiliary database is created and the specified tables or table partitions are recovered into it until the specified point in time.
3. A Data Pump export dump file that contains the recovered tables or table partitions is generated from the auxiliary database.
4. Optionally, the dump file is imported into the target instance. If the dump file is not imported as part of the recovery process, it must be manually imported later using the Data Pump Import utility.
5. Optionally, the recovered tables or table partitions are renamed in the target database.

Perform recovery of index and read-only tablespaces, temp file

The common factor between a read only tablespace, a temporary tablespace and a tablespace that contains *only* indexes is that all three can be recovered without the application of redo. The specifics of why this is the case for each differs:

- A temporary tablespace never requires redo to be applied.
- A read-only tablespace generates no redo after being set to read-only.
- An index tablespace generates redo, but the information can be re-created without the application of redo logs.

This begs the question of what the Oracle certification means by having these under the 'RMAN' recovery section of the exam. RMAN <u>certainly</u> is not used when recovering a lost temp tablespace and often is not used for the other two. If it is used, then they are recovered in a fashion that is identical to other types of tablespaces, so there is no reason to break them out to a separate chapter. The recovery of all three types of tablespaces is covered in later sections under user-managed backup and recovery.

Restore a database to a new host

Restoring a database to a new host is a procedure that is used either to test out disaster recovery procedures or to permanently move a database to a new host. It is not the method that should be used to create a copy of an existing database. Restoring a database to a new host will result in a database with the same DBID as the original. When creating a copy of an existing database, the DUPLICATE command should be utilized. An RMAN DUPLICATE operation will assign a new DBID to the database it creates, allowing it to be registered in the same recovery catalog as the original database.

There are several steps to prepare for the restoration:

- Record the DBID of source database.
- Copy the source database initialization parameter file to the new host using OS commands.

- Ensure that RMAN is not connected to the recovery catalog. Otherwise, metadata about the restored data files will be stored in the recovery catalog which will interfere with future attempts to restore and recover the primary database.
- Ensure that backups used for the restore operation are accessible on the restore host.
- If this is a trial restore of the production database, then perform one of the following actions:
- If the fast recovery area of the new database is in a different location from the source, set DB_RECOVERY_FILE_DEST to the new location.
- If the fast recovery area will be the same physical location as the production database, set DB_UNIQUE_NAME in the test database instance to be different from the source database.

Once the above steps are completed, the disk backups must be restored to the new host. If the database will be moved to the new host using data file copies or backup sets on disk, the files must be transferred files manually to the new host:

1. Start RMAN and connect to a target database and recovery catalog.
2. Run a LIST command to see a listing of backups of the data file and control file autobackups.
3. Copy the backups to the new host with an operating system utility.

The steps to restore the database on a new host are:

1. Ensure that the backups from the above steps are accessible on the new host.
2. Configure the ORACLE_SID on the new host.

   ```
   % setenv ORACLE_SID ocpdb2
   ```

3. Start RMAN on the new host and connect to the target database without connecting to the recovery catalog.

```
% rman NOCATALOG
RMAN> CONNECT TARGET /
```

4. Set the DBID and start the database instance without mounting the database.

```
SET DBID 1470242087;
STARTUP NOMOUNT
```

5. Restore and edit the server parameter file. Assuming the control file autobackup feature was enabled, the server parameter file is included in the backup. Allocate a channel to the media manager and restore the server parameter file:

```
RUN
{
ALLOCATE CHANNEL c1 DEVICE TYPE sbt PARMS '...';
SET CONTROLFILE AUTOBACKUP FORMAT FOR DEVICE TYPE DISK TO
'/tmp/%F';
RESTORE SPFILE
TO PFILE '?/oradata/test/initocpdb2.ora'
FROM AUTOBACKUP;
SHUTDOWN ABORT;
}
```

6. Edit the restored initialization parameter file to correct any location-specific parameters.
7. Restart the instance with the edited initialization parameter file.

```
STARTUP FORCE NOMOUNT
    PFILE='?/oradata/test/initocpdb2.ora';
```

8. Restore the control file from an autobackup and then mount the database.

```
RUN
{
ALLOCATE CHANNEL c1 DEVICE TYPE sbt PARMS '...';
RESTORE CONTROLFILE FROM AUTOBACKUP;
ALTER DATABASE MOUNT;
}
```

9. Catalog the data file copies using their new file names:

```
CATALOG START WITH '/oracle/oradata/ocpdb2/';
```

Alternately, specify files individually:

```
CATALOG DATAFILECOPY
'/oracle/oradata/ocpdb2/system01.dbf',
'/oracle/oradata/ocpdb2/undotbs01.dbf',
'/oracle/oradata/ocpdb2/tools01.dbf',
'/oracle/oradata/ocpdb2t/users01.dbf';
```

10. Start a SQL*Plus session on the new database and query the database file names recorded in the control file. The recorded file names will be what existed on the original host. You can query V$ views to obtain this information:

```
SPOOL LOG '/tmp/ocpdb2_dbfiles.out'
SELECT file# AS "File/Grp#", name
FROM   v$datafile
UNION
SELECT group#, member
FROM   v$logfile;
SPOOL OFF
EXIT
```

11. Create an RMAN restore and recovery script. It must include the following steps:
    a. For each data file that is restored to a different path than it had on the source host, a SET NEWNAME command must be used to specify the new path.
    b. For each online redo log that will be created at a different location, the SQL ALTER DATABASE RENAME FILE command must be used to specify the path name on the destination host.
    c. Perform a SET UNTIL operation to limit recovery to the end of the archived redo logs.
    d. Restore and recover the database.
    e. Run the SWITCH DATAFILE ALL command so that the control file recognizes the new path names as the official new names of the data files.

12. The following example RMAN script can perform the restore and recovery operation:

```
RUN
{
# allocate a channel to the tape device
ALLOCATE CHANNEL c1 DEVICE TYPE sbt PARMS '...';
# rename the data files and online redo logs
SET NEWNAME FOR DATAFILE 1 TO
'?/oradata/ocpdb2/system01.dbf';
SET NEWNAME FOR DATAFILE 2 TO
'?/oradata/ocpdb2/undotbs01.dbf';
SET NEWNAME FOR DATAFILE 7 TO '?/oradata/ocpdb2/tools01.dbf';
SET NEWNAME FOR DATAFILE 8 TO '?/oradata/ocpdb2/users01.dbf';
ALTER DATABASE RENAME FILE '/u03/oracle/dbs/redo01.log'
TO '?/oradata/ocpdb2/redo01.log';
ALTER DATABASE RENAME FILE '/u03/oracle/dbs/redo02.log'
TO '?/oradata/ocpdb2/redo02.log';
# Do a SET UNTIL to prevent recovery of the online logs
SET UNTIL SCN 234567;
# restore the database and switch the data file names
RESTORE DATABASE;
SWITCH DATAFILE ALL;
# recover the database
RECOVER DATABASE;
}
EXIT
```

13. Execute the script created in the previous step.

```
% rman TARGET / NOCATALOG
RMAN> @ocpdb2_test.rman
```

14. Open the restored database with the RESETLOGS option.

```
ALTER DATABASE OPEN RESETLOGS;
```

Recover using incrementally updated backups

The incrementally updated backup feature allows for a very efficient backup strategy. Incrementally updated backups have the following features:

- A level 0 data file copy is required as a base. This copy has either a system-defined or user-defined tag.

- Periodically, level 1 differential backups are created with the same tag as the level 0 data file copy. The BACKUP FOR RECOVER OF COPY command specifies that an incremental backup contains only blocks changed since the most recent incremental backup with the same tag.
- The incremental backups are periodically applied to the level 0 data file copy. This process 'rolls forward' the data file copy to contain more recent changes. If it is required for a restore operation it will require less media recovery.

When performing media recovery, RMAN will examine the restored files to determine if any of them can be recovered using an incremental backup. If it is an option, RMAN will always choose incremental backups over archived redo logs. Applying changes to a datafile at a block level is faster than applying redo. There is no need for RMAN to restore a base incremental backup of a data file in order to apply incremental backups to the data file during recovery. This makes it possible to restore data file image copies and recover them with incremental backups.

Switch to image copies for fast recovery

One option to reduce database recovery time is to use incrementally updated backups. In this strategy, an image copy of each data file is created. Periodically the image copy is rolled forward by making and applying a level 1 incremental backup. If the image files need to be used for recovery, the only redo that needs to be applied is whatever redo has been generated since the last incremental backup.

Incrementally Updating Backups

This process avoids the overhead of making full image copy backups of datafiles, while minimizing media recovery time. If incremental changes are created and applied by a daily backup script, there will never be more than 1 day of redo to apply during media recovery. After the incremental changes have been made to a given backup data file, it will be identical to the datafile at the time of the most recently applied incremental level 1 backup.

- Create a full image copy backup of a data file with a specified tag.
- At regular intervals, make a level 1 differential incremental backup of the data file with the same tag as the base data file copy.
- Apply the incremental backup to the most recent backup with the same tag.

To create incremental backups for use in an incrementally updated backup strategy, use the BACKUP ... FOR RECOVER OF COPY WITH TAG form of the BACKUP command. The script following is a very basic example of implementing a strategy based on incrementally updated backups.

```
RUN
{
  RECOVER COPY OF DATABASE
    WITH TAG 'incr_update';
  BACKUP
    INCREMENTAL LEVEL 1
    FOR RECOVER OF COPY WITH TAG 'incr_update'
    DATABASE;
}
```

Perform disaster recovery

Disaster recovery assumes that the entire database has been lost, including all datafiles, the recovery catalog database, all current control files, all online redo log files, and all parameter files. Recovering the database in the event of a loss like this requires:

- Backups of all datafiles
- All archived redo logs generated after the creation time of the oldest backup that you intend to restore

- At least one control file autobackup
- A record of the DBID of the database

In this recovery, it is assumed that the server hardware the database was on has been damaged beyond repair. A full backup exists and the Oracle software has been installed on a new host with the same directory structure. The four requirements listed above have been met.

To recover the database on the new host:

1. If possible, restore or re-create all relevant network files such as tnsnames.ora and listener.ora and a password file.
2. Start RMAN and connect to the target database instance using operating system authentication.

   ```
   RMAN> CONNECT TARGET /
   ```

3. Specify the DBID for the target database with the SET DBID command.

   ```
   SET DBID 343487540;
   ```

4. Issue the STARTUP NOMOUNT command.
5. Allocate a channel to the media manager and then restore the server parameter file from autobackup.

   ```
   RUN
   {
   ALLOCATE CHANNEL c1 DEVICE TYPE sbt;
   RESTORE SPFILE FROM AUTOBACKUP;
   }
   ```

6. Restart the instance with the restored server parameter file.

   ```
   STARTUP FORCE NOMOUNT;
   ```

7. Write a command file to perform the restore and recovery operation, and then execute the command file. The command file should do the following:
   o Allocate a channel to the media manager.
   o Restore a control file autobackup.
   o Mount the restored control file.

- o Catalog any backups not recorded in the repository with the CATALOG command.
- o Restore the datafiles to their original locations.
- o Recover the datafiles. RMAN stops recovery when it reaches the log sequence number specified.

```
RMAN> RUN
{
ALLOCATE CHANNEL t1 DEVICE TYPE sbt;
RESTORE CONTROLFILE FROM AUTOBACKUP;
ALTER DATABASE MOUNT;
RESTORE DATABASE;
RECOVER DATABASE;
}
```

8. If recovery was successful, then open the database and reset the online logs:

```
ALTER DATABASE OPEN RESETLOGS;
```

Using Oracle Secure Backup

Configure and use Oracle Secure Backup

Oracle Secure Backup is a media manager solution from Oracle. It serves as a media management layer for RMAN through the SBT interface. Oracle Secure Backup is designed to protect data as it is backed up through the file system to tape. It supports major tape drives and tape libraries in SAN, Gigabit Ethernet, and SCSI environments. The Oracle Secure Backup Cloud Module can also provide integrated Oracle Database backup to third-party cloud storage. Oracle Secure Backup comes in two editions:

- **Oracle Secure Backup** -- This version supports distributed environments consisting of multiple servers. It provides advanced data protection requirements including encryption, rotation of tapes between multiple locations, and protection of NAS devices.
- **Oracle Secure Backup Express** -- This edition is available free with the Oracle Database. It is the same core product, but the Express edition is limited to a single host with one direct-attached tape drive. It also has some restrictions on the usage of advanced features.

There is also the Oracle Secure Backup Cloud Module. This is independent of the Oracle Secure Backup tape management editions. The cloud module provides Oracle Database backup to cloud storage using Recovery Manager (RMAN). It can be used in addition to the Oracle Secure Backup tape management solution or other third-party media-management products.

The basic steps to configure Oracle Secure Backup for use with RMAN follow. For more details on these steps, read the Oracle Secure Backup Installation and Configuration Guide.

1. Configure RMAN access to the Oracle Secure Backup SBT.
2. Create an Oracle Secure Backup user preauthorized for RMAN operations.

3. Create media families for data files and archived redo logs. This is optional, but recommended. If no media families are created, the RMAN-DEFAULT media family will be used.
4. Optionally, configure database backup storage selectors or RMAN media management parameters.

In order for Oracle Secure Backup to honor SBT requests, the user making the request must be preauthorized for RMAN backup on that host. The preauthorized Oracle Secure Backup user must meet two sets of requirements.

- The user must be mapped to operating system privileges that allow them to access the files to be backed up or restored.
- The user must be assigned to an Oracle Secure Backup class possessing the rights to access Oracle backups (set to owner, class, or all) and to perform Oracle backups and restores.

Only a single Oracle Secure Backup user can be preauthorized on a particular host. It is possible to have multiple RMAN users who can start backup or restore operations. It is also possible to preauthorize an Oracle Secure Backup user for command-line (obtool) operations. Users with this capability can utilize backup and restore scripts. It is possible to configure a preauthorized user during installation of the Oracle Secure Backup software. After installation a user can be configured using either the Oracle Secure Backup Web tool or the mkuser command in obtool.

Using Flashback Technologies

Describe the Flashback technologies

Configure a database to use Flashback technologies

There are a number of different capabilities that Oracle includes under the 'Flashback' umbrella. The methods used to implement them likewise make use of several different technologies. The common factor of all the Oracle Flashback features is that they allow database administrators to either view data as it existed at a previous point in time or to change data in the database to match what existed at an earlier point in time. That said, the various Flashback technologies and how to configure them for use follow

Flashback Table

By default, when a table is dropped, the database does not immediately remove the space associated with the table. Instead, the database renames it and places the table and any associated objects that were dropped in a recycle bin. If it is determined that the table was dropped in error, it can be recovered at a later date. The FLASHBACK TABLE statement is used to restore the table.

The recycle bin is a data dictionary table that contains information required to recover dropped objects. The dropped objects themselves remain where they were before being dropped and still occupy the same amount of disk space. Dropped objects also continue to count against user space quotas until they are explicitly purged or are purged by the database due to tablespace space constraints. The Oracle recycle bin is enabled by default, so there is no configuration required to use this feature.

Flashback Query

Flashback Query, Flashback Version Query and Flashback Transaction Query all make use of undo records to show data as it existed in the past. Flashback Transaction Query also gives information about transactions that have altered data. Oracle databases will always have an undo tablespace, so these features can be used without any configuration. The size of the undo tablespace will affect how far back in time it is possible to view data and transactions. The next chapter on undo retention will deal more with that.

Flashback Database

Oracle's Flashback Database feature allows you to set the database back to an earlier time in order to correct problems caused by logical data corruption or user errors within a designated time window. Flashback Database is much more efficient than performing a point-in-time recovery and does not require a backup and restore operation. Flashback Database is accessible through the RMAN command FLASHBACK DATABASE or the SQL statement FLASHBACK DATABASE.

To enable Flashback Database, the database must have a Fast Recovery Area configured and a flashback retention target set. This target specifies how far in the past it should possible to rewind the database. Flashback Database uses its own logging mechanism, creating flashback logs and storing them in the fast recovery area. The database must be set up in advance to create flashback logs in order to take advantage of this feature. Once configured, at regular intervals, the database copies images of each altered block in every data file into the flashback logs. These block images can later be used to reconstruct the data file contents to any moment for which logs exist. In addition to the flashback logs, redo logs on disk or tape must be available for the entire time period spanned by the flashback logs. The range of SCNs for which there is currently enough flashback log data to support the FLASHBACK DATABASE command is called the flashback database window.

If the Fast Recovery Area does not contain sufficient space for recovery files such as archived redo logs and other backups needed for the retention policy, the database may delete the flashback logs starting from the earliest SCNs. The flashback retention target does not guarantee that Flashback Database is available for the full period. A larger Fast Recovery Area may be required in this case.

Guarantee undo retention

Any time that automatic undo management is enabled, there is an undo retention period. This is the minimum amount of time that the database will try to keep old undo information from being overwritten. The undo retention period is based on the undo tablespace size and system activity. It is possible to use the UNDO_RETENTION initialization parameter to specify a minimum undo retention period.

It the undo tablespace is fixed size, the value of UNDO_RETENTION is ignored. The database automatically uses system activity and undo tablespace size to tune the undo retention period for the best possible retention. For an undo tablespace set to AUTOEXTEND, the database will attempt to honor the specified UNDO_RETENTION period. When space is low, the tablespace will auto-extend (up to the MAXSIZE) instead of overwriting unexpired undo information. If the MAXSIZE is reached, the database may not be able to meet the UNDO_RETENTION value. The minimum undo retention period (in seconds) can be set in two ways:

- Set UNDO_RETENTION in the initialization parameter file.

```
UNDO_RETENTION = 2000
```

- The UNDO_RETENTION value can be modified dynamically using the ALTER SYSTEM statement.

```
ALTER SYSTEM SET UNDO_RETENTION = 3000;
```

The effect of an UNDO_RETENTION parameter change can only be honored if the current undo tablespace has sufficient space.

When using a fixed-size undo tablespace, the Undo Advisor is valuable for estimating the optimum size. It can be accessed through Oracle Enterprise Manager Express or through DBMS_ADVISOR. The Undo Advisor uses AWR data to create its analysis, so there must be sufficient workload statistics available for it to make accurate recommendations. When using the Undo Advisor, two values must be estimated:

- The length of the expected longest running query.
- The longest interval required for Oracle Flashback operations

The larger of these two values is used as input to the Undo Advisor. The Undo Advisor does not alter the size of the undo tablespace, it only offers a recommended size. You must use ALTER DATABASE statements to change the tablespace data file size. The following example changes an undo tablespace with a file called undotbs.dbf to a fixed size of 400MB.

```
ALTER DATABASE DATAFILE '/u01/oracle/dbs/undotbs.dbf' RESIZE 400M;
ALTER DATABASE DATAFILE '/u01/oracle/dbs/undotbs.dbf' AUTOEXTEND OFF;
```

The RETENTION_GUARANTEE clause is used to guarantee the success of long-running queries or Oracle Flashback operations. When enabled, the specified minimum undo retention is guaranteed. Oracle will never overwrite unexpired undo data even when doing so means that transactions fail from lack of space in the undo tablespace. When retention guarantee is disabled (the default), the database can overwrite unexpired undo when space is low. The RETENTION GUARANTEE clause can be specified for an undo tablespace at create time with either the

CREATE DATABASE or CREATE UNDO TABLESPACE statement. The clause can be used to modify an existing tablespace using the ALTER TABLESPACE statement. Retention guarantee is disabled with the RETENTION NOGUARANTEE clause.

Use Flashback to query data

Use Flashback Query

Oracle Flashback Query allows a prior time to be specified when executing a query against the database. The query will return results as they would have appeared at that time. This can be used to recover from an unwanted change in the recent past by selecting a target time before the error and executing a query to retrieve the lost or damaged data.

The Oracle Flashback Query capability is implemented via the AS OF clause in a SELECT statement. When the AS OF clause is included, Oracle retrieves data as it existed at an earlier point in time. The AS OF clause must explicitly reference a past time through a time stamp or System Change Number (SCN). When a timestamp is used, the time will be accurate to within three seconds. If greater accuracy is required, an SCN should be utilized. The query will return committed data that was current at the specified time/SCN. The following example retrieves the row for employee with the ID 107 at an earlier point in time:

```
SELECT *
FROM   hr.employees
AS OF TIMESTAMP
    TO_TIMESTAMP('2014-03-14 12:30:00', 'YYYY-MM-DD HH:MI:SS')
WHERE employee_id = 107;
```

If that record had been accidentally deleted from the table, it could be recovered with the following statement:

```
INSERT INTO hr.employees
(SELECT *
 FROM   hr.employees
 AS OF TIMESTAMP
    TO_TIMESTAMP('2014-03-14 12:30:00', 'YYYY-MM-DD HH:MI:SS')
 WHERE employee_id = 107);
```

Use Flashback Version Query

Flashback Version Query is used to retrieve metadata and historical data for a specific interval. The interval can be specified by two timestamps or by two SCNs. The metadata returned includes the start and end time a version existed, type of DML operation used to create it, and the identity of the transaction that created each row version. The VERSIONS BETWEEN clause of a SELECT statement is used to generate a Flashback Version Query. The syntax of the VERSIONS BETWEEN clause is: VERSIONS {BETWEEN {SCN | TIMESTAMP} start AND end}.

The pseudocolumns returned by a Flashback version query are:

- **VERSIONS_START[SCN/TIME]** -- Starting System Change Number (SCN) or TIMESTAMP when the row version was created. NULL if version is from before the start value.
- **VERSIONS_END[SCN/TIME]** -- SCN or TIMESTAMP when the row version expired. If NULL, then either the row version was current at the time of the query or the row is for a DELETE operation.
- **VERSIONS_XID** -- Identifier of the transaction that created the row version.
- **VERSIONS_OPERATION** -- Operation performed by the transaction: I for insertion, D for deletion, or U for update. The version is that of the row that was inserted, deleted, or updated.

A given row version is valid starting at VERSIONS_START* up to, but not including, VERSIONS_END*. That is, it is valid for any time 't' such that VERSIONS_START* <= t < VERSIONS_END*. The following three updates were issued against the EMPLOYEES table, with a pause in-between.

```
UPDATE employees SET salary = 97000
WHERE emp_last='McCoy';
UPDATE employees SET salary = 102000
WHERE emp_last='McCoy';
UPDATE employees SET salary = 105000
WHERE emp_last='McCoy';
COMMIT;
```

Then the following Flashback Versions query was run against employees:

```
SELECT versions_starttime, versions_endtime,
       versions_xid, versions_operation AS OP,
       salary
  FROM employees
  VERSIONS BETWEEN TIMESTAMP
     TO_TIMESTAMP('22-FEB-14 11.46.00PM','DD-MON-YY HH:MI:SSAM')
  AND TO_TIMESTAMP('22-FEB-14 11.52.00PM','DD-MON-YY HH:MI:SSAM')
  WHERE emp_last = 'McCoy';
```

```
VERSIONS_STARTTIME     VERSIONS_ENDTIME       VERSIONS_XID      OP SALARY
-------------------    --------------------   ----------------  -- ------
22-FEB-14 11.51.08PM                          09000900A9010000  U  105000
22-FEB-14 11.49.50PM   22-FEB-14 11.51.08PM   04001A003F010000  U  102000
22-FEB-14 11.49.02PM   22-FEB-14 11.49.50PM   03002100A2010000  U   97000
                       22-FEB-14 11.49.02PM                          93500
```

From the results above, you see the three updates against the table, each increasing the salary column value. It's clear when each salary value started and ended (save the initial value for which the start time was outside the window, and the final value which is current (and therefore has no end time). You can use VERSIONS_XID with Oracle Flashback Transaction Query to locate the metadata for any of the three transactions. This will include the SQL required to undo the row change and the user responsible for the change.

Use Flashback Transaction Query

Oracle Flashback Transaction allows a transaction to be reversed. Oracle will determine the dependencies between transactions and create a compensating transaction to reverse the unwanted change. The result is a state as if the transaction and any dependent transactions had never happened.

A Flashback Transaction Query is used to retrieve metadata and historical data for a single transaction or for all transactions in a supplied interval. The data is generated from the static data dictionary view FLASHBACK_TRANSACTION_QUERY. The Flashback Transaction Query creates a column UNDO_SQL. The SQL text in this field is the logical opposite of the DML operation performed by the transaction shown. The code from this field can usually reverse the original transaction within reason (e.g. a SQL_UNDO INSERT operation would be unlikely to insert a row back at the same ROWID from which it was deleted). As a general rule, Oracle Flashback Transaction Query is used in conjunction with an Oracle Flashback Version Query that provides transaction IDs.

```
SELECT operation, start_scn, commit_scn, logon_user
  FROM flashback_transaction_query
    WHERE xid = HEXTORAW('09000900A9010000');

OPERATION    START_SCN COMMIT_SCN LOGON_USER
-----------  --------- ---------- ------------
UNKNOWN         393394     393463 OCPGURU
BEGIN           393394     393463 OCPGURU
```

The following statement uses Oracle Flashback Version Query as a subquery to associate each row version with the LOGON_USER responsible for the row data change.

```
SELECT xid, logon_user
  FROM flashback_transaction_query
    WHERE xid IN (
      SELECT versions_xid
      FROM employees VERSIONS BETWEEN TIMESTAMP
        TO_TIMESTAMP('22-FEB-14 11.40.00 PM',
                     'DD-MON-YY HH:MI:SS AM') AND
        TO_TIMESTAMP('22-FEB-14 11.56.00 PM',
                     'DD-MON-YY HH:MI:SS AM'));
```

You can use the DBMS_FLASHBACK.TRANSACTION_BACKOUT procedure to roll back a transaction and its dependent transactions while the database remains online. Transaction backout uses undo data to create and execute the compensating transactions to return the affected data to its original state. TRANSACTION_BACKOUT does not commit the DML operations that it performs as part of transaction backout. However, it does hold all the required locks on rows and tables in the right form to prevent other dependencies from entering the system. To make the transaction backout permanent, you must explicitly commit the transaction.

In order to configure a database for the **Oracle Flashback Transaction Query** feature, the database must be running in ARCHIVELOG mode. In addition, the database administrator must enable supplemental logging.

```
ALTER DATABASE ADD SUPPLEMENTAL LOG DATA;
```

To perform Oracle Flashback Query operations, the administrator must grant appropriate privileges to the user who will be performing them. For Oracle Flashback Query, the administrator can do either of the following:

- To allow access to specific objects during queries, grant FLASHBACK and SELECT privileges on those objects.
- To allow queries on all tables, grant the FLASHBACK ANY TABLE privilege.

For Oracle Flashback Transaction Query, the administrator will need to grant the SELECT ANY TRANSACTION privilege. To allow execution of undo SQL code retrieved by an Oracle Flashback Transaction, the administrator will need to grant: SELECT, UPDATE, DELETE, and INSERT privileges for the appropriate tables. Finally, the administrator will need to grant the user EXECUTE privileges on the DBMS_FLASHBACK Package.

Flash back a transaction

The following example updates a record in the AIRCRAFT_FLIGHTS table. It then locates the transaction ID using a Flashback versions query. The transaction ID can be used to locate the SQL required to undo the transaction from the UNDO_SQL column of a Flashback Transaction Query. The text in the UNDO_SQL column is then executed to reverse the original transaction.

```
UPDATE aircraft_flights
SET    flight_id = 'Flight 081109'
WHERE  flt_id = 1600;
1 rows updated.

SELECT versions_xid, versions_operation AS OP, flight_id
  FROM aircraft_flights
  VERSIONS BETWEEN TIMESTAMP
      TO_TIMESTAMP('26-MAY-15 11.03.00PM','DD-MON-YY HH:MI:SSAM')
  AND TO_TIMESTAMP('26-MAY-15 11.05.00PM','DD-MON-YY HH:MI:SSAM')
  WHERE flt_id = 1600;

VERSIONS_XID     OP FLIGHT_ID
---------------- -- ------------
02001F0034030010 U  Flight 081109


SELECT undo_sql
  FROM flashback_transaction_query
    WHERE xid = HEXTORAW('02001F0034030010');

UNDO_SQL
-----------------------------------------------------------
update "OCPGURU"."AIRCRAFT_FLIGHTS" set "FLIGHT_ID" =
'Flight 081108' where ROWID = 'AAALRXAAEAAABLhABX';


update "OCPGURU"."AIRCRAFT_FLIGHTS"
set "FLIGHT_ID" = 'Flight 081108'
where ROWID = 'AAALRXAAEAAABLhABX';
1 rows updated.
```

Perform Flashback Table operations

Perform Flashback Table

By default, when a table is dropped, the database does not immediately remove the space associated with the table. Instead, the database renames it and places the table and any associated objects that were dropped in a recycle bin. If it is determined that the table was dropped in error, it can be recovered at a later date. The FLASHBACK TABLE statement can be used to restore the table.

The recycle bin is a data dictionary table that contains information required to recover dropped objects. The dropped objects themselves remain where they were before being dropped and still occupy the same amount of disk space. Dropped objects also continue to count against user space quotas until they are explicitly purged or are purged by the database due to tablespace space constraints.

When a tablespace including its contents is dropped, the recycle bin does not come into play. The storage where the objects were no longer exists. The database purges any entries in the recycle bin for objects that were located in the tablespace. If the recycle bin is disabled, dropped tables and their dependent objects are simply dropped. They must be recovered by other means, such as recovering from backup. The recycle bin is enabled by default.

The FLASHBACK TABLE ... TO BEFORE DROP statement is used to recover objects from the recycle bin. When recovering a table, you must specify either the system-generated name of the table in the recycle bin or the original table name. An optional RENAME TO clause lets you rename the table as you recover it. The USER_RECYCLEBIN view can be used to obtain the system-generated name. To use the FLASHBACK TABLE ... TO BEFORE DROP statement, you need the same privileges required to drop the table.

Restore tables from the recycle bin

The following example creates a test table, FB_DROP_TEST, drops it, and then restores it using the FLASHBACK TABLE capability.

```
CREATE TABLE fb_drop_test (
col1    NUMBER);
table FB_DROP_TEST created.

INSERT INTO fb_drop_test VALUES (1);
1 rows inserted.

DROP TABLE fb_drop_test;
table FB_DROP_TEST dropped.

SELECT * FROM fb_drop_test;
Error report -
SQL Error: ORA-00942: table or view does not exist
00942. 00000 -  "table or view does not exist"

FLASHBACK TABLE fb_drop_test TO BEFORE DROP;
table FB_DROP_TEST succeeded.

SELECT * FROM fb_drop_test;
     COL1
----------
     1
```

When performing the FLASHBACK TABLE operation, it is possible to rename the table. This might be used if a new table has already been created with the same name since the original was dropped. The following example demonstrates using the RENAME option:

```
DROP TABLE fb_drop_test;
table FB_DROP_TEST dropped.

FLASHBACK TABLE fb_drop_test TO BEFORE DROP
RENAME TO fb_drop_test2;
table FB_DROP_TEST succeeded.

SELECT * FROM fb_drop_test2;
     COL1
----------
     1
```

Describe and use Flashback Data Archive

Use Flashback Data Archive

Oracle's Flashback Data Archive feature allows you to store table-level change history for extended periods of time. It provides the ability to track all transactional changes to a table over its lifetime. The Flashback Data Archive functionality is useful to maintain compliance with record storage policies and audit reports. It is possible to have multiple Flashback Data Archives in a single database, one of which can be (although it is not required), specified as the default for the database. Each Flashback Data Archive in a database is configured with a retention time that determines how long data stored in that particular archive is to be retained.

Flashback archiving is off for any table by default. You can enable flashback archiving for a table if all of the following are true:

- You have the FLASHBACK ARCHIVE object privilege on the Flashback Data Archive that you want to use for that table.
- The table you want to archive is not nested, clustered, temporary, remote, or external.
- The table does not contain LONG or nested columns.

Once flashback archiving is enabled for a table, you can disable it only if you either have the FLASHBACK ARCHIVE ADMINISTER system privilege or you are logged into the database with SYSDBA privileges. While flashback archiving is enabled for a table, some DDL statements are not allowed on it and will generate an ORA-55610 error. The following operations are disallowed:

- ALTER TABLE statement that includes an UPGRADE TABLE clause, with or without an INCLUDING DATA clause
- ALTER TABLE statement that moves or exchanges a partition or subpartition operation
- DROP TABLE statement

Flashback Data Archive can be the solution to any number of business requirements. Many government agencies and organizations require that data be kept for a set number of years before being deleted. The settings of a Flashback Data Archive can be specifically configured to meet these requirements. After the specified time period has expired, the data will automatically be aged out of the archive – effectively 'shredding' it without requiring direct intervention. It can help in satisfying some of the storage requirements for such legislative acts as Sarbanes-Oxley and HIPAA. It can provide a source of data for audits. Flashback data archive can also be used as a simple method to recover accidentally altered or deleted data.

A Flashback Data Archive is created using the CREATE FLASHBACK ARCHIVE statement. If you are logged on with SYSDBA privileges, you can also specify that this is the default Flashback Data Archive for the system. When creating a new flashback data archive, you must specify the following:

- Name of the Flashback Data Archive
- Name of the first tablespace of the Flashback Data Archive
- Retention time (number of days that Flashback Data Archive data for the table is guaranteed to be stored)
- (Optional) Maximum amount of space that the Flashback Data Archive can use in the first tablespace. The default is unlimited.

Create a default Flashback Data Archive named fda1 using a maximum of 15 Gigs of tablespace fda_tbs1. The data will be retained for two years:

```
CREATE FLASHBACK ARCHIVE DEFAULT fda1
TABLESPACE fda_tbs1 QUOTA 15G RETENTION 2 YEAR;
```

Create a Flashback Data Archive named fda2 that uses tablespace fda_tbs2, whose data will be retained for three years:

```
CREATE FLASHBACK ARCHIVE fda2
TABLESPACE fda_tbs2 RETENTION 3 YEAR;
```

Using the ALTER FLASHBACK ARCHIVE statement, you can change the retention time of a Flashback Data Archive; purge some or all of its data; and add, modify, or remove tablespaces. If you are logged on with SYSDBA privileges, you can also make a specific archive the default Flashback Data Archive for the system.

- Make Flashback Data Archive fla1 the default Flashback Data Archive:

```
ALTER FLASHBACK ARCHIVE fda1 SET DEFAULT;
```

- Add an additional 5Gigs quota of tablespace fda_tbs1 to Flashback Data Archive fda1:

```
ALTER FLASHBACK ARCHIVE fda1
ADD TABLESPACE da_tbs1 QUOTA 5G;
```

- Add unlimited quota on tablespace fda_tbs3 to Flashback Data Archive fda1:

```
ALTER FLASHBACK ARCHIVE fda1 ADD TABLESPACE tbs3;
```

- Change the retention time for Flashback Data Archive fda1 to four years:

```
ALTER FLASHBACK ARCHIVE fda1 MODIFY RETENTION 4 YEAR;
```

- Purge all historical data older than one day from Flashback Data Archive fda1:

```
ALTER FLASHBACK ARCHIVE fda1
PURGE BEFORE TIMESTAMP (SYSTIMESTAMP - INTERVAL '1' DAY);
```

You can drop a Flashback Data Archive with the DROP FLASHBACK ARCHIVE statement. This statement will delete its historical data, but will not drop the tablespace the archive was stored on. To remove Flashback Data Archive fda1 and all its historical data:

```
DROP FLASHBACK ARCHIVE fda1;
```

Flashback archiving is disabled for all tables by default. If a flashback data archive exists in the database, and you have the FLASHBACK ARCHIVE privilege on it, you can enable flashback archiving for a table. To enable flashback archiving for a table, you use the FLASHBACK ARCHIVE clause in either a CREATE TABLE or ALTER TABLE statement. It's possible to set the specific Flashback Data Archive where the data for the table will be stored in the FLASHBACK ARCHIVE clause. If no clause is provided, the default Flashback Data Archive for the database will be used. Some examples of making tables use flashback archiving are:

- Create table dept and use the default Flashback Data Archive:

```
CREATE TABLE dept (DEPTNO NUMBER(4) NOT NULL,
                   DEPTNAME VARCHAR2(10))
FLASHBACK ARCHIVE;
```

- Create table employee and use the Flashback Data Archive fda1:

```
CREATE TABLE dept (DEPTNO NUMBER(4) NOT NULL,
                   DEPTNAME VARCHAR2(10))
FLASHBACK ARCHIVE fda1;
```

- Enable flashback archiving for the table dept and use the default Flashback Data Archive:

```
ALTER TABLE dept FLASHBACK ARCHIVE;
```

- Enable flashback archiving for the table dept and use the Flashback Data Archive fda1:

```
ALTER TABLE dept FLASHBACK ARCHIVE fda1;
```

- Disable flashback archiving for the table dept:

```
ALTER TABLE dept NO FLASHBACK ARCHIVE;
```

The following views in the data dictionary are specific to the Flashback Data Archive:

- DBA_FLASHBACK_ARCHIVE_TABLES
- DBA_FLASHBACK_ARCHIVE
- DBA_FLASHBACK_ARCHIVE_TS

Use DBMS_FLASHBACK_ARCHIVE package

The DBMS_FLASHBACK_ARCHIVE package provides a number of subprograms that extend the functionality of the Flashback Data Archive functionality of Oracle. One of the more common uses is to allow DDL changes to be made to a table that has had flashback archive enabled. Once Flashback Data Archive has been enabled for a table, users are prevented from issuing any DDL statements on it. The following example will disassociate the DEPT table from its history table:

```
EXEC DBMS_FLASHBACK_ARCHIVE.DISASSOCIATE_FBA('HR','DEPT');
```

Once the above command has been executed, it is possible to make DDL changes to the DEPT table (for example adding a column) that would have generated an error because of the associated history table. Once the DDL has been completed, the following command will reassociate the table with its history table:

```
EXEC DBMS_FLASHBACK_ARCHIVE.REASSOCIATE_FBA('HR','DEPT')
```

There are a number of subprograms available in the DBMS_FLASHBACK_ARCHIVE package, including:

- **ADD_TABLE_TO_APPLICATION** -- Takes an application name and adds a table to the application as a security table.
- **CREATE_TEMP_HISTORY_TABLE** -- Creates a table called TEMP_HISTORY with the correct definition in schema.

- **DISABLE_APPLICATION** -- Takes an application name and marks a table in it as a security table.
- **DISABLE_ASOF_VALID_TIME** -- Disables session level valid-time flashback.
- **DISASSOCIATE_FBA** -- Disassociates the given table from the flashback data archive.
- **DROP_APPLICATION** -- Takes an application name and removes it from the list of applications.
- **ENABLE_APPLICATION** -- Takes an application name and enables Flashback Data Archive on all the security tables for this application.
- **ENABLE_AT_VALID_TIME** -- Enables session level valid time flashback.
- **EXTEND_MAPPINGS** -- Extends time mappings to times in the past.
- **GET_SYS_CONTEXT** -- Gets the context previously selected by the SET_CONTEXT_LEVEL Procedure.
- **IMPORT_HISTORY** -- Imports history from a table called TEMP_HISTORY in the given schema.
- **LOCK_DOWN_APPLICATION** -- Takes an application name and makes all the security tables read-only. The group called SYSTEM cannot be locked.
- **PURGE_CONTEXT** -- Purges the context to be saved selected by the SET_CONTEXT_LEVEL Procedure.
- **REASSOCIATE_FBA** -- Reassociates the given table with the flashback data archive.
- **REGISTER_APPLICATION** -- Takes an application name and optionally a Flashback Data Archive, and registers an application for database hardening.
- **REMOVE_TABLE_FROM_APPLICATION** -- Takes an application name and marks a table in it as no longer being a security table.
- **SET_CONTEXT_LEVEL** -- Defines how much of the user context is to be saved.

Using Flashback Database

Perform Flashback Database

Configure Flashback Database

Oracle's Flashback Database feature allows you to set the database back to an earlier time in order to correct problems caused by logical data corruption or user errors within a designated time window. Flashback Database is much more efficient than performing a point-in-time recovery and does not require a backup and restore operation. Flashback Database is accessible through the RMAN command FLASHBACK DATABASE or the SQL statement FLASHBACK DATABASE.

To enable Flashback Database, the database must have a Fast Recovery Area configured and a flashback retention target set. This target specifies how far in the past it should possible to rewind the database. Flashback Database uses its own logging mechanism, creating flashback logs and storing them in the fast recovery area. The database must be set up in advance to create flashback logs in order to take advantage of this feature. Once configured, at regular intervals, the database copies images of each altered block in every data file into the flashback logs. These block images can later be used to reconstruct the data file contents to any moment for which logs exist. In addition to the flashback logs, redo logs on disk or tape must be available for the entire time period spanned by the flashback logs. The range of SCNs for which there is currently enough flashback log data to support the FLASHBACK DATABASE command is called the flashback database window.

If the Fast Recovery Area does not contain sufficient space for recovery files such as archived redo logs and other backups needed for the retention policy, the database may delete the flashback logs starting from the earliest SCNs. The flashback retention target does not guarantee that Flashback Database is available for the full period. A larger Fast Recovery Area may be required in this case.

Flashback Database has the following limitations:

- It can only undo changes to a data file made by Oracle Database. It cannot be used to repair media failures, or recover from accidental deletion of data files.
- It cannot undo a shrink data file operation.
- If the database control file is restored from backup or re-created, all accumulated flashback log information is discarded.
- If you Flashback Database to a target time at which a NOLOGGING operation was in progress, block corruption is likely in the database objects and datafiles affected by the NOLOGGING operation.

A normal restore point simply assigns a restore point name to an SCN or specific point in time. It functions as an alias for this SCN. If you use flashback features or point-in-time recovery, the restore point name can be used instead of a time or SCN. Normal restore points eventually age out of the control file if not manually deleted, so they require no ongoing maintenance. The following commands support the use of restore points:

- RECOVER DATABASE and FLASHBACK DATABASE commands in RMAN
- FLASHBACK TABLE statement in SQL

A guaranteed restore point also serves as an alias for an SCN in recovery operations. However, guaranteed restore points never age out of the control file and must be explicitly dropped. It ensures that you can use Flashback Database to rewind a database to the restore point SCN, even if the generation of flashback logs is not enabled. When enabled, a guaranteed restore point enforces the retention of flashback logs all the way back in time to the guaranteed SCN.

In order to enable Flashback Database, you must first ensure the database instance is open or mounted. If the instance is mounted, then the database must be shut down cleanly unless it is a physical standby database.

1. Optionally, set the DB_FLASHBACK_RETENTION_TARGET to the length of the desired flashback window in minutes. The default is 1 day (1440 minutes).
2. Enable the Flashback Database feature for the whole database:

```
ALTER DATABASE FLASHBACK ON;
```

3. Optionally, disable flashback logging for specific tablespaces.

To disable Flashback Database logging, you must issue the following command on a database instance that is either in mount or open state:

```
ALTER DATABASE FLASHBACK OFF;
```

Maintaining flashback logs does not impose significant overhead on a database instance. Changed blocks are written to the flashback logs at relatively infrequent, regular intervals, to limit processing and I/O overhead. Optimizing performance is primarily a matter of ensuring that the writes occur as fast as possible.

- Use a fast file system for your fast recovery area, preferably without operating system file caching.
- Configure enough disk spindles for the file system that holds the fast recovery area.
- If the storage system used to hold the fast recovery area does not have nonvolatile RAM, then try to configure the file system on striped storage volumes with a relatively small stripe size such as 128 KB.
- For large databases, set the initialization parameter LOG_BUFFER to at least 8 MB.

There are several database views that allow you to monitor the impact of flashback logs on the database. The V$FLASHBACK_DATABASE_LOG view allows you to monitor the Flashback Database retention target and how much space is being used by the flashback logs in the Fast Recovery Area.

- **OLDEST_FLASHBACK_SCN** -- Lowest system change number (SCN) in the flashback data, for any incarnation.
- **OLDEST_FLASHBACK_TIME** -- Time of the lowest SCN in the flashback data, for any incarnation.
- **RETENTION_TARGET** -- Target retention time (in minutes).
- **FLASHBACK_SIZE** -- Current size (in bytes) of the flashback data.
- **ESTIMATED_FLASHBACK_SIZE** -- Estimated size of flashback data needed for the current target retention.

The V$FLASHBACK_DATABASE_STAT view displays statistics for monitoring the I/O overhead of logging flashback data. It also displays the estimated flashback space needed based on previous workloads.

- **BEGIN_TIME** -- Beginning of the time interval.
- **END_TIME** -- End of the time interval.
- **FLASHBACK_DATA** -- Number of bytes of flashback data written during the interval.
- **DB_DATA** -- Number of bytes of database data read and written during the interval.
- **REDO_DATA** -- Number of bytes of redo data written during the interval.
- **ESTIMATED_FLASHBACK_SIZE** -- Value of ESTIMATED_FLASHBACK_SIZE in V$FLASHBACK_DATABASE_LOG at the end of the time interval.

The V$RECOVERY_FILE_DEST view displays information about the disk quota and current disk usage in the fast recovery area.

- **NAME** -- Location name. This is the value specified in the DB_RECOVERY_FILE_DEST initialization parameter.
- **SPACE_LIMIT** -- Maximum amount of disk space (in bytes) that the database can use for the fast recovery area. This is the value specified in the DB_RECOVERY_FILE_DEST_SIZE initialization parameter.
- **SPACE_USED** -- Amount of disk space (in bytes) used by fast recovery area files created in current and all previous fast

recovery areas. Changing fast recovery areas does not reset SPACE_USED to 0.

- **SPACE_RECLAIMABLE** -- Total amount of disk space (in bytes) that can be created by deleting obsolete, redundant, and other low priority files from the fast recovery area.
- **NUMBER_OF_FILES** -- Number of files in the fast recovery area.

Perform Flashback Database

If a database has been configured for flashback logging as described in the previous section, it is possible use the FLASHBACK DATABASE command to return the database contents to points in time within the flashback window. The database must be mounted when the FLASHBACK DATABASE is issued. If restore points have been created for the database, they make flashback database operations simpler. However, they are not required. The steps to rewind a database with Flashback Database are:

1. Start RMAN and connect to a target database.
2. Ensure that the database is in a mounted state.

```
SHUTDOWN IMMEDIATE;
STARTUP MOUNT;
```

3. Run the FLASHBACK DATABASE command. Following are three different forms of the command:

```
FLASHBACK DATABASE TO SCN 571340;
FLASHBACK DATABASE TO RESTORE POINT GOOD_TIMES;
FLASHBACK DATABASE TO TIMESTAMP TO_DATE('28-MAY-2015
01:00:00',
                                    'DD-MON-YYYY
HH24:MI:SS');
```

4. After performing the Flashback Database, open the database read-only in SQL*Plus and execute some queries to verify the database contents.

```
ALTER DATABASE OPEN READ ONLY;
```

5. Once satisfied with the results, issue the following sequence of commands to shut down and then open the database:

```
SHUTDOWN IMMEDIATE;
STARTUP MOUNT;
ALTER DATABASE OPEN RESETLOGS;
```

Transporting Data

Describe and use transportable tablespaces and databases

Transport tablespaces between databases using image copies or backup sets

It is possible to transport tablespaces between servers using RMAN's transport tablespace capability. The RMAN TRANSPORT TABLESPACE command will create a transportable tablespace set. This set contains data files for a one or more tablespaces plus an export file that contains the structural metadata for included tablespaces. The export file is generated by Data Pump Export rather than by RMAN. The RMAN TRANSPORT TABLESPACE command does not require access to the live data files from the tablespaces to be transported. It creates the tablespace set from database backups (either image copies or backup sets). It is also possible to specify a target point in time, SCN, or restore point for the set to be exported so long at that time exists within the recovery window.

In order to create a tablespace set with the TRANSPORT TABLESPACE operation, a backup of all needed tablespaces and archived redo log files must be accessible to RMAN. The transport process occurs in the following steps:

1. RMAN starts an auxiliary instance on the same host as the source database. This instance is used to perform the restore and recovery of the tablespaces.
2. RMAN restores a backup of the source database control file to serve as the auxiliary instance control file.
3. RMAN restores auxiliary set and transportable set data files from the backups of the source database. The auxiliary set includes files that are required for the tablespace transport but which are not part of the transportable tablespace set. It typically includes the SYSTEM and SYSAUX tablespaces, temp files, and data files containing rollback or undo segments.

4. RMAN performs database point-in-time recovery (DBPITR) at the auxiliary instance as of the target time specified for the TRANSPORT TABLESPACE command. When a target time is not specified, the recovery uses all available redo.

5. RMAN opens the auxiliary database with the RESETLOGS options.

6. RMAN places the transportable set tablespaces of the auxiliary instance into read-only mode. It then executes Data Pump Export in transportable tablespace mode to create the export dump file for the transportable set.

7. If the preceding steps are successful, then RMAN shuts down the auxiliary instance and deletes all files created during the operation except for the transportable set files, the Data Pump Export file, and the sample import script.

The following limitations apply to transporting tablespaces:

- The source and the destination databases must use compatible database character sets.
- The destination database cannot contain a tablespace of the same name. If it does, you must rename either the tablespace to be transported or the one in the destination database.
- Objects with underlying objects (such as materialized views) or contained objects (such as partitioned tables) are not transportable unless all of the underlying or contained objects are in the tablespace being transported.
- Transportable tablespaces cannot transport tables with TIMESTAMP WITH TIMEZONE (TSTZ) data across platforms with different time zone file versions.
- Transportable tablespaces cannot transport encrypted tablespaces or tablespaces containing tables with encrypted columns.
- Administrative tablespaces, such as SYSTEM and SYSAUX, cannot be included in a transportable tablespace set.
- Tablespaces that do not use block encryption but that contain tables with encrypted columns cannot be transported.

Transport databases using data files or backup sets

The transportable database feature is essentially an extension of the transportable tablespaces feature that allows Data Pump to handle tablespaces that cannot be transported. When performing a full database export, Data Pump has a new full transportable export option. A full transportable export is performed when the TRANSPORTABLE=ALWAYS parameter is specified along with the FULL parameter. This functionality exports all objects and data required to create a complete copy of the database. Two data movement methods are performed by Data Pump depending on whether the tablespaces are transportable or not:

- **Non-transportable tablespaces** -- Tablespaces like SYSTEM and SYSAUX that cannot be transported have both their metadata and data unloaded into the dump file set, using direct path unload and external tables.
- **Transportable tablespaces** -- For transportable tablespaces, only metadata is unloaded into the dump file set. The contents of the tablespaces are moved when the data files are copied to the target database.

There are several restrictions for performing a full transportable export, including:

- The DATAPUMP_EXP_FULL_DATABASE privilege is required to perform this operation.
- The default tablespace of the user performing the export must not be set to one of the tablespaces being transported.
- If the database being exported contains either encrypted tablespaces or tables with encrypted columns, the ENCRYPTION_PASSWORD parameter must be supplied.
- If there are encrypted tablespaces in the source database, the source and target databases must be on platforms with the same endianness.
- If the source platform and the target platform are of different endianness, then you must convert the data being transported so that it is in the format of the target platform.

- A full transportable export is not restartable.
- All objects with storage that are selected for export must have all of their storage segments either entirely within administrative, non-transportable tablespaces (SYSTEM / SYSAUX) or entirely within user-defined, transportable tablespaces. Storage for a single object cannot straddle the two kinds of tablespaces.

The new functionality can be used to move a non-CDB into a pluggable database (PDB) or to move a PDB into another PDB. Full transportable operations can reduce both the export time and import times required for a full export. When this option is used, table data does not need to be unloaded and reloaded and index structures in user tablespaces do not need to be re-created. The full transportable feature is ideal for moving a database to a new computer system or upgrading to a new release of Oracle.

Transport data across platforms

It is possible to transport tablespaces from an Oracle database on one platform to an Oracle database on a different platform. If the source and destination platforms have the same endian format, it is possible to simply copy the associated files from one platform to the other using operating system commands. The RMAN CONVERT command is required when transporting tablespaces when the endian formats are different between the source and destination platforms. If the entire database is being moved, even if the platforms have the same endian format, any data files with undo information must be converted using RMAN.

Tablespace conversion is performed using the RMAN CONVERT TABLESPACE command on the **source** host only. The command will generate output files in the correct format for the destination platform. The data files in the source database are not altered by the CONVERT command.

The RMAN CONVERT DATAFILE command can be used to convert files on the **destination** host only. Because the data files are not associated with any given tablespace on the destination, individual files must be specified by name in RMAN.

The list of available platforms and their respective endian formats are available from the V$TRANSPORTABLE_TABLESPACE view:

```
SELECT platform_id, platform_name, endian_format
FROM   v$transportable_platform
WHERE  platform_name LIKE '%Linux%';

PLATFORM_ID PLATFORM_NAME                 ENDIAN_FORMAT
----------- --------------------------- --------------
         10 Linux IA (32-bit)           Little
         11 Linux IA (64-bit)           Little
          9 IBM zSeries Based Linux     Big
         13 Linux x86 64-bit            Little
         18 IBM Power Based Linux       Big
```

Duplicating a Database

Choose a technique for duplicating a database

From an active database, connected to the target and auxiliary instances

Advantages:

- Active duplication can be performed for a database even if backups of it do not exist.
- Requires less disk space on the destination because data is transferred directly from the source database to the destination database.
- RMAN can employ unused block compression while creating backups to reduce the size of backups that are transported over the network.

Disadvantages/Requirements:

- Because active duplication copies mounted or online database files over the network to the auxiliary instance it will generate considerable network traffic during the duplication process.
- The source database must run processes that are used in transferring the files to the auxiliary host. This will negatively affect the performance of the source database and production workload.
- Requires that the target and auxiliary instances use the same password as the source database.
- Requires that a recovery catalog exist.

From backup, connected to the target and auxiliary instances

Advantages:

- Backup files can be transferred to the destination host prior to starting the duplicate operation. This will eliminate the problem of network traffic during the duplication process.
- The performance impact on the source database during the duplication operation is reduced because source database does not need to run processes for transferring files to the auxiliary host.
- The target and auxiliary instances do not need to use the same password as the source database.

Disadvantages/Requirements:

- Requires that backups of for the source database exist.
- Requires more disk space on the destination host if backups are transferred there.
- The backup files on the destination host must have the same file specification as they had on the source host.

From backup, connected to the auxiliary instance, not connected to the target, but with recovery catalog connection

Advantages:

- Backup files can be transferred to the destination host prior to starting the duplicate operation. This will eliminate the problem of network traffic during the duplication process.
- The target and auxiliary instances do not need to use the same password as the source database.
- Useful when network connections from the auxiliary host to the source database are restricted or prone to intermittent disruptions.
- In duplication without a TARGET connection, the source database is unaffected by the duplication.

Disadvantages/Requirements:

- Requires that backups of for the source database exist.
- Requires more disk space on the destination host if backups are transferred there.
- The backup files on the destination host must have the same file specification as they had on the source host.
- Requires that a recovery catalog exist.

From backup, connected to the auxiliary instance, not connected to the target and the recovery catalog

Advantages:

- Backup files can be transferred to the destination host prior to starting the duplicate operation. This will eliminate the problem of network traffic during the duplication process.
- The target and auxiliary instances do not need to use the same password as the source database.
- Useful when network connections from the auxiliary host to the source database are restricted or prone to intermittent disruptions.
- In duplication without a TARGET connection, the source database is unaffected by the duplication.

Disadvantages/Requirements:

- Requires that backups of for the source database exist.
- Requires more disk space on the destination host if backups are transferred there.
- The backup files on the destination host must have the same file specification as they had on the source host.
- Must supply the location of the backups to be used via the BACKUP LOCATION clause.

Duplicate a database with RMAN

The RMAN DUPLICATE command is used to copy all or a subset of the data in a source database. Once created, the duplicate database will function independently from the source database. There are several cases in which it can be useful to create a duplicate database:

- Test backup and recovery procedures
- Test an upgrade to a new release of Oracle Database
- Test the effect of applications on database performance
- Create a standby database
- Generate reports without impacting performance on the source database

When the DUPLICATE command creates a copy of the source database, it can be one of the following:

- **A duplicate database** -- This is a copy of the source database (or a subset of the source database) with a unique DBID. Because it has a unique DBID, the copy is independent of the source and can be registered in the same recovery catalog.
- **A standby database** -- A standby database acts as a backup for the source (or primary) database. It is not assigned a new DBID and the standby is continually updated by applying archived redo log files from the primary database.

If a database is copied using operating system utilities rather than the DUPLICATE command, the DBID of the copy will always be the same as the original database. It is not possible to register the copy in the same recovery catalog with the original unless the DBID is changed with the DBNEWID utility.

RMAN supports two basic types of duplication: active database duplication and backup-based duplication. When backup-based duplication is used, it can be performed with or without either of the following connections:

- Target Database
- Recovery catalog

When performing active database duplication, a connection to both is required.

Create a backup-up based duplicate database

The following DUPLICATE example does not include FROM ACTIVE DATABASE clause. Omitting this clause instructs RMAN to perform backup-based duplication. The files will be copied to the new host using the same directory structure as the source database. The NOFILENAMECHECK option is required because the source database files have the same names as the duplicate database files. The DB_NAME of the duplicate database will be DBMINUS10.

```
DUPLICATE TARGET DATABASE TO dbminus10
SPFILE
NOFILENAMECHECK
UNTIL TIME 'SYSDATE-10';
```

RMAN will automatically perform the following steps:

- Copy the server parameter file to the destination host.
- Restart the auxiliary instance with the server parameter file.
- Copy all necessary database files and archived redo logs over the network to the destination host.
- Recover the database to a point ten days in the past.
- Open the database with the RESETLOGS option to create the online redo log.

Duplicate a database based on a running instance

The following example will perform active duplication using the pull
method (the default) using backup sets. The files will be copied to the new
host using the same directory structure as the source database. The
NOFILENAMECHECK option is required because the source database files
have the same names as the duplicate database files. The PASSWORD FILE
option tells RMAN to copy the password file to the destination host. The
DB_NAME of the duplicate database will be DBCOPY.

```
DUPLICATE TARGET DATABASE TO dbcopy
FROM ACTIVE DATABASE
PASSWORD FILE
SPFILE
NOFILENAMECHECK;
```


RMAN will automatically perform the following steps:

- Copy the server parameter file to the destination host.
- Restart the auxiliary instance with the server parameter file.
- Copy all necessary database files and archived redo logs over the
  network to the destination host.
- Recover the database.
- Open the database with the RESETLOGS option to create the
  online redo log.

Monitoring and Tuning of RMAN Operations

Tune RMAN performance

Interpret RMAN error stacks

RMAN reports errors as they occur. If RMAN is unable to perform failover to another channel to complete a particular job step, it will report a summary of the errors after all job sets complete. It is possible to determine whether RMAN encountered an error by searching the RMAN output for the string RMAN-00569. This is message number for the error stack banner which will precede all RMAN errors. If the output does not contain RMAN-00569, there are no errors. Typically, the following types of error codes occur in RMAN message stacks:

- Errors prefixed with RMAN-
- Errors prefixed with ORA-
- Errors preceded by the line Additional information:

When interpreting RMAN Error Stacks the following tips and suggestions can assist:

- The messages should be read from the bottom up, because this is the order in which RMAN issues the messages. The lowest one or two errors in the stack are generally the most informative.
- Look for the RMAN-03002 or RMAN-03009 message immediately following the error banner. These messages indicate which command failed.
- Refer to Oracle Database Error Messages for further information about the messages.

The following is an example of an RMAN error stack. An attempt was made to backup the OCP_USERS tablespace and the following message was generated:

```
Starting backup at 24-MAY-15
using channel ORA_DISK_1
RMAN-00571:
===========================================================
RMAN-00569: =============== ERROR MESSAGE STACK FOLLOWS
===============
RMAN-00571:
===========================================================
RMAN-03002: failure of backup command at 05/24/2015 12:31:19
RMAN-20202: tablespace not found in the recovery catalog
RMAN-06019: could not translate tablespace name "OPC_USERS"
```

The RMAN-03002 error indicates that the BACKUP command failed. Based on the last two messages in the stack, it is obvious that the problem was caused by the OCP_USERS tablespace being misspelled in the backup command.

Diagnose performance bottlenecks

It is possible to use the V$BACKUP_SYNC_IO and V$BACKUP_ASYNC_IO views to locate the source of backup or restore bottlenecks.

- **V$BACKUP_SYNC_IO** -- Contains rows when the I/O is synchronous to the process (or thread on some platforms) performing the backup.
- **V$BACKUP_ASYNC_IO** -- Contains rows when the I/O is asynchronous. Asynchronous I/O is obtained either with I/O processes or because it is supported by the underlying operating system.

Despite the fact that these are dynamic performance views, the results of a backup or restore job remain in memory until the database instance shuts down. This allows the views to be queried even after the backup or restore job has completed. When a backup or restore operation is going to or coming from a tape, it is possible to determine whether the tape is streaming as follows:

1. Start SQL*Plus and connect to the target database.
2. Query the EFFECTIVE_BYTES_PER_SECOND column in the V$BACKUP_SYNC_IO or V$BACKUP_ASYNC_IO view.

If the value of EFFECTIVE_BYTES_PER_SECOND is less than the raw capacity of the hardware, then the tape is not streaming. When the value is greater than the raw capacity of the hardware, the tape may be streaming. The effects of compression can cause the EFFECTIVE_BYTES_PER_SECOND value to be greater than the speed of actual I/O.

Identifying specific bottlenecks with synchronous I/O is difficult because all synchronous I/O acts a bottleneck to the process. The only metric for tuning synchronous I/O is comparing the rate (in bytes per second) with the device's maximum throughput rate. When the rate is lower than the maximum specified for the device specifies, it might be worthwhile to tune tuning this aspect of the backup and restore process. The steps to determine the rate of synchronous I/O are:

1. Start SQL*Plus and connect to the target database.
2. Query the DISCRETE_BYTES_PER_SECOND column in the V$BACKUP_SYNC_IO view to display the I/O rate.

If there is data in V$BACKUP_SYNC_IO, then asynchronous I/O is not enabled or disk I/O slaves are not being used.

When working with asynchronous I/O, there are two types of waits:

- **Long waits** -- This is the number of times a backup or restore process told the operating system to wait until an I/O was complete.
- **Short waits** -- This is the number of times the backup or restore process made an operating system call to poll for I/O completion in a nonblocking mode.

The steps to determine the rate of asynchronous I/O are:

1. Start SQL*Plus and connect to the target database.
2. Query the LONG_WAITS and IO_COUNT columns in the V$BACKUP_SYNC_IO view to display the I/O rate.

One way to identify an asynchronous I/O bottleneck is to locate the data file that has the largest ratio for LONG_WAITS divided by IO_COUNT. The following query is an example of this:

```
SELECT long_waits / io_count, filename
FROM    v$backup_async_io
WHERE   long_waits / io_count > 0
ORDER BY long_waits / io_count DESC;
```

Tune RMAN backup performance

There are a number of different factors involved in RMAN performance. This section covers many different ways of increasing RMAN performance, reducing the load it places on the database, or both.

RATE

The RMAN commands ALLOCATE and CONFIGURE CHANNEL both have a RATE parameter. This is used to specify the bytes per second that are read on a channel. It is intended to set an upper limit for bytes read in order to prevent RMAN from consuming excessive disk bandwidth. This ensures that there is disk bandwidth available for other database operations. If the backup is not streaming to tape, the RATE parameter should not be set.

Large Pool

RMAN is one of the several users of the large pool. The total size of the pool must be sufficient for all the processes that use it. This is especially true if the DBWR_IO_SLAVES parameter has been set. The value of the LARGE_POOL_SIZE initialization parameter should be set or increased if the database reports an error in the alert log stating that there is insufficient memory to start I/O slaves. The error message will be similar to the following:

```
ksfqxcre: failure to allocate shared memory means sync I/O will be
used whenever async I/O to file not supported natively
```

To set the large pool size:

1. Start SQL*Plus and connect to the target database.
2. Set the LARGE_POOL_SIZE initialization parameter in the target database.
3. The ALTER SYSTEM SET statement can be used to set the parameter dynamically.
4. ALTER SYSTEM SET LARGE_POOL_SIZE = 512M scope=both;
5. Restart the RMAN backup.

Multiplexing

When performing an incremental backup, RMAN will only back up blocks that have changed since a previous backup that is part of the same strategy. If block change tracking is not enabled, RMAN must scan the entire data file for changed blocks. The changed blocks are written to output buffers as RMAN finds them. If relatively few blocks changed while RMAN is making an SBT backup, the output buffers may not fill fast enough to keep the tape drive streaming. In these cases, it is possible to improve backup performance by adjusting the level of multiplexing. This is the number of input files that are simultaneously read and written to the same RMAN backup piece. The level of multiplexing is determined by the smaller of the number of input files placed in each backup set and the MAXOPENFILES setting on the channel.

Tuning the Copy and Write Phases

There are several options for tuning the Copy and Write phases depending on the circumstances. Some alternatives for improving this are:

- If the performance issue is with a full backup, consider using incremental backups. Incremental level 1 backups write only the changed blocks from data files to tape. If there is a bottleneck when writing to tape, this will reduce the impact on the overall backup strategy.
- For backups that use the basic compression algorithm, consider using the Advanced Compression Option.
- On a database host with multiple CPUs and a backup using binary compression, try increasing the number of channels.
- For an encrypted backup, change the encryption to AES128, which is the least CPU-intensive algorithm.
- If RMAN is backing up files to ASM, then increase the number of channels up to a maximum of 16.

You can use the DURATION parameter of the BACKUP command to limit the amount of time a given backup job is given to run. To specify a backup duration:

```
BACKUP
DURATION 4:00
TABLESPACE users;
```

The above command will generate an error if the backup does not complete inside the window. If the keyword PARTIAL is specified, RMAN does not report an error but rather displays a message showing which files are not backed up. If the BACKUP command is part of a RUN block, then the remaining commands in the RUN block continue to execute. Specifying FILESPERSET of 1 will save each file as its own backup set. If the window closes before the backup is complete, only the current set (one file) is lost. The following example prevents RMAN from issuing an error and minimizes lost work when a backup partially completes:

```
BACKUP
DURATION 4:00 PARTIAL
TABLESPACE users
FILESPERSET 1;
```

Minimizing Backup Load and Duration

When using DURATION you can run the backup with the maximum possible performance, or run as slowly as possible while still finishing within the allotted time, to minimize the performance impact of backup tasks. To maximize performance, use the MINIMIZE TIME option with DURATION.

```
BACKUP
DURATION 4:00 PARTIAL
MINIMIZE TIME
DATABASE
FILESPERSET 1;
```

When MINIMIZE LOAD is specified, RMAN monitors the progress of the running backup, and periodically estimates how long the backup will take to complete at its present rate. If RMAN estimates that the backup will finish before the end of the backup window, then it slows down the rate of backup so that the full available duration is used. This reduces the overhead on the database associated with the backup. To extend the backup to use the full time available, use the MINIMIZE LOAD option:

```
BACKUP
DURATION 4:00 PARTIAL
MINIMIZE LOAD
DATABASE
FILESPERSET 1;
```

When an RMAN channel accesses a disk for read or write operations, the I/O is either synchronous or asynchronous. When performing synchronous I/O, a server process can perform only one task at a time. When using asynchronous I/O, a server process can begin an I/O operation and then perform some other task while waiting for the I/O to complete. It is also possible to start additional I/O operations without having to wait for the first to complete. When reading from an ASM disk group, you should use asynchronous disk I/O if possible.

Disk I/O Slaves

Many operating systems support asynchronous I/O natively. If an operating system does not support native asynchronous I/O, the database can use special I/O slave processes to simulate it. The availability of disk I/O slaves is controlled by setting the DBWR_IO_SLAVES initialization parameter. By default, the value is 0 and I/O server processes are not used. Set DBWR_IO_SLAVES to enable RMAN to perform asynchronous I/O if and only if your disk does not support asynchronous I/O natively. Any nonzero value for DBWR_IO_SLAVES causes a fixed number of disk I/O slaves to be used for backup and restore, which simulates asynchronous I/O. To enable disk I/O slaves:

1. Start SQL*Plus and connect to the target database.
2. Shut down the database.
3. Set DBWR_IO_SLAVES initialization parameter to a nonzero value.
4. Restart the database.

Tape I/O Slaves

The initialization parameter BACKUP_TAPE_IO_SLAVES specifies whether or not RMAN uses slave processes. Tape devices can only be accessed by a single process at one time, so RMAN uses only the number of slaves necessary for the number of tape devices. If set to true, RMAN will allocate tape buffers from the SGA. When the LARGE_POOL_SIZE initialization parameter is also set, then RMAN allocates buffers from the large pool. When BACKUP_TAPE_IO_SLAVES is set to false, RMAN allocates tape buffers from the PGA. When making use of I/O slaves, set the LARGE_POOL_SIZE initialization parameter to dedicate space for these large memory allocations. This prevents RMAN I/O buffers from competing with the library cache for SGA memory.

Using Automatic Storage Management

Use Automatic Storage Management

Explain Automatic Storage Management (ASM)

Oracle Automatic Storage Management (ASM) is a storage solution for Oracle Database files. It acts as a volume manager to provide a file system for the exclusive use of the database. When using ASM, partitioned disks are assigned to ASM with specifications for striping and mirroring. When making use of Automatic Storage Management, in addition to any database instances that exist, there will be an instance dedicated to ASM. Oracle ASM also makes use of the Oracle Managed Files (OMF) feature. OMF automatically creates files in the locations designated, as well as naming them. It also removes the files automatically when tablespaces or files are deleted from within Oracle. The ASM instance exists to manage the disk space and distribute the I/O load across multiple drives to optimize performance. ASM provides several benefits over using standard data files:

- Simplifies operations such as creating databases and managing disk space
- Distributes data across physical disks to provide uniform performance
- Rebalances data automatically after storage configuration changes

An Oracle ASM instance uses the same basic technology as an Oracle Database instance. The System Global Area (SGA) and background processes of an ASM instance are similar to those of Oracle Database. The SGA for an ASM instance is much smaller than a database instance and has fewer internal components because the ASM instance has fewer functions. The only function of an ASM instance is to mount disk groups and make the associated file available to database instances. There is no database instance mounted by Oracle ASM instances. The logical storage elements of an Oracle ASM instance are:

- **ASM Disks** -- A storage device that is provisioned to an Oracle ASM disk group. It can be a physical disk or partition, a Logical Unit Number (LUN) from a storage array, a logical volume, or a network-attached file.
- **ASM Disk Groups** -- A collection of Oracle ASM disks managed as a logical unit.
- **ASM Files** -- A file stored in an Oracle ASM disk group. The database can store data files, control files, online redo log files, and other types of files as Oracle ASM files.
- **ASM Extents** -- The raw storage used to hold the contents of an Oracle ASM file. An ASM file consists of one or more file extents and an ASM extent consists of one or more ASM allocation units.
- **ASM Allocation Units** -- The fundamental unit of allocation within a disk group.
- **ASM Instances** -- A special Oracle instance that manages Oracle ASM disks. They manage the metadata of the disk group and provide file layout information to the database instances.

Oracle ASM supports the majority of file types required by the database. The list below shows the most commonly used file types and default template that provides the attributes for file creation. Oracle ASM cannot directly support some administrative file types on disk groups. These include trace files, audit files, alert logs, export files, and core files.

- **Control files** -- CONTROLFILE
- **Data files** -- DATAFILE
- **Redo log files** -- ONLINELOG
- **Archive log files** -- ARCHIVELOG
- **Temporary files** -- TEMPFILE
- **Data file backup pieces** -- BACKUPSET
- **Archive log backup piece** -- BACKUPSET
- **Persistent initialization parameter file (SPFILE)** -- PARAMETERFILE
- **Flashback logs** -- FLASHBACK
- **Data Pump dumpset** -- DUMPSET

Fully Qualified File Name Form

Whenever a file is created in ASM, Oracle Managed Files automatically generates a fully qualified file name for it. The fully qualified filename represents a complete path name in the Oracle ASM file system. You can use a fully qualified file name for referencing existing Oracle ASM files in Oracle ASM operations, except for disk group creation. A fully qualified file name has the following form:

+diskgroup/dbname/filetype/filetypetag.file.incarnation.

The definitions of the individual elements are:

- **+diskgroup** -- The disk group name preceded by a plus sign. The plus sign (+) is equivalent to the root directory for the Oracle ASM file system.
- **dbname** -- The DB_UNIQUE_NAME of the database to which the file belongs.
- **filetype** -- The Oracle file type and can be one of the file types shown in Table 7–3.
- **filetypetag** -- Type-specific information about the file.
- **file.incarnation** -- The file/incarnation pair, used to ensure uniqueness.

An example of a fully qualified Oracle ASM filename is:

+data/ocpdb/controlfile/Current.221.46544321

The file creation request does not specify the fully qualified filename. It supplies an alias or just a disk group name. Oracle ASM then creates the file in the correct Oracle ASM path based on the file type. ASM then assigns an appropriate fully qualified filename. If an alias is specified in the creation request, ASM creates the alias and points it to the fully qualified filename. ASM file creation requests are either single or multiple file creation requests.

Alias Filenames

Alias filenames can be used for referencing existing files and creating new ASM files. Alias names consist of the disk group name preceded by a plus sign followed by a name string. Alias filenames use a hierarchical directory structure, with the slash (/) or backslash (\) character separating name components. Aliases must include the disk group name. They cannot exist at the root level (+). When a file is created with an alias, both the alias and fully-qualified names are recorded and you can access the file with either name. Alias filenames do not (and cannot) end in a dotted pair of numbers. Examples of alias filenames include:

- +data/ocpdb/control_file_main
- +data/ocpdb/control_file_bkup
- +fra/recover/second.dbf

The example below creates an undo tablespace with a data file that has an alias name, and with attributes that are set by the user-defined template my_undo_template. This example assumes that the **ocpdb** directory has been created in disk group **data**.

```
CREATE UNDO TABLESPACE ocpundo
DATAFILE '+data/ocpdb/ocp_undo_ts' SIZE 200M;
```

If an alias is used to create the data file, it is not an Oracle Managed Files (OMF) file. This means that the file will not be automatically deleted when the tablespace is dropped. To drop the file manually after the tablespace has been dropped, use the following SQL statement:

```
ALTER DISKGROUP data DROP FILE '+data/ocpdb/ocp_undo_ts';
```

Set up initialization parameter files for ASM and database instances

When an Oracle instance starts, it makes use of an initialization parameter file to determine many of the database settings that will be used. At minimum, this file must specify the DB_NAME parameter. If the file contains nothing else, all other parameters will be set to default values. There are two types of parameter file that Oracle can use: a text-based parameter file that is read-only to the Oracle instance (PFILE), or a binary file that the instance can both read from and write to (SPFILE). When an instance stats, Oracle uses the following steps to locate an initialization parameter file. It will use the first file it locates:

1. It looks for spfile[SID].ora
2. It looks for spfile.ora
3. It looks for init[SID].ora

The recommended option is to utilize the binary file. It is called a server parameter file or spfile. Unlike the other options, with a spfile, you can change initialization parameters using ALTER SYSTEM commands and have those changes persist across a database shutdown and startup. The spfile also provides a method by which Oracle can self-tune. A spfile can be created manually from your text-based initialization file. Alternately, DBCA can automatically generate one when the database is created. When a server parameter file does not exist, the instance will start using a text initialization parameter file. At startup, the instance initially searches for a server parameter file in a default location. Only if it does not find one will the instance will search for a text initialization parameter file. It's also possible to bypass an existing server parameter file by naming a PFILE as a STARTUP argument.

The default file name for the text initialization parameter file is init[SID].ora. For a database with a SID of oraprod, the default filename would be initoraprod.ora. The default location under Unix and Linux is in the ORACLE_HOME/dbs directory. Under MS Windows, the file would be stored in ORACLE_HOME\database by default.

Many of the database initialization parameters can be dynamically changed using the ALTER SYSTEM statement. For instances using a spfile, such changes can persist across shutdowns. However, if you are using a text initialization parameter file, any changes made via ALTER SYSTEM are effective only for the current instance. You must update them manually in the initialization parameter file to make them permanent.

The text initialization parameter file contains name/value pairs in one of the following forms:

- **Single-Value Parameters** – parameter_name=value
- **Multiple-Value Parameters** – parameter_name=(value[,value] ...)

Multiple-value parameters can also be entered on multiple lines using the same format as a single parameter. If a single-value parameter appears on more than one line in the file, only the last value will be used.

Some initialization parameters derive their values from the values of other parameters. As a general rule, the values for derived parameters should not be altered. However, if they are explicitly set, then the specified value will override the calculated value. An example of a derived parameter is SESSIONS. This parameter is calculated from the value of the PROCESSES parameter. Unless SESSIONS is set explicitly, when the value of PROCESSES changes, then the default value of SESSIONS changes as well.

The host operating system will determine the valid values or value ranges of some initialization parameters. The DB_BLOCK_BUFFERS parameter indicates the number of data buffers in main memory. The maximum allowable value for this parameter depends on the operating system. In addition, the size of data block buffers, set by DB_BLOCK_SIZE, defaults to 8K under most operating systems.

Common Initialization Parameters

The following are all commonly set initialization parameters. These and other initialization parameters are listed in more detail in the Oracle 12c Reference Manual.

- **DB_NAME** – Determines the local component of the database name.
- **DB_DOMAIN** – Indicates the domain (logical location) within a network structure. This parameter is optional. The combination of the DB_NAME and DB_DOMAIN must create a database name that is unique within a network.
- **CONTROL_FILES** – Specifies one or more control filenames for the database. Control files are generated at the time a database is created using the names specified by the CONTROL_FILES parameter. If you do not include CONTROL_FILES in the initialization parameter file, Oracle will create a control file in the same directory as the initialization parameter file, using a default operating system–dependent filename.
- **PROCESSES** – Determines the maximum number of OS processes that can connect to Oracle simultaneously. At minimum, this parameter must have a minimum value of one for each background process plus one for each user process.
- **MEMORY_TARGET** – Sets a target memory size for the instance. The total memory used by the instance will remain reasonably constant, based on the supplied value. The instance will automatically distribute memory between the system global area (SGA) and the instance program global area (instance PGA).
- **SGA_TARGET** – If MEMORY_TARGET is not set, you can enable the automatic shared memory management feature by setting the SGA_TARGET parameter to a nonzero value. This parameter sets the total size of the SGA. Oracle will automatically tune the SGA components as needed.
- **SGA_MAX_SIZE** – Specifies the maximum size of the System Global Area for the lifetime of the instance. If you do not specify SGA_MAX_SIZE, then Oracle Database selects a default value that is the sum of all components specified or defaulted at the time of initialization.

- **PGA_AGGREGATE_TARGET** – Allows you to control the total amount of memory dedicated to the instance PGA.
- **UNDO_MANAGEMENT** – When set to AUTO or null, this parameter enables automatic undo management. When set to MANUAL, undo management will use manual mode.
- **UNDO_TABLESPACE** – This parameter is optional, and valid only in automatic undo management mode. The parameter specifies the name of an undo tablespace. It is used only when the database has multiple undo tablespaces.
- **DB_BLOCK_SIZE** – Sets the standard block size for the database. The standard block size is used for the SYSTEM tablespace and will be used for other tablespaces by default. Oracle can support up to four additional nonstandard block sizes.
- **DIAGNOSTIC_DEST** – Used to determine the location of the Automatic Diagnostic Repository.
- **LOG_ARCHIVE_DEST_n** – Determines where to write Archived Redo Logs.
- **OPEN_CURSORS** – Sets the maximum number of open cursors for an individual session.
- **SESSIONS** – Sets the maximum number of sessions that can connect to the database.

Displaying Database Parameters

You can determine the values of instance parameters in from either SQL*Plus or SQL Developer. Parameter values can be determined by querying the V$PARAMETER view:

```
SELECT name, value
FROM   v$parameter
WHERE  name LIKE '%size%';

NAME                            VALUE
------------------------------- ----------
sga_max_size                    1073741824
shared_pool_size                0
large_pool_size                 0
java_pool_size                  0
streams_pool_size               0
shared_pool_reserved_size       18454937
java_max_sessionspace_size      0
db_block_size                   8192
```

You can also use the "show parameter" command to display one or more parameters. The parameter name given in the command is treated as a wildcard. Any parameters for which the supplied value is a part of the name will be displayed:

```
show parameter pool_size

NAME                         TYPE          VALUE
-------------------------    -----------   -----
global_context_pool_size     string
java_pool_size               big integer   0
large_pool_size              big integer   0
olap_page_pool_size          big integer   0
shared_pool_size             big integer   0
streams_pool_size            big integer   0
```

If you give a complete parameter name, only the one parameter will be returned:

```
show parameter large_pool_size

NAME                         TYPE          VALUE
-------------------------    -----------   -----
large_pool_size              big integer   0
```

You can use the "show spparameter" command to view parameter values that have been specified in the server parameter file. Since there is nothing in the value column below, the parameter value has not been specified in the file:

```
show spparameter shared_pool_reserved_size

SID NAME                         TYPE          VALUE
--- -------------------------    -----------   ------
*   shared_pool_reserved_size    big integer
```

The following database views can be used to locate information about database parameters.

- **V$PARAMETER** – Displays the values of initialization parameters in effect for the current session.
- **V$PARAMETER2** – Similar to V$PARAMETER. However it is easier to distinguish list parameter values in this view because each list parameter value appears in a separate row.
- **V$SYSTEM_PARAMETER** – Displays the values of initialization parameters in effect for the instance.
- **V$SPPARAMETER** – Displays the current contents of the SPFILE. It returns FALSE values in the ISSPECIFIED column if an SPFILE is not being used by the instance.

Altering Initialization Parameter Values

There are two broad classes of initialization parameters: static and dynamic. Static parameters affect the entire database and can only be modified by changing the PFILE or SPFILE and require a database shutdown before they will take effect. Dynamic parameters can be altered while the instance is running and will take effect without requiring a shutdown. Dynamic parameters can be further subdivided into session and system-level parameters:

- **Session-level parameters** – Affect only a single session. These can be altered using the ALTER SESSION command and will only affect the session in which that command is executed. The changed values expire as soon as that session is closed.
- **System-level parameters** – Affect the entire database and all sessions. They can be set with the ALTER SYSTEM command and can either be temporary or permanent.

You can use the ALTER SYSTEM statement with the SET clause to alter initialization parameter values. When doing so, there is a second optional SCOPE clause that determines the scope of the change. For instances that are not using a server parameter file, only the SCOPE=MEMORY is a valid option. Permanent parameter changes will have to be made by manually altering the text-based parameter file.

- **SCOPE = SPFILE** – The change is applied in the server parameter file only. No change is made to the current instance. The change is effective at the next startup and is persistent. This scope can be used with either static or dynamic parameters.
- **SCOPE = MEMORY** – The change is applied in memory only. The change is made to the current instance and is effective immediately. The change is not persistent because the server parameter file is not updated. This scope is only valid for dynamic parameters.
- **SCOPE = BOTH** – The change is applied in both the server parameter file and memory. The change is made to the current instance and is effective immediately. The effect is persistent because the server parameter file is updated. This scope is only valid for dynamic parameters.

There are two more optional modifiers that add additional functionality to the ALTER SYSTEM command:

- **COMMENT** – For instances using a server parameter file, this clause can be used with the SPFILE and BOTH options to add a comment to the SPFILE along with the changed parameter (i.e. 'Changed on 4/28/2012 by Matt Morris').
- **DEFERRED** – This keyword is valid for dynamic parameters with the MEMORY and BOTH options for parameters that are session-specific. The change will be made effective only for future sessions.

ASM Initialization Parameters

When installing Oracle ASM in a standalone configuration, Oracle Universal Installer creates a server parameter file for the Oracle ASM instance. The ASM SPFILE is stored in a disk group during installation. For a clustered Oracle ASM environment, OUI creates a single, shared SPFILE for Oracle ASM in a disk group. It's possible to use an SPFILE or a text-based initialization parameter file (PFILE) as the Oracle ASM instance parameter file. Oracle recommends that the Oracle ASM SPFILE is placed in a disk group.

You can set ASM parameters using the Oracle ASM Configuration Assistant (ASMCA). Some parameters can be set after database creation using Oracle Enterprise Manager or SQL ALTER SYSTEM or ALTER SESSION statements. The Oracle ASM* parameters use suitable defaults for most environments. Any parameters that have names prefixed with Oracle ASM* cannot be used in database instance parameter files. There are several database initialization parameters that are also valid for an Oracle ASM instance and the default values for these are appropriate in most cases. Some of parameters for ASM instances are:

- **ASM_DISKGROUPS** -- Specifies a list of disk groups that an Oracle ASM instance mounts at startup. The default value of the ASM_DISKGROUPS parameter is a NULL string.
- **ASM_DISKSTRING** -- Specifies a comma-delimited list of strings that limits the set of disks that an Oracle ASM instance discovers. The discovery strings can include wildcard characters.
- **ASM_POWER_LIMIT** -- Specifies the default power for disk rebalancing in a disk group. The range of values is 0 to 1024. The default value is 1. A value of 0 disables rebalancing.
- **ASM_PREFERRED_READ_FAILURE_GROUPS** -- Specifies the failure groups that should be preferentially read by the given instance. Generally used for clustered Oracle ASM instances and its value can be different on different nodes.
- **DB_CACHE_SIZE** -- Determines the size of the buffer cache. Not required when using automatic memory management.
- **DIAGNOSTIC_DEST** -- Specifies the directory where diagnostics for an instance are located. The default value is the $ORACLE_BASE directory.
- **INSTANCE_TYPE** -- Set to ASM for an ASM instance.
- **LARGE_POOL_SIZE** -- Specifies the size of the LARGE_POOL memory area. Not required when using automatic memory management.
- **PROCESSES** -- This parameter affects Oracle ASM, but the default value is usually suitable.

- **SHARED_POOL_SIZE** -- Determines the amount of memory required to manage the instance. The setting for this parameter is also used to determine the amount of space that is allocated for extent storage. Not required when using automatic memory management.

Administer ASM diskgroups

An ASM disk group consists of multiple disks and is the fundamental object that Oracle ASM manages. Disk groups contain the information required to manage drive space. The sub-components of disk groups include disks, files, and allocation units. A given file is contained within a single disk group. However, a disk group can contain files from several databases. A single database can use files from multiple disk groups.

Disk Group Attributes

Disk group attributes are parameters that are bound to a disk group rather than an Oracle ASM instance. Some of the more common attributes are below. Refer to the Oracle ASM Administrator's Guide for more details.

- **ACCESS_CONTROL.ENABLED** -- This attribute determines whether Oracle ASM File Access Control is enabled for a disk group. The value can be true or false. The default is false. This attribute can only be set when altering a disk group.
- **ACCESS_CONTROL.UMASK** -- This attribute determines which permissions are masked out on the creation of an Oracle ASM file for the user that owns the file, users in the same user group, and others not in the user group. This attribute applies to all files on a disk group.
- **AU_SIZE** -- A file extent consists of one or more allocation units. An Oracle ASM file consists of one or more file extents. When you create a disk group, you can set the Oracle ASM allocation unit size with the AU_SIZE disk group attribute. The values can be 1, 2, 4, 8, 16, 32, or 64 MB, depending on the specific disk group compatibility level.

- **COMPATIBLE.ASM** -- This attribute controls the format of data structures for ASM metadata in the given disk group. The ASM software version must be equal or greater than this value in order to be able to access the disk group. The COMPATIBLE.ASM attribute must always be greater than or equal to COMPATIBLE.RDBMS for the same disk group. For example, you can set COMPATIBLE.ASM for the disk group to 11.0 and COMPATIBLE.RDBMS for the disk group to 10.1. In this case, the disk group can be managed only by ASM software with a version of 11.0 or higher. However, any database client of version 10.1 or higher can use the disk group. If you will be increasing both parameters, the COMPATIBLE.ASM value must be increased first.
- **COMPATIBLE.RDBMS** -- This dictates the format of messages that are exchanged between the Automatic Storage Management instance and the database instance. This parameter set the minimum database client release that may access a given disk group. You can set different values of this parameter on diskgroups within the same ASM instance for multiple database clients running at different compatibility settings.
- **CONTENT.TYPE** -- Identifies the disk group type: data, recovery, or system. The type value determines the distance to the nearest neighbor disk in the failure group where Oracle ASM mirrors copies of the data. The default value is 'data' which specifies a distance of 1 to the nearest neighbor disk. A value of 'recovery' specifies a distance of 3 to the nearest neighbor disk and a value of 'system' specifies a distance of 5.
- **DISK_REPAIR_TIME** -- Determines the amount of time that a disk can be unavailable due to a transient failure before to being dropped permanently from the diskgroup. To use this parameter, both the compatible.rdbms and compatible.asm attributes must be set to at least 11.1. You cannot set this attribute when creating a disk group, but you can alter the DISK_REPAIR_TIME attribute in an ALTER DISKGROUP ... SET ATTRIBUTE statement to change the default value. If both compatible.rdbms and compatible.asm are set to at least 11.1, then the default is 3.6 hours. If either parameter is less than 11.1, the disk is dropped immediately if it becomes inaccessible. The time can be specified in units of minutes by using the letter M or hours by using the letter H. If you provide a number with no unit, then the default is hours. The default attribute value can be changed while bringing the disk

offline by using an ALTER DISKGROUP ... DISK OFFLINE statement and the DROP AFTER clause. If a disk is taken offline using the current value of DISK_REPAIR_TIME, and the value of this attribute for the diskgroup is subsequently changed with the ALTER DISKGROUP ... SET ATTRIBUTE statement, then the changed value is used by ASM in determining when to drop the disk.

CREATE DISKGROUP

The CREATE DISKGROUP SQL statement is used to create disk groups. When creating a disk group, you specify the following information:

- A unique name to the disk group.
- The redundancy level of the disk group. For Oracle ASM to mirror files, specify the redundancy level as NORMAL REDUNDANCY (2-way mirroring by default for most file types) or HIGH REDUNDANCY (3-way mirroring for all files). Specify EXTERNAL REDUNDANCY if you do not want mirroring by Oracle ASM.
- The disks that are to be formatted as Oracle ASM disks belonging to the disk group.
- Optionally specify the disks as belonging to specific failure groups.
- Optionally specify the type of failure group.
- Optionally specify disk group attributes, such as software compatibility or allocation unit size.

The SQL statement below creates a disk group named data with normal redundancy. It consists of two failure groups: fg1 or fg2 with three disks in each failure group. The data disk group is typically used to store database data files.

```
CREATE DISKGROUP data NORMAL REDUNDANCY
FAILGROUP fg1 DISK
'/devices/diska1' NAME diska1,
'/devices/diska2' NAME diska2,
'/devices/diska3' NAME diska3
FAILGROUP fg2 DISK
'/devices/diskb1' NAME diskb1,
'/devices/diskb2' NAME diskb2,
'/devices/diskb3' NAME diskb3
```

```
ATTRIBUTE 'au_size'='2M',
'compatible.asm' = '12.1',
'compatible.rdbms' = '12.1';
```

ALTER DISKGROUP

The ALTER DISKGROUP SQL statement enables you to alter a disk group configuration. It is possible to add, resize, or drop disks while the database remains online. Multiple operations in a single ALTER DISKGROUP statement are both possible and recommended. Grouping operations in a single ALTER DISKGROUP statement can reduce rebalancing operations. Oracle ASM automatically rebalances a disk group when its configuration changes. The V$ASM_OPERATION view allows you to monitor the status of rebalance operations. The following command adds two more disks to the data diskgroup.

```
ALTER DISKGROUP data ADD DISK
'/devices/diska4' NAME diska4,
'/devices/diska5' NAME diska5;
```

When rebalancing a disk group, if the POWER clause is not specified in an ALTER DISKGROUP statement, or if a rebalance is executed implicitly because a disk has been added or dropped, the ASM_POWER_LIMIT initialization parameter determines the power used. The value of this parameter can be adjusted dynamically. Higher power values will cause a rebalance operation to complete faster, but consumes more processing and I/O resources. The default value of 1 minimizes disruption to other applications.

Execute SQL commands with ASM file names

It is possible to use ASM filenames in the file specification clause of SQL statements. If a file is being created for the first time, the creation form of an ASM filename should be used. If the file already exists, the reference context form of the filename must be used. If a file is being re-created, the REUSE keyword must be included in the SQL statement. The following example creates a tablespace called SCRATCH_TS in a SQL statement:

```
CREATE TABLESPACE scratch_ts DATAFILE '+dgroup1' SIZE 400M AUTOEXTEND
ON;
```

The tablespace SCRATCH_TS will be created and with a single 400 megabyte datafile in the disk group dgroup1. The datafile is set to auto-extensible with an unlimited maximum size.

Perform startup and shutdown for ASM instances

An Oracle ASM instance is started much like an Oracle database instance with some minor differences. When starting an Oracle ASM instance, note the following:

You must set the ORACLE_SID environment variable to the Oracle ASM system identifier (SID). The default Oracle ASM SID for a single-instance database is +ASM, and the default SID for Oracle ASM for an Oracle RAC node is +ASMnode_number where node_number is the number of the node. The ORACLE_HOME environment variable must be set to the Grid Infrastructure home where Oracle ASM was installed.

- The initialization parameter file must contain the following entry: INSTANCE_TYPE = ASM. This indicates that it is an Oracle ASM instance rather than a database instance.
- When you run the STARTUP command, rather than trying to mount and open a database, this command attempts to mount Oracle ASM disk groups.

An ASM instance interprets SQL*Plus STARTUP command parameters differently than a database instance.

- **FORCE** -- Issues a SHUTDOWN ABORT to the Oracle ASM instance before restarting it.
- **MOUNT or OPEN** -- Mounts the disk groups specified in the ASM_DISKGROUPS initialization parameter. This is the default. An OPEN state for an ASM instance doesn't really exist. If supplied, this parameter is simply treated as MOUNT.
- **NOMOUNT** -- Starts up the Oracle ASM instance without mounting any disk groups.
- **RESTRICT** -- Starts up an instance in restricted mode. Only users with both the CREATE SESSION and RESTRICTED SESSION system privileges can connect.

The SYSASM operating system privilege and the OSASM operating system group allow storage responsibilities to be assigned to System Administrators without granting high-level access to the Oracle database itself. Users can be created in the ASM instance and granted the SYSASM privilege. This allows them to connect to the ASM instance and perform administration tasks. Similarly, assigning an operating system user to the OSASM group would allow then to connect as SYSASM using OS authentication.

```
$ export ORACLE_SID=+ASM
$ sqlplus / as sysasm

CREATE USER asm_admin IDENTIFIED by badpassword_nobiscuit;
User created.

SQL> GRANT SYSASM TO asm_admin;


SQLPLUS /NOLOG
SQL> CONNECT asm_admin AS SYSASM
Enter password: badpassword_nobiscuit
Connected to an idle instance.
```

```
SQL> STARTUP
ASM instance started
Total System Global Area 71303168 bytes
Fixed Size 1069292 bytes
Variable Size 45068052 bytes
ASM Cache 25165824 bytes
ASM disk groups mounted
```

Shutting Down an Oracle ASM Instance

An ASM instance is shut down using the SHUTDOWN command in SQL*Plus just as with a database instance. As with startup, you must ensure that the ORACLE_SID environment variable is set to the Oracle ASM SID before connecting to SQL*Plus. Before you shut down an ASM instance, you should shut down all database instances that use it. You should also dismount all file systems mounted on Oracle ASM Dynamic Volume Manager volumes before attempting to shut down the ASM instance.

To shut down an Oracle ASM instance, perform the following steps:

```
SQLPLUS /NOLOG
SQL> CONNECT asm_admin AS SYSASM
Enter password: badpassword_nobiscuit
Connected.
SQL> SHUTDOWN NORMAL
```

The SHUTDOWN modes when used with an Oracle ASM instance are:

- **NORMAL** -- The instance waits for any in-progress SQL to complete before dismounting all of the disk groups and shutting down. The instance also waits for all currently connected users to disconnect from the instance. If any database instances are connected to the ASM instance, then the SHUTDOWN command aborts and returns an error. NORMAL is the default mode.
- **IMMEDIATE or TRANSACTIONAL** -- The instance waits for any in-progress SQL to complete before dismounting all of the disk groups and shutting down the Oracle ASM instance. It does not wait for users currently connected to the instance to disconnect. If any database instances are connected to the Oracle ASM

instance, then the SHUTDOWN aborts with an error. ASM instances have no transactions, so TRANSACTIONAL and IMMEDIATE are equivalent.

- **ABORT** -- The instance immediately shuts down without the orderly dismount of disk groups. This requires recovery on the next Oracle ASM startup. Any database instances that are connected to the Oracle ASM instance will also perform a shutdown abort because their storage will no longer be available.

Use the ASMCMD command-line interface

The ASM command-line utility (ASMCMD) allows ASM disk identification, disk bad block repair, and backup and restore operations of your ASM environment for faster recovery, among other capabilities. Three of the most important of the ASMCMD commands are md_backup, md_restore, and chkdg. The md_backup and md_restore commands were both covered in earlier chapters.

chkdg

The ASMCMD chkdg is used to checks the metadata of a disk group and optionally repair it. The syntax of the chkdg command is:

```
chkdg [--repair] diskgroup
```

The following example checks and repairs the dgroupMain disk group.

ASMCMD [+] > chkdg --repair dgroupMain

Set up ASM fast mirror resynch

Fast mirror resynch is an Automated Storage Management feature that allows a disk group to restore redundancy quickly after a transient disk failure. When using ASM with disk group redundancy on a version prior to 11g (or with compatibility set lower than 11g), if a disk cannot be accessed, it is taken offline and almost immediately dropped. To restore redundancy, the mirror extent copies are resynchronized in the remaining drives of the disk group. This resynchronization is an extremely costly operation.

When ASM fast mirror resynch is used, if a transient disk failure occurs, the failed drive is automatically taken offline. However, it is not <u>dropped</u> until a predetermined period of time has expired. This time period is set by a new disk group attribute: DISK_REPAIR_TIME. During the time that the drive is offline, ASM tracks modified extents in the disk group. If access to the drive is restored before the drive is dropped, only the modified extents must be resynchronized. Restoring the redundancy is much faster using this process than the pre-11g behavior. Fast mirror resynch can only help when the drive failure is transient – a brief power loss, a loose cable, and so forth. If the drive fails such that there is a loss of data or data corruption, fast mirror resynch cannot help.

DISK_REPAIR_TIME

The default value of the DISK_REPAIR_TIME attribute is 3.6 hours. You may change this by issuing the command:

```
ALTER DISKGROUP dgroupMain SET ATTRIBUTE 'disk_repair_time'='5h';
```

Note that if you provide a number for this attribute with no modifier, the default time increment is hours. You can also take drives offline and set the DISK_REPAIR_TIME if performing maintenance. The following example takes disk D2_001 offline and drops it after five minutes.

```
ALTER DISKGROUP dgroupMain OFFLINE DISK D2_001 DROP AFTER 5m;
```

Alternately, you can offline the disk and leave the drop time equal to the DISK_REPAIR_TIME attribute:

```
ALTER DISKGROUP dgroupMain OFFLINE DISK D2_001;
```

You can determine the current setting of the DISK_REPAIR_TIME attribute for the diskgroups in your ASM instance from the V$ASM_ATTRIBUTE view:

```
SELECT group_number, name, value
FROM   v$asm_attribute
WHERE name='disk_repair_time';

GROUP_NUMBER NAME                 VALUE
------------ -------------------- ------------
           1 disk_repair_time     3.6h
           2 disk_repair_time     3.6h
```

Use RMAN to migrate your database to ASM

It is possible to use RMAN to migrate data to Oracle ASM whether or not RMAN is being used as the primary backup tool. Only a single RMAN database backup is required to perform the migration. So long as there is sufficient disk space to contain the entire database both in Oracle ASM and alternative storage systems, a database can be migrated directly into Oracle ASM. In cases where there is not sufficient storage, one option is to back the database up to tape; create an Oracle ASM disk group that uses the disk space previously used by the database files; and finally restore the database from tape to Oracle ASM.

The following steps are required to prepare the database for migration to Oracle ASM Using RMAN:

1. Back up the database
2. Back up the server parameter file
3. Disable Oracle Flashback Database.

Once the above steps are complete, the following steps must be performed to complete the migration of the database to Oracle ASM:

1. Restore files to Oracle ASM
2. Recover the database
3. Optionally migrate the fast recovery area to Oracle ASM.

The steps above are broken out in much greater detail in the "Automatic Storage Management Administrator's Guide" under the chapter: "Overview of Oracle ASM Data Migration".

Performing User-Managed Backup and Recovery

Perform user-managed backup and recovery

Describe the backup mode

When performing user-managed backups of the datafiles for an online read-write tablespace while the database is open, it is required that the tablespace first be placed into backup mode. Any time that a tablespace is online and writable, it is possible for the database writer (DBWR) to be updating the file at the same time that the operating system utility is copying it. When this happens, it is possible for the utility to read a block while it is in a partially-updated state. In this case, the block that is copied to the backup media would contain some newer data and some older data. This type of logical corruption is known as a fractured block. Fractured blocks are not consistent with any SCN and Oracle does not normally store sufficient information to repair them.

This situation can be resolved by placing datafiles into backup mode with the ALTER DATABASE or ALTER TABLESPACE statement with the BEGIN BACKUP clause. Once a tablespace has been put into backup mode, Oracle writes the before image for an entire block to the redo stream before making changes to it. The changes made to the block are also stored in the online redo log. Backup mode also freezes the data file checkpoint until the file is removed from backup mode. During recovery, the before image can be used to repair fractured blocks.

RMAN itself does not require extra logging or backup mode because it knows the format of data blocks and will never back up fractured blocks. RMAN also does not need to freeze the data file header checkpoint. It is aware of the order in which the blocks are read, so it can always capture a known good checkpoint.

Back up and recover a control file

There are two ALTER DATABASE commands that can be used to back up a control file. You can back up the control file to a binary file using the following statement:

```
ALTER DATABASE BACKUP CONTROLFILE TO '/oracle/backup/control.bkp';
```

Alternately, the following command writes a SQL script to a trace file that can be used to reproduce the control file. The alert log will contain the name and location of the trace file.

```
ALTER DATABASE BACKUP CONTROLFILE TO TRACE;
```

Finally, for a user managed backup while the database is shut down, you can use operating system commands to copy the control file.

If the control file has been multiplexed and any of the copies is still usable, recovering is simply a matter of copying the undamaged file into the locations specified by the CONTROL_FILES parameter. However, if a permanent media failure has damaged all control files of a database but you have a backup of the control file, the following procedure will allow you to restore a backup control file. If possible, restore the backup control file to the original location to avoid having to specify new control file locations in the initialization parameter file.

1. If the instance is still running, shut it down:

    ```
    SQL> SHUTDOWN ABORT
    ```

2. Correct the hardware problem that caused the media failure.
3. Restore the backup control file to all locations specified in the CONTROL_FILES parameter in the server parameter file or initialization parameter file. For example, if /u01/oradata/trgt/ctrl01.dbf and /u02/oradata/trgt/ctrl02.dbf are the control file locations listed in the server parameter file, then use an operating system utility to restore the backup control file to these locations:

```
% cp /backup/ctrl01.dbf /u01/oradata/trgt/ctrl01.dbf
% cp /backup/ctrl02.dbf /u02/oradata/trgt/ctrl02.dbf
```

4. Start a new instance and mount the database. For example, enter:

```
SQL> STARTUP MOUNT
```

5. Begin recovery by executing the RECOVER command with the USING BACKUP CONTROLFILE clause. Specify UNTIL CANCEL if you are performing incomplete recovery. For example, enter:

```
SQL> RECOVER DATABASE USING BACKUP CONTROLFILE UNTIL CANCEL
```

6. Apply the prompted archived logs.
7. Open the database with the RESETLOGS option after finishing recovery:

```
SQL> ALTER DATABASE OPEN RESETLOGS;
```

Recover from a lost temp file

If one of more files belonging to the temporary tablespace is lost, any SQL statements that require space in the temporary tablespace will generate an error. If the database is up and you would like to recreate the file immediately, you can do so by creating a new datafile and dropping the old one as follows:

```
SQL> ALTER TABLESPACE temp ADD TEMPFILE
'/u01/app/oracle/oradata/orcl/temp02.dbf' SIZE 50M;
SQL> ALTER TABLESPACE temp DROP TEMPFILE
'/u01/app/oracle/oradata/orcl/temp01.dbf';
```

If the loss or damage to the datafile occurred while the database is down, simply starting the instance will automatically recreate the datafile. If Oracle detects a missing datafile on startup, it will issue the commands to recreate it. You will see a message in the alert log such are:

```
Re-creating tempfile /u01/app/oracle/oradata/orcl/temp01.dbf
```

If the file damage occurred while the database is started, but you would prefer to have the recovery done automatically (and assuming that restarting the database is an option), then shutting down and restarting the instance will recreate the file.

Recover from a lost redo log group

If all members of an online redo log group are damaged, the recovery process depends on the type of online redo log group affected and the whether or not the database is in archivelog mode. If the damaged online redo log group is current and active, then it is needed for crash recovery; otherwise, it is not. You can determine the status of the group associated with the damage files from V$LOGFILE:

```
SELECT group#, status, member
FROM   v$logfile;

GROUP#    STATUS        MEMBER
-------   -----------   ---------------------
0001                    /oracle/dbs/log1a.f
0001                    /oracle/dbs/log1b.f
0002      INVALID       /oracle/dbs/log2a.f
0002      INVALID       /oracle/dbs/log2b.f
0003                    /oracle/dbs/log3a.f
0003                    /oracle/dbs/log3b.f
```

You can determine which groups are active from the V$LOG view:

```
SELECT group#, status, archived
FROM   v$log;

GROUP#   STATUS      ARCHIVED
------   ---------   -----------
 0001    INACTIVE    YES
 0002    ACTIVE      NO
 0003    CURRENT     NO
```

If all members of an inactive online redo log group are damaged, then the procedure depends on whether it is possible to repair the media problem that damaged the group. If the failure is transient, then fix the problem. The log writer will reuse the redo log group when required. For permanent failures, the damaged redo log group will halt normal database operation when the database tries to use it. The damaged group must be reinitialized manually by issuing the ALTER DATABASE CLEAR LOGFILE statement.

If all members of an active (but not current) log group are damaged and the database is still running, issue the ALTER SYSTEM CHECKPOINT statement. If the checkpoint is successful, then the redo log group will become inactive. At this point you can follow the steps for an inactive online redo log group. If the checkpoint is unsuccessful, or the database has halted, then depending on the archiving mode you must follow the recovery procedures corresponding to the current log group.

The current log group is the one LGWR is currently writing to. If a LGWR I/O operation fails, then LGWR terminates and the instance is terminated. In this case, you must restore a backup, perform incomplete recovery, and open the database with the RESETLOGS option.

Recovering from the Loss of Active Logs in NOARCHIVELOG Mode

If the media failure is temporary, then correct the problem so that the database can reuse the group when required.

- Restore the database from a consistent, whole database backup (data files and control files).
- Mount the database:
- To allow the database to reset the online redo logs, you must first mimic incomplete recovery:

```
RECOVER DATABASE UNTIL CANCEL
CANCEL
```

- Open the database using the RESETLOGS option:

  ```
  ALTER DATABASE OPEN RESETLOGS;
  ```

- Shut down the database consistently.

  ```
  SHUTDOWN IMMEDIATE
  ```

- Make a whole database backup.

Recovering from Loss of Active Logs in ARCHIVELOG Mode

- Begin incomplete media recovery, recovering up through the log before the damaged log.
- Ensure that the current name of the lost redo log can be used for a newly created file. If not, then rename the members of the damaged online redo log group to a new location.
- Open the database using the RESETLOGS option:

  ```
  ALTER DATABASE OPEN RESETLOGS;
  ```

Recover from the loss of a password file

If the Oracle password file is lost or damaged, it must be recreated using the orapwd command-line utility. When a new password file is created, orapwd prompts for the SYS password and stores the result in the created password file. The Oracle password file is required to support the administrative privileges SYSDBA and SYSOPER. If this file is lost or damaged, it must be recreated using the orapwd command-line utility. When a new password file is created, orapwd prompts for the SYS password and stores the result in the created password file. The syntax of the ORAPWD command is as follows:

```
ORAPWD FILE=filename [ENTRIES=numusers] [FORCE={Y|N}]
[IGNORECASE={Y|N}]
```

The command arguments of orapwd follow. For all parameters, there are no spaces permitted around the equal sign (=) character.

- **FILE** --Name to assign to the password file. You must supply a complete path. If you supply only a file name, the file is written to the current directory.
- **ENTRIES** -- Maximum number of entries (user accounts) to permit in the file. This is optional.
- **FORCE** -- If Y, permits overwriting an existing password file. This is optional.
- **IGNORECASE** -- If Y, passwords are treated as case-insensitive. This is optional.
- **FORMAT** -- When this argument is set to 12 (the default), ORAPWD creates a database password file in Oracle Database 12c format. The 12c format is required for the file to support SYSBACKUP, SYSDG, and SYSKM administrative privileges. If this argument is set to legacy, then ORAPWD creates a database password file that only supports SYSDBA and SYSOPER privileges.

The following command creates a password file named orapworcl that allows up to 40 privileged users with different passwords.

```
orapwd FILE=orapworcl ENTRIES=40
```

Perform user-managed complete database recovery

Complete database recovery is normally performed when one or more datafiles become damaged or lost. In a complete database recovery, all available redo logs will be applied to recover the database to the current SCN. The following recovery makes these assumptions:

- The current control file is available.
- You have backups of all needed data files.
- All necessary archived redo logs are available.

The basic steps to perform complete recovery while the database is not open follow. You can recover either all damaged data files in one operation or perform individual recovery of each damaged data file in separate operations.

1. If the database is open, query V$RECOVER_FILE to determine which data files must be recovered and why they must be recovered.
2. Query the V$ARCHIVED_LOG and V$RECOVERY_LOG views to determine which archived redo log files are needed.
3. If some archived logs must be restored, restore the required archived redo log files to the location specified by LOG_ARCHIVE_DEST_1.
4. If the database is open, then shut it down.
5. If the files are permanently damaged, then identify the most recent backups for the damaged files. Restore only the data files damaged by the media failure: do not restore undamaged data files or any online redo log files.
6. Use an operating system utility to restore the data files to their default location or to a new location if there is a media failure that cannot be fixed.
7. Connect to the database with administrator privileges. Then start a new instance and mount, but do not open, the database.
8. If you restored one or more damaged data files to alternative locations, then update the control file of the database to reflect the new data file names.
9. Issue a statement to recover the database, tablespace, or data file. For example, enter one of the following RECOVER commands:

```
RECOVER AUTOMATIC DATABASE
RECOVER AUTOMATIC TABLESPACE users
RECOVER AUTOMATIC DATAFILE '?/oradata/trgt/users01.dbf'
```

10. If no archived redo logs are required for complete media recovery, then the database applies all necessary online redo log files and terminates recovery.
11. After recovery terminates, open the database for use

Perform user-managed incomplete database recovery

This section describes steps to perform an incomplete recovery. When performing an incomplete recovery you must recover all damaged data files in a single operation.

1. If the database is open, query V$RECOVER_FILE to determine which data files must be recovered and why they must be recovered.
2. Query the V$ARCHIVED_LOG and V$RECOVERY_LOG views to determine which archived redo log files are needed.
3. If some archived logs must be restored, restore the required archived redo log files to the location specified by LOG_ARCHIVE_DEST_1.
4. If the database is open, then shut it down.
5. If the files are permanently damaged, then identify the most recent backups for the damaged files. Restore only the data files damaged by the media failure: do not restore undamaged data files or any online redo log files.
6. Use an operating system utility to restore the data files to their default location or to a new location if there is a media failure that cannot be fixed.
7. Connect to the database with administrator privileges. Then start a new instance and mount, but do not open, the database.
8. If you restored one or more damaged data files to alternative locations, then update the control file of the database to reflect the new data file names.
9. Begin cancel-based recovery by issuing the following command in SQL*Plus:

   ```
   RECOVER DATABASE UNTIL CANCEL
   ```

10. Continue applying redo log files until the last log has been applied to the restored data files, then cancel recovery by executing the following command:

    ```
    CANCEL
    ```

11. Open the database with the RESETLOGS option. You must always reset the logs after incomplete recovery or recovery with a backup control file.

12. After opening the database with the RESETLOGS option, check the alert log to determine whether the database detected inconsistencies between the data dictionary and the control file.

Multitenant Environment

Multitenant Container and Pluggable Database Architecture

Describe multitenant architecture

Oracle 12c introduced a radical new architecture with the Multitenant option. The new architecture allows for Oracle to be provisioned as a 'Container' database (CDB) that can host multiple 'Pluggable' databases (PDBs), each of which can be added and removed from the CDB. Existing legacy Oracle databases can be adapted to become pluggable databases. The new PDBs in turn can continue to be accessed by other tiers without having to make changes to legacy applications.

There are a number of advantages to the Multitenant architecture, including:

- **Database Consolidation** -- Multiple pluggable databases can be stored in a single container database. When in a CDB, they share a single set of background processes, server and system memory while still maintaining complete separation of the data in each PDB. There is no added maintenance overhead or mingling of data as is the case with Virtual Private Databases. This makes it possible to store many more PDBs on a given hardware platform than individual Oracle databases using the legacy architecture.
- **Reduced Costs** -- Consolidating multiple databases can dramatically reduce the costs associated with hardware. In addition, a container database with a dozen PDBs requires considerably less maintenance than twelve individual databases. The result requires fewer personnel to maintain.
- **Rapid Implementation** -- Pluggable databases make it very easy to migrate or implement data and code. It requires very little time to plug a PDB into a CDB, unplug it, and then plug the PDB into a different CDB.

- **Simplified Management** -- With multiple PDBs in a single container database, it is simpler for database administrators to monitor and manage the physical database. There is only a single set of database files and one instance to maintain. This simplifies both backup strategies and disaster recovery scenarios.
- **Separation of administrative duties** -- Multitenant user accounts are either common, which allows them to connect to any container on which they have privileges, or local, and can only connect to a single PDB. DBA duties in turn can be split between CDB-level and PDB-level. CDB administrators use a common account to manage the CDB. PDB administrators use local accounts to manage individual PDBs. Privileges exist only in the container for which they are granted. A local user on one PDB does not have privileges on other PDBs within the same CDB.
- **Simplified Tuning** -- Monitoring and tuning one database is much easier than monitoring and tuning a dozen databases.
- **Simplified Patching** -- Patching/upgrading a single database is much easier than doing so for a dozen databases.

The multitenant architecture is what allows an Oracle database to act as a container database that includes zero, one, or many PDBs. A container is a collection of schemas, objects, and related structures stored in a multitenant container database. A container is either a PDB or the root container (also called the root). Each PDB appears logically to an application as a separate database. Within a CDB, each PDB container must have a unique ID and name. PDBs isolate data and operations so that from the perspective of a user or application accessing it through Oracle Net, each PDB appears as if it were a traditional database.

Every container database has the following containers:

- **One root** -- The root container stores Oracle-supplied metadata (such as the source code for Oracle-supplied PL/SQL packages) and common users. A common user is a database user known in every container. The root container is named CDB$ROOT. All PDBs belong to the root. User data should never be stored in the root and the system-supplied schemas should never be altered. It is possible, however, to create common users and roles for database administration.

- **One seed PDB** -- The seed PDB is a system-supplied template that can be used to create new PDBs. The seed PDB is named PDB$SEED. You cannot add or modify objects in PDB$SEED.

- **Zero or more user-created PDBs** -- User-created PDBs are the entities that contain the data and code required for a specific set of features. No PDBs exist at the time the CDB is initially created. PDBs are added to the container database as needed. PDBs must be uniquely named within a CDB, and follow the same naming rules as service names. Moreover, because a PDB has a service with its own name, a PDB name must be unique across all CDBs whose services are exposed through a specific listener.

Explain pluggable database provisioning

Part of Enterprise Manager Cloud Control's Provisioning capability includes the ability to manipulate pluggable databases. EM Cloud Control enables administrators to manage the entire PDB lifecycle. This includes provisioning CDBs, provisioning PDBs (from the seed or from an unplugged PDB), cloning existing PDBs, migrating non-CDBs as PDBs, and unplugging PDBs. From EM Cloud control, it is possible to provision PDBs in several different ways:

- Create a new PDB within a CDB
- Cloning an existing PDB
- Migrating existing non-CDBs to a CDB as PDBs
- Plugging an unplugged PDB into a CDB

The first two of the above operations create a new pluggable database and attach it to an existing Container Database. The second two simply attach an existing database to a CDB. When a PDB becomes part of a CDB, it runs under the umbrella of the CDB, sharing the instance, undo tablespace and various other functionality that will be described in the following topics.

Creating Multitenant Container Databases and Pluggable Databases

Create and configure a CDB

The steps involved in creating a container database are very much like those required to create a standard Oracle database. Prior to creating the CDB, you must take into account what the database will be used for and plan accordingly. Some of the recommended pre-creation actions include:

- Plan the tables and indexes for the pluggable databases (PDBs) that will be contained in the CDB and estimate the amount of space they will require.
- Plan the layout of the underlying operating system files for the CDB.
- Plan for the number of background processes that the CDB will require.
- Determine the global database name for the CDB to be set by the DB_NAME and DB_DOMAIN initialization parameters.
- Develop a backup and recovery strategy to protect the CDB from failure.
- Select an appropriate character set.
- Determine the appropriate initial size for the SYSAUX tablespace.

Before a new CDB can be created, the following prerequisites must be met:

- Oracle 12c must be installed with the database compatibility level set to at least 12.0.0.
- Sufficient memory must be available to start the Oracle Database instance.
- Sufficient disk storage space must be available for the planned PDBs.

The container database creation prepares several operating system files to work together as a CDB. A CDB can be created either during or after

Oracle Database software installation. A CDB can be created either with the Database Configuration Assistant (DBCA) or with the CREATE DATABASE SQL statement. Oracle strongly recommends using the Database Configuration Assistant (DBCA) method. DBCA is a much easier method for doing so and the CDB is ready to use as soon as DBCA completes.

The Database Configuration Assistant can be launched by the Oracle Universal Installer or launched as a standalone tool at any time after Oracle Database installation. It is possible to create a CDB in interactive mode or noninteractive/silent mode. The interactive mode provides a graphical interface and guided workflow for the CDB creation process. Noninteractive mode enables you to script the creation of the CDB. Once the CDB has been created, DBCA can be used to plug new PDBs into it or unplug existing ones.

If you decide to use the CREATE DATABASE statement to create a CDB, there are additional actions that must be completed before the CDB will be operational. Namely, the standard PL/SQL packages must be installed and required views created against the data dictionary tables. The catcdb.sql script must be executed to perform these actions.

Create a PDB using different methods

Prior to creating a PDB, several prerequisites must be met:

- The CDB must exist.
- The CDB must be in read/write mode.
- The current user must be a common user whose current container is the root.
- The current user must have the CREATE PLUGGABLE DATABASE system privilege.

- A PDB name must be selected that is unique to the CDB it will be plugged into and all the CDBs whose instances are reached through a specific listener.
- PDBs created in an Oracle Data Guard configuration with a physical standby database, have additional requirements. Reference the Oracle Data Guard Concepts and Administration manual for more information.

There are four different methods for creating a pluggable database (PDB) in a multitenant container database (CDB):

- **Using the seed** -- The files associated with the seed are copied to a new location and associated with the new PDB.
- **Cloning an existing PDB** -- An existing PDB can be cloned and plugged into the CDB. The PDB to be used as the source can either be in the local CDB or in a remote CDB. All of the files associated with the source PDB are copied to a new location and associated with the new PDB.
- **Plugging in an unplugged PDB** -- The XML metadata file that describes an unplugged PDB plus its associated files are plugged into the CDB.
- **Converting a non-CDB** -- The DBMS_PDB package can create an unplugged PDB from an Oracle Database 12c non-CDB. The newly-created PDB can then be plugged into a CDB.

All four techniques make use of the CREATE PLUGGABLE DATABASE statement at some point. This statement is used for both copying a database and for plugging a PDB in to a CDB as required. The statement has optional clauses that can be used to set several aspects of the PDB:

- **Storage** – The STORAGE clause specifies the amount of storage that can be used by all tablespaces that belong to the PDB and the amount of storage in the default temporary tablespace shared by all PDBs that can be used by sessions connected to the PDB. If STORAGE UNLIMITED is set, or if there is no STORAGE clause, the PDB has no storage limits.

- **File Locations** -- There are three clauses that affect the file names used for a PDB. The PATH_PREFIX clause can be used to ensure that a PDB's files reside in a specific directory and its subdirectories when relative paths are used for directory objects and certain initialization parameters. The FILE_NAME_CONVERT clause specifies the names of the PDB's files after the PDB is plugged into the CDB. The SOURCE_FILE_NAME_CONVERT clause specifies the names of a PDB's files before the PDB is plugged into the CDB.

- **Temp File Reuse** -- The TEMPFILE REUSE clause specifies that an existing temp file in the target location is reused if one exists. If this clause is specified, and there is no temp file in the target location, Oracle will create a new temp file. If the clause is not specified, Oracle will attempt to create a new temp file for the PDB. If a file exists with the same name as the new temp file in the target location, an error will be generated, and the PDB creation will fail.

Creating a PDB Using the Seed

The CREATE PLUGGABLE DATABASE statement can be used to create a PDB in a CDB using the files of the seed. When creating a new PDB from the seed, a PDB administrator must be specified in the CREATE PLUGGABLE DATABASE statement. The new database will be created with two tablespaces: SYSTEM and SYSAUX. The administrator is created as a local user in the PDB and granted the PDB_DBA role. To create a PDB from the seed:

- In SQL*Plus, ensure that the current container is the root.
- Run the CREATE PLUGGABLE DATABASE statement, and specify a local administrator for the PDB. Specify other clauses when they are required.
- Open the new PDB in read/write mode that that Oracle can complete the integration of the new PDB into the CDB.
- Back up the PDB.

An example of this method (with none of the optional clauses) is:

```
CREATE PLUGGABLE DATABASE ocp_pdb ADMIN USER ocp_adm IDENTIFIED BY
password;
```

Cloning a PDB

The CREATE PLUGGABLE DATABASE statement can be used to clone a PDB. When cloning an existing PDB, the FROM clause will specify the source PDB to be cloned. The source PDB can be in the local CDB or in a remote CDB. In order to clone a PDB, the current user must have the CREATE PLUGGABLE DATABASE system privilege in both the root and the source PDB and the source PDB must be open in read-only mode. To clone a PDB:

- In SQL*Plus, ensure that the current container is the root.
- Run the CREATE PLUGGABLE DATABASE statement, and specify the source PDB in the FROM clause. Specify other clauses when they are required.
- Open the new PDB in read/write mode.
- Back up the PDB.

An example of the syntax for cloning a PDB is:

```
CREATE PLUGGABLE DATABASE pdb2 FROM pdb1
PATH_PREFIX = '/u02/oracle/pdb2'
FILE_NAME_CONVERT = ('/u01/oracle/pdb1/', '/u02/oracle/pdb2/');
```

Plugging an Unplugged PDB into a CDB

This technique uses the XML metadata file of an existing PDB along with its associated files to plug it into the CDB. The USING clause of the CREATE PLUGGABLE DATABASE statement specifies the XML metadata file. The XML file in turn contains the locations of the PDB's files. To plug in an unplugged PDB:

- In SQL*Plus, ensure that the current container is the root.
- (Optional) Run the DBMS_PDB.CHECK_PLUG_COMPATIBILITY function to determine whether the unplugged PDB is compatible with the CDB.
- Run the CREATE PLUGGABLE DATABASE statement, and specify the XML file in the USING clause. Specify other clauses when they are required.
- Open the new PDB in read/write mode.
- Back up the PDB.

An example of the syntax for plugging in an unplugged PDB is:

```
CREATE PLUGGABLE DATABASE ocp_pdb USING '/u01/usr/ocp_pdb.xml'
NOCOPY TEMPFILE REUSE;
```

Creating a PDB Using a Non-CDB

It is possible to move a non-CDB into a PDB via three different methods:

- **DBMS_PDB** -- The DBMS_PDB package can be used to generate an XML metadata file. This file describes the database files of the non-CDB . It can then be plugged into a CDB using the XML file as described above. In order to use this technique, the non-CDB must be from an Oracle 12c Database. Older databases must be upgraded to Oracle Database 12c in order to use this technique.
- **Oracle Data Pump** -- With this method, Oracle Data Pump is used to export the data from the non-CDB database so that it can then be imported into a PDB.
- **Goldengate replication** -- In this method data is replicated from the non-CDB to a PDB. When the PDB catches up with the non-CDB, you fail over to the PDB.

Unplug and drop a PDB

Unplugging a PDB disassociates it from the CDB. This might be done in order to move the PDB to a different CDB or because there is no longer a need for the PDB to be available. When a PDB is unplugged, the ALTER PLUGGABLE DATABASE statement will specify an XML file to contain metadata about the PDB after it is unplugged. The XML file will be created by the operation and will contain information that will allow a CREATE PLUGGABLE DATABASE statement on a target CDB to plug in the PDB.

The unplug operation makes some changes in the PDB's data files, including recording the PDB was successfully unplugged. An unplugged PDB is still part of the CDB, and will be included in an RMAN backup of the entire CDB. To completely remove the PDB from the CDB, it must be dropped. The only operation supported on an unplugged PDB is to drop it. An unplugged PDB cannot be plugged back into the same database unless it is dropped. In order to unplug a PDB, the following prerequisites must be met:

- The user must be connected to the root with the SYSDBA or SYSOPER administrative privilege.
- The PDB must have been opened at least once.
- The PDB must be closed.

To unplug a PDB:

1. In SQL*Plus, connect to the root as SYSDBA or SYSOPER.
2. Run the ALTER PLUGGABLE DATABASE statement with the UNPLUG INTO clause, and specify the PDB to unplug and the name and location of the PDB's XML metadata file. The following statement unplugs the PDB ocp_pdb and creates the ocp_pdb.xml metadata file in the /oracle/data/ directory:

```
ALTER PLUGGABLE DATABASE ocp_pdb
  UNPLUG INTO '/oracle/data/ocp_pdb.xml';
```

The DROP PLUGGABLE DATABASE statement is used to drop a PDB. A PDB might be dropped in order to move it to another CDB or when it is no longer needed. When a PDB is dropped, the control file of the CDB is modified to eliminate all references to it. And archived redo log files and backups that are associated with the PDB are not removed by the DROP statement. Oracle Recovery Manager (RMAN) can be used to remove them. When a PDB is dropped, it is possible to either keep or delete the data files associated with it by using one of the following clauses:

- **KEEP DATAFILES** -- This is the default, and retains the data files. The PDB's temp file is removed even when KEEP DATAFILES is specified because it is no longer needed.
- **INCLUDING DATAFILES** -- This option removes the data files from disk. For a PDB that was created with the SNAPSHOT COPY clause, INCLUDING DATAFILES must be specified when dropping the PDB.

In order to drop a PDB, the following prerequisites must be met:

- The PDB must be in mounted mode, or it must be unplugged.
- The user must be connected to the root with the SYSDBA or SYSOPER administrative privilege.

To drop a PDB:

1. In SQL*Plus, connect to the root as SYSDBA or SYSOPER.
2. Run the DROP PLUGGABLE DATABASE statement and specify the PDB to drop.

```
DROP PLUGGABLE DATABASE ocpdb
INCLUDING DATAFILES;
```

Migrate a non-CDB to a PDB database

It is possible to move a non-CDB into a PDB via three different methods:

- **DBMS_PDB** -- The DBMS_PDB package can be used to generate an XML metadata file. This file describes the database files of the non-CDB. It can then be plugged into a CDB using the XML file as described above. In order to use this technique, the non-CDB must be from an Oracle 12c Database. Older databases must be upgraded to Oracle Database 12c in order to use this technique.
- **Oracle Data Pump** -- With this method, Oracle Data Pump is used to export the data from the non-CDB database so that it can then be imported into a PDB.
- **Goldengate replication** -- In this method data is replicated from the non-CDB to a PDB. When the PDB catches up with the non-CDB, you fail over to the PDB.

This section will deal with using the DBMS_PDB.DESCRIBE procedure of the DBMS_PDB package. Oracle Data Pump is discussed in a later section and GoldenGate is outside the scope of this exam.

To move a non-CDB into a PDB using the DBMS_PDB package, the CDB must be in a transactionally-consistent state. In addition, it must be placed in read-only mode. Once the non-CDB is read-only, connect to the database, and execute the DBMS_PDB.DESCRIBE procedure. This procedure will construct an XML file that describes the non-CDB. The following example will generate an XML file named ocp_db.xml in the /u01/oracle directory:

```
BEGIN
DBMS_PDB.DESCRIBE(
  pdb_descr_file => '/u01/oracle/ocp_db.xml');
END;
/
```

Once the procedure has completed and the XML file has been created, the XML file and the non-CDB's database files can be plugged into a CDB. Shut down the non-CDB and then issue the CREATE PLUGGABLE DATABASE statement with the appropriate clauses, for example:

```
CREATE PLUGGABLE DATABASE ncdb USING '/u01/oracle/ocp_db.xml'
COPY
FILE_NAME_CONVERT = ('/u01/oracle/dbs/', '/u02/oracle/ocp_db/');
```

Before opening the new PDB for the first time, you must run the ORACLE_HOME/rdbms/admin/noncdb_to_pdb.sql script. This script is only required when converting non-CDB databases into a PDB.

```
@$ORACLE_HOME/rdbms/admin/noncdb_to_pdb.sql
```

After running the script, the new PDB must be opened in read/write mode for Oracle Database to complete the integration of the new PDB into the CDB. An error is returned if you attempt o open the PDB in read-only mode. Once the database has been opened in read-write mode, you should immediately take a backup of the new PDB.

Managing CDBs and PDBs

Establish connections to a CDB/PDB

Client applications connecting to a CDB can access the root of a PDB through database services. Database services have an optional PDB property. When a PDB is created, a new default service with the same name as the PDB will be created automatically. If Oracle Net Services is configured properly, it is possible to use the service name to access the PDB using the easy connect syntax or the net service name from the tnsnames.ora file. When a connection is submitted using a service with a non-null PDB property, the user name for the session is resolved in the context of the specified PDB. If no service is specified or a service name with a NULL PDB property is used, the user name will be resolved in the context of the root.

If two or more CDBs on the same computer system use the same listener and they contain two or more PDBs with the same service name, using that service name will connect randomly to one of the PDBs using it. All service names for PDBs should be unique on a given system, or each CDB should use a separate listener.

It is possible to connect to a container by using the SQL*Plus CONNECT command. Alternately, it is possible to switch into a container with an ALTER SESSION SET CONTAINER SQL statement. The CONNECT command can be used to connect either to the root or to a PDB in a CDB. Any of the following techniques are valid for connecting to the root using the SQL*Plus CONNECT command:

- Local connection
- Local connection with operating system authentication
- Database connection using easy connect
- Database connection using a net service name
- Remote database connection using external authentication

In order for a user to connect to the root, they must be a common user and that user must have been granted CREATE SESSION privilege in the root. To connect to the root using the SQL*Plus CONNECT command, you must start SQL*Plus with the /NOLOG argument:

```
sqlplus /nolog
```

Once in SQL*Plus, you can connect to the root by various methods:

- Connecting with a Local Connection
  ```
  connect username/password
  ```

- Connecting with Operating System Authentication
  ```
  connect / as sysdba
  ```

- Connecting with a Net Service Name
  ```
  connect username/password@ocp_db
  ```

Either of the following techniques can be used to connect to a PDB with the SQL*Plus CONNECT command:

- Database connection using easy connect
- Database connection using a net service name

In order to connect to a PDB, a user must be a common user of the CDB with CREATE SESSION granted either commonly or locally in the PDB, or a local user in the PDB with CREATE SESSION granted. Only a user with SYSDBA, SYSOPER, SYSBACKUP, or SYSDG privilege can connect to a PDB that is in mounted mode. To connect to a PDB using the SQL*Plus CONNECT command, you must start SQL*Plus with the /NOLOG argument:

```
sqlplus /nolog
```

The following command connects to the candidate local user in the ocp_db PDB:

```
CONNECT candidate@ocp_db
```

When a session is connected to a container as a common user, the following statement can be used to switch to a different container:

```
ALTER SESSION SET CONTAINER = container_name
```

The container_name, can be any one of the following:

- CDB$ROOT to switch to the root
- PDB$SEED to switch to the seed
- A PDB name to switch to the PDB

Start up and shut down a CDB and open and close PDBs

Unless being operated in a Real Application Clusters environment, a CDB runs with a single instance. You need to be connected to the root of the CDB with SYSDBA privileges in order to start the instance. The startup process for a CDB instance is same as that for non-CDB databases. STARTUP NOMOUNT, STARTUP MOUNT, and STARTUP OPEN all function in a CDB and have the effect on the Container Database that they would on a non-CDB. However, the status of the PDBs within the CDB is not always the same. Once the instance has been started, you may use the V$PDBS view to determine the status of PDBs.

- **NOMOUNT** -- When the CDB is in NOMOUNT status, the instance is started, but the PDBs have no status. Querying the V$PDBS view will return no rows.

- **MOUNT** -- When the CDB is in MOUNT status, the control files for the instance will be opened. The Root and all of the PDBs will be in a status of MOUNTED.
- **OPEN** -- When the CDB is initially set to OPN, the root will be opened. The SEEB PDB will be opened in read-only mode. All other PDBs in the CDB will still be in MOUNTED status.

Once the CDB is opened, it is possible to open the PDBs individually or all at once:

```
ALTER PLUGGABLE DATABASE ocp_db OPEN;
ALTER PLUGGABLE DATABASE ALL OPEN;
```

A CDB instance is shut down in the same fashion that a non-CDB instance is. To shut the instance down, the following requirements must be met:

- It must be mounted or open
- The current user must be a common user with SYSDBA, SYSOPER, SYSBACKUP, or SYSDG administrative privilege
- The current container must be the root.

The open mode of a PDB can be altered using the ALTER PLUGGABLE DATABASE SQL statement or the SQL*Plus STARTUP command. The possible modes for PDBs are:

- **OPEN READ WRITE** -- This mode allows queries and user transactions to proceed and allows users to generate redo logs.
- **OPEN READ ONLY** -- This mode allows queries but does not allow user changes.
- **OPEN MIGRATE** -- This mode allows you to run database upgrade scripts on the PDB. A PDB is in this mode after an ALTER DATABASE OPEN UPGRADE is run.
- **MOUNTED** -- A PDB is in mounted mode behaves like a non-CDB in mounted mode. No changes are allowed to objects and it is accessible only to database administrators.

When the current container is the root, an ALTER PLUGGABLE DATABASE statement with a pdb_change_state clause modifies the open mode of the specified PDBs. When a PDB is opened using the ALTER PLUGGABLE DATABASE OPEN statement, READ WRITE is the default unless the PDB belongs to a CDB that is used as a physical standby database, in which case READ ONLY is the default. The PDBs to be modified by the ALTER statement can be specified in the following ways:

- List one or more PDBs separated by commas.
- Specify ALL to modify all of the PDBs.
- Specify ALL EXCEPT to modify all of the PDBs, except for the PDBs listed.

Some examples of this statement are:

```
ALTER PLUGGABLE DATABASE ocp_db, test_db OPEN READ WRITE;

ALTER PLUGGABLE DATABASE ocp_db OPEN READ ONLY RESTRICTED;

ALTER PLUGGABLE DATABASE ALL OPEN READ WRITE;
```

When the current container is the root it is also possible to use the STARTUP PLUGGABLE DATABASE command to open a single PDB. The STARTUP PLUGGABLE DATABASE statement has the following options:

- **FORCE** -- Closes an open PDB before re-opening it in read/write mode.
- **RESTRICT** -- Enables only users with the RESTRICTED SESSION system privilege in the PDB to access the PDB.
- **OPEN** -- Opens the PDB in either read/write mode or read-only mode. You can specify OPEN READ WRITE or OPEN READ ONLY. When no option is specified, READ WRITE is the default.

Some examples of this statement are:

```
STARTUP PLUGGABLE DATABASE ocp_db OPEN

STARTUP PLUGGABLE DATABASE ocp_db RESTRICT
```

```
STARTUP PLUGGABLE DATABASE ocp_db OPEN READ ONLY

STARTUP PLUGGABLE DATABASE ocp_db FORCE
```

The ALTER PLUGGABLE DATABASE can also be used to close one or more PDBs. To close a PDB, connect to the root as SYSOPER or SYSDBA and issue an ALTER PLUGGABLE DATABASE CLOSE statement, specifying the PDB or PDBs to be closed. If the command is issued with the IMMEDIATE keyword, transactions in the selected PDBs are rolled back and the sessions disconnected. If the IMMEDIATE keyword is omitted, the statement hangs until all sessions have disconnected from the PDB. All of the data files of the PDB will be closed and it will be inaccessible to users. When connected to PDB, issuing a SHUTDOWN IMMEDIATE is equivalent to ALTER PLUGGABLE DATABASE CLOSE.

Some examples of this statement are:

```
ALTER PLUGGABLE DATABASE ocp_db, test_db CLOSE;

ALTER PLUGGABLE DATABASE ALL CLOSE;

ALTER PLUGGABLE DATABASE ALL EXCEPT test_db CLOSE IMMEDIATE;
```

Evaluate the impact of parameter value changes

A CDB will contain only a single SPFILE no matter how many PDBs it contains. Any initialization parameters specified at the root level apply to the root and will be the default value for any PDBs it contains. Many (but not all) initialization parameters can also be set at the PDB level. The parameters that are modifiable for PDBs can be located with the following query:

```
SELECT name
FROM   v$system_parameter
WHERE  ispdb_modifiable = 'TRUE'
ORDER BY name;
```

Any of the initialization parameters listed by this query that are not set independently for a PDB will be inherited from the parameter value set at the root. Values from the list can be set at the PDB level with the ALTER SYSTEM command. When the SCOPE is set to SPFILE or BOTH, the values will be retained across PDB close/open and across bouncing the CDB instance. Parameters set at this level will also travel with clone and unplug/plug operations. Any initialization parameters that do not show up in the above query can be set for the root only.

It is possible to use the ALTER SYSTEM statement to dynamically alter a PDB. Not all possible ALTER SYSTEM statements can be executed from a PDB. Any statements that affect the entire CDB must be run by a common user in the root. When the current container is a PDB, a user with the proper privileges can execute the following ALTER SYSTEM statements:

- ALTER SYSTEM FLUSH SHARED_POOL
- ALTER SYSTEM FLUSH BUFFER_CACHE
- ALTER SYSTEM ENABLE RESTRICTED SESSION
- ALTER SYSTEM DISABLE RESTRICTED SESSION
- ALTER SYSTEM SET USE_STORED_OUTLINES
- ALTER SYSTEM SUSPEND
- ALTER SYSTEM RESUME
- ALTER SYSTEM CHECKPOINT
- ALTER SYSTEM CHECK DATAFILES
- ALTER SYSTEM REGISTER
- ALTER SYSTEM KILL SESSION
- ALTER SYSTEM DISCONNECT SESSION
- ALTER SYSTEM SET initialization_parameter (for a subset of initialization parameters)

The new CON_ID column in the V$PARAMETER view contains the ID of the container to which the data pertains. Possible values include:

- **0** -- This value is used for rows containing data that pertain to the entire CDB. This value is also used for rows in non-CDBs.
- **1** -- This value is used for rows containing data that pertain to only the root
- **n** -- Where n is the applicable container ID for the rows containing data

Managing Storage in a CDB and PDBs

Manage permanent and temporary tablespaces in CDB and PDBs

Tablespaces in a multitenant environment serve the same purpose and for the most part are treated in the same fashion as tablespaces in a non-CDB. The syntax for creating and altering tablespaces is largely unchanged. There are a few considerations for tablespaces in a CDB:

- A permanent tablespace can be associated with only one container.
- When you create a tablespace in a container, the tablespace is associated with that container.
- A CDB can have only one active undo tablespace or one active undo tablespace for each instance of an Oracle RAC CDB.
- There is one default temporary tablespace for an entire CDB. The root and the PDBs can use this temporary tablespace. Optionally, each PDB can also have its own temporary tablespace.

Because a permanent tablespace can be associated with only a single container, each container must have its own default permanent tablespace. They cannot be shared between containers. Users connected to a given container who are not explicitly assigned a tablespace will use that container's default permanent tablespace. When connected to the CDB, the command to set the default permanent tablespace would be:

```
ALTER DATABASE DEFAULT TABLESPACE tbs_users_cdb;
```

While connected to a PDB, the 'ALTER DATABASE' command is still retained for backward compatibility, but the preferred command would be:

```
ALTER PLUGGABLE DATABASE DEFAULT TABLESPACE tbs_users_pdb;
```

The current settings for the default tablespaces can be determined by querying the database_properties view:

```
SELECT property_name, property_value
FROM   database_properties
WHERE  property_name like '%TABLESPACE';

PROPERTY_NAME                      PROPERTY_VALUE
----------------------------       --------------
DEFAULT_TEMP_TABLESPACE            TEMP2
DEFAULT_PERMANENT_TABLESPACE       USERS
```

A CDB will have only a single default temporary tablespace (or tablespace group). In order to create or modify this temporary tablespace, the current container must be the root. It is possible to have additional temporary tablespaces in the root, and to assign specific users to them. Likewise, each PDB can contain one default temporary tablespace and additional temporary tablespaces that can be assigned specific users. When a PDB is unplugged from a CDB, its temporary tablespaces are also unplugged.

Managing Security in a CDB and PDBs

Manage common and local users

A common user is a database user that has the same identity in the root and in every existing and future PDB. Common users can connect to and perform operations within the root, and within any PDB in which they have been granted privileges. A user connected to the root can perform certain operations, such as ALTER PLUGGABLE DATABASE, CREATE USER, CREATE ROLE, that affect other pluggable databases. However, most privileges can only be exercised within the current container. Users must first switch to the PDB where the action is to be taken, and then exercise their privileges from there. For example, a common user cannot query tables or views in a PDB when it is not the current container.

Creating a common user account:

- You must be connected to the root and have the commonly granted CREATE USER system privilege.
- The session's current container must be CDB$ROOT.
- The name of the common user must start with C## or c## and contain only ASCII or EDCDIC characters.
- To explicitly designate a user account as a common user, in the CREATE USER statement, specify CONTAINER=ALL. When logged into the root, if the CONTAINER clause is omitted, CONTAINER=ALL is implied.

No objects should be created in the schemas of common users. They cannot be shared across PDB boundaries and can cause problems during plug-in and unplug operations. The following example creates a common user account and grants the user the SET CONTAINER and CREATE SESSION privileges (common users must have these privileges to navigate between containers):

```
CREATE USER c##ocp_admin
   IDENTIFIED BY password
   DEFAULT TABLESPACE ts_cdb_users
   QUOTA 100M ON ts_cdb_users
   TEMPORARY TABLESPACE temp_ts
   CONTAINER = ALL;
GRANT SET CONTAINER, CREATE SESSION
   TO c##ocp_admin CONTAINER = ALL;
```

Creating a local user account:

Local user accounts exist only in the PDB that they are created in. They cannot connect to or be granted privileges in other PDBs. It is possible, of course, to create a user of the same name in multiple PDBs, but the accounts share nothing except the name. To create a local user account:

- You must be connected to the PDB in which you want to create the account, and have the CREATE USER privilege.
- The name of the local user must not start with C## or c##.
- The clause CONTAINER=CURRENT can be included in the CREATE USER statement to explicitly specify the user as a local user. When connected to a PDB, if the clause is omitted, CONTAINER=CURRENT is implied.

```
CREATE USER ocp_user
   IDENTIFIED BY password
   DEFAULT TABLESPACE ts_pdb_users
   QUOTA 100M ON ts_pdb_users
   TEMPORARY TABLESPACE temp_ts
   PROFILE ocp_profile
   CONTAINER = CURRENT;
```

Manage common and local privileges

Common users and local users can grant privileges to one another. A given privilege (i.e. CREATE ANY TABLE) is neither common nor local by itself. If CREATE ANY TABLE is granted commonly, then it becomes a common privilege, and if granted locally, it becomes a local privilege.

Commonly granted privileges:

- A privilege that is granted commonly can be used in every existing and future container.
- Only common users can grant privileges commonly, and only to a common user or a common role.
- The grantor must be connected to the root and must specify CONTAINER=ALL in the GRANT statement.
- Can include system and object privileges.
- Should never be granted to PUBLIC.

Locally granted privileges:

- A privilege granted locally can be used only in the container in which it was granted, even when granted in the root.
- Both common users and local users can grant privileges locally.
- A common user and a local user can grant privileges to other common or local roles.
- The grantor must be connected to the container and must specify CONTAINER=CURRENT in the GRANT statement.
- Any user can grant a privilege locally to any other user or role (both common and local) or to the PUBLIC role.

The CONTAINER clause in a GRANT or REVOKE statement determines where a privilege is granted to or revoked from. When the CONTAINER is set to ALL, the statement applies the privilege to all existing and future containers. Using CURRENT in the clause will apply the privilege to the local container. The value will default to CURRENT if the clause is omitted except when connected to the root, when the default will be ALL. The following example grants the CREATE TABLE privilege to common user c##ocp_admin. After the grant, the user will be able to use the privilege in all existing and future containers.

GRANT CREATE TABLE TO c##ocp_admin CONTAINER=ALL;

Manage common and local roles

Common roles are created in the root and are known in all existing and future containers. All Oracle-supplied predefined roles are common roles. Local roles exist in only the PDB they were created in and can only be used there. Local roles cannot have any commonly granted privileges.

- Common users can both create and grant common roles to other common and local users.
- A common role can be granted to a common user either commonly or locally.
- If a common role is granted to a local user, the privileges from the role apply only to the local user's PDB.
- Local users cannot create common roles
- Local users can grant common roles to common and local users.

If the following requirements are met, commonly granted privileges that have been made to a common role apply in the root and all current and future PDBs to which the grantor can connect:

- Both the grantor and the grantee are common users.
- The grantor possesses the commonly granted SET CONTAINER privilege and the ADMIN OPTION for the common role.
- The GRANT statement contains the CONTAINER=ALL clause.

The name given to user-created common roles must start with C## or c## and contain only ASCII or EDCDIC characters (the C## rule does not apply to Oracle-supplied roles, such as DBA or RESOURCE). When the role is created, the CONTAINER clause must be set to ALL. Except when logged in to the root, omitting this clause from the CREATE ROLE statement creates a local role in the current PDB. If the CONTAINER clause is omitted when logged in to the root, by default the role is created as a common role. The following example creates the c##ocp_admin common role:

```
CREATE ROLE c##ocp_admin CONTAINER=ALL;
```

Enable common users to access data in specific PDBs

The CONTAINER clause of a GRANT statement can be used to grant a privilege to a specific PDB in a multitenant environment. When a privilege is granted while connected to the root, setting CONTAINER to the PDB name applies the privilege to the specified PDB only. The following example would grant the SELECT ANY TABLE privilege to common user c##hr_admin to the ocp_pdb PDB while connected to the root:

```
GRANT SELECT ANY TABLE TO c##ocp_admin CONTAINER=ocp_pdb;
```

Except while connected to the root, omitting the CONTAINER clause applies the privilege to the local container. If a GRANT statement for an object is made by a local user while connected to a given PDB, then the privilege is applied to that PDB only. Either of the following statements would grant the SELECT ANY TABLE privilege to common user c##ocp_admin to the ocp_pdb PDB while connected to that PDB:

```
GRANT SELECT ANY TABLE TO c##ocp_admin;
GRANT SELECT ANY TABLE TO c##ocp_admin CONTAINER=CURRENT;
```

Container Data Objects

A container data object is a table or view that contains information about multiple containers and possibly the CDB as a whole. In a multitenant environment, the X$ tables and the V$, GV$ and CDB_* views are examples of container data objects. Querying these objects can return information about the root and every PDB in the container database. It is possible to restrict data pertaining to one or more containers when common users perform queries of these objects. This may be necessary to avoid exposing sensitive information about specific PDBs to common users. All container data objects have a CON_ID column that indicates which container a particular row references. This column can contain the following values:

- **0** -- Whole CDB, or non-CDB
- **1** -- CDB$ROOT
- **2** -- PDB$SEED
- **Other #s** -- User-Created PDBs

In order to enable common users to access data about specific PDBs, they must be assigned the appropriate CONTAINER_DATA value. This is done by executing an ALTER USER statement from the root. The following example enables the common user c##ocp_admin to view information pertaining to the CDB$ROOT, OCP_PDB, and DEV_PDB containers in all container data objects accessible to that user, for the V$SESSION view.

```
ALTER USER c##ocp_admin
SET CONTAINER_DATA = (CDB$ROOT, OCP_PDB, DEV_PDB)
FOR V$SESSION CONTAINER=CURRENT;
```

The CONTAINER = CURRENT clause must be specified. When connected to the root, CONTAINER=ALL is the default for the ALTER USER statement, but modification of the CONTAINER_DATA attribute must be restricted to the root.

Managing Availability

Perform backups of a CDB and PDBs

There is a full range of capabilities for backing up Oracle databases in a
multitenant environment through RMAN and Enterprise Manager Cloud
Control. If is possible to back up and recover a complete CDB, just the root
of the CDB, or to back up any or all of the PDBs. It is also possible to back
up and recover individual tablespaces and data files in a single PDB.
Backing up each element of a container database individually (the root
and each PDB) is functionally equivalent in terms of recoverability to
backing up the entire CDB.

The steps for backing up an entire CDB are equivalent to performing a full
database backup of a non-CDB. When the entire CDB is backed up, RMAN
backs up the root, all the PDBs, and the archived redo logs. From the
resulting backup, it is possible to recover the whole CDB, the root only, or
combination of PDBs contained in the CDB backup. To back up a CDB, you
must start RMAN and connect to the root of the CDB as a common user
with the SYSBACKUP or SYSDBA privilege and to a recovery catalog (if
used). The database must be either mounted or open. You can then issue
the appropriate backup options from the RMAN prompt:

Back up the entire CDB:

```
RMAN> BACKUP DATABASE;
```

Back up the database, switch the online redo logs, and include archived
logs in the backup:

```
RMAN> BACKUP DATABASE PLUS ARCHIVELOG;
```

Back Up the Root

```
RMAN> BACKUP DATABASE ROOT;
```

Back Up a PDB

There are two approaches to backing up a PDB with RMAN:

- Connect to the root and then issue the BACKUP PLUGGABE DATABASE command from the RMAN prompt. This method can be used to back up one or more PDBs.

  ```
  RMAN> BACKUP PLUGGABLE DATABASE ocprep;

  RMAN> BACKUP PLUGGABLE DATABASE ocprep, testdb;
  ```

- Connect to the PDB and then issue the following command from the RMAN prompt:

  ```
  RMAN> BACKUP DATABASE;
  ```

Recover PDB from PDB datafiles loss

When recovering a container database, it is possible to recover the entire CDB, only the root, only a single PDB, or just a portion of a PDB such as a tablespace or datafile. When the whole CDB is recovered, the root and all PDBs are recovered in a single operation.

To recover the entire CDB, you use the RMAN commands RESTORE and RECOVER. RMAN will automatically restore the backups of any required archived redo logs during the recovery operation. If the backup is stored on a media manager, then any required channels must be configured so that RMAN can access the backup files. You must start RMAN and connect to the root of the CDB as a common user with the SYSBACKUP or SYSDBA privilege and to a recovery catalog (if used). The following commands will restore and recover the entire CDB:

```
RESTORE DATABASE;
RECOVER DATABASE;
```

You can automatically delete any archived redo logs that were restored from disk for the recovery operation (once they are no longer needed for recovery) by using the following command:

```
RECOVER DATABASE DELETE ARCHIVELOG;
```

It is _possible_ to recover only the root if a user error or data corruption occurs that is specific to the root. However, Oracle strongly recommends that you recover all PDBs after recovering the root. This will eliminate the possibility of introducing metadata inconsistencies among the root and the PDBs. As a general rule, it is preferable to recover the whole CDB. To recover the root, you must be connected to the root from RMAN as a common user with the SYSDBA or SYSBACKUP privilege and the CDB must be in MOUNT mode.

- If required, use the CONFIGURE command to configure the default device type and automatic channels.
- Restore and recover the root with the following commands:

```
RESTORE DATABASE ROOT;
RECOVER DATABASE ROOT;
```

- Examine the output from RMAN to verify that media recovery was successful. Oracle strongly recommends at this point that you recover all of the PDBs, including the seed. To do this, issue the RESTORE PLUGGABLE DATABASE and RECOVER PLUGGABLE DATABASE commands.

```
RESTORE PLUGGABLE DATABASE 'PDB$SEED', ocprep, testdb;
RECOVER PLUGGABLE DATABASE 'PDB$SEED', ocprep, testdb;
```

- Examine the output from RMAN to verify that media recovery was successful. If it was successful, open the CDB and all PDBs.

```
ALTER DATABASE OPEN;
ALTER PLUGGABLE DATABASE ALL OPEN;
```

Administrators can perform a complete recovery on a given PDB, or multiple PDBs without affecting operations of other open PDBs in the same container database. It is possible to recover a PDB in RMAN while connected to the root or while connected to the PDB. While connected to the root, you would use the RESTORE PLUGGABLE DATABASE and RECOVER PLUGGABLE DATABASE commands (as demonstrated previously). With these commands, you can recover multiple pluggable databases at once. When connected to the PDB you would use the RESTORE DATABASE and RECOVER DATABASE commands. Only one PDB can be recovered at a time using this method. The following steps will recover the ocprep PDB while connected to the root from RMAN as a common user with the SYSDBA or SYSBACKUP privilege:

- Close the PDBs to be recovered.

```
ALTER PLUGGABLE DATABASE ocprep CLOSE;
```

- If the PDB has missing data files an error will occur and the PDB cannot be closed. You must connect to the PDB with missing data file(s) and take them offline so that the PDB can be closed. The following command takes the data file 8 offline:

```
ALTER PLUGGABLE DATABASE DATAFILE 8 OFFLINE;
```

- If required, use the CONFIGURE command to configure the default device type and automatic channels.
- Restore and recover the PDB with the following commands:

```
RESTORE PLUGGABLE DATABASE ocprep;
RECOVER PLUGGABLE DATABASE ocprep;
```

- If any data files were taken offline in Step 2, bring these data files back online, for example:

```
ALTER PLUGGABLE DATABASE DATAFILE 8 ONLINE;
```

- Examine the output from RMAN to verify that media recovery was successful. If it was successful, open the PDB(s).

```
ALTER PLUGGABLE DATABASE ocprep OPEN;
```

To recover a single PDB while connected to it, you connect to the PDB from RMAN as a local user with SYSDBA system privilege.

- Close the PDB.

  ```
  ALTER PLUGGABLE DATABASE CLOSE;
  ```

- If the PDB has missing data files an error will occur and the PDB cannot be closed. You must connect to the PDB with missing data file(s) and take them offline so that the PDB can be closed. The following command takes the data file 8 offline:

  ```
  ALTER DATABASE DATAFILE 8 OFFLINE;
  ```

- If required, use the CONFIGURE command to configure the default device type and automatic channels.
- Restore and recover the PDB with the following commands:

  ```
  RESTORE DATABASE;
  RECOVER DATABASE;
  ```

- If any data files were taken offline in Step 2, connect to that PDB and bring these data files back online, for example:

  ```
  ALTER DATABASE DATAFILE 8 ONLINE;
  ```

- Examine the output from RMAN to verify that media recovery was successful. If it was successful, open the PDB(s).

  ```
  ALTER PLUGGABLE DATABASE OPEN;
  ```

Use Data Recovery Advisor

Oracle's Data Recovery Advisor is a data corruption repair function integrated with Support Workbench, database health checks and RMAN. It can display data corruption problems, assess their extent and impact, recommend repair options, and automate the repair process. In the context of Data Recovery Advisor, a health check is a diagnostic procedure run by the Health Monitor to assess the state of the database or its components. Health checks are invoked reactively when an error occurs and can also be invoked manually. Data Recovery Advisor can diagnose failures such as the following:

- Components such as data files and control files that are not accessible by the database.
- Physical corruptions such as block checksum failures and invalid block header field values.
- Inconsistencies such as a data file that is older than other database files.
- I/O failures such as hardware errors, operating system driver failures, and exceeding operating system resource limits.

In some cases, the Data Recovery Advisor may be able to detect or handle logical corruptions. As a general rule, detecting and repairing logical corruptions will require assistance from Oracle Support Services.

Failures

A failure is a persistent data corruption detected by a health check. They are usually detected reactively when a database operation encounters corrupted data and generates an error. This will automatically invoke a health check in the database. The check will search the database for failures related to the error and record any findings in the Automatic Diagnostic Repository. Data Recovery Advisor can generate repair advice and repair failures only after failures have been detected by the database and stored in the ADR. Data Recovery Advisor can report on and repair failures such as inaccessible files, physical and logical block corruptions, and I/O failures. All failures are assigned a priority: CRITICAL, HIGH, or LOW, and a status of OPEN or CLOSED.

- **CRITICAL** priority failures require immediate attention because they make the whole database unavailable. Typically, critical failures bring down the instance and are diagnosed during the subsequent startup.
- **HIGH** priority failures make a database partially unavailable or unrecoverable, and usually have to be repaired in a reasonably short time.
- **LOW** priority indicates that failures can be ignored until more important failures are fixed.

DRA Repairs

Data Recovery Advisor allows you to view repair options. Repairs might involve the use of block media recovery, datafile media recovery, or Oracle Flashback Database. In general, Data Recovery Advisor presents both automated and manual repair options. If appropriate, you can choose an automated repair option in order to perform a repair. In an automated repair, Data Recovery Advisor performs the repair, verifies the repair success, and closes the relevant failures.

The recommended workflow for repairing data failures from RMAN is to run the following commands in sequence during an RMAN session: LIST FAILURE to display failures, ADVISE FAILURE to display repair options, and REPAIR FAILURE to fix the failures.

LIST FAILURE

The LIST FAILURE command displays failures against which you can run the ADVISE FAILURE and REPAIR FAILURE commands.

```
RMAN> LIST FAILURE;
List of Database Failures
=========================
Failure ID Priority Status  Time Detected Summary
---------- ---- ---- ------- ----
274        HIGH     OPEN    21-FEB-14     One or more non-system
                                          datafiles are missing
329        HIGH     OPEN    21-FEB-14     Datafile 1:
                                          '/u01/oradata/prod/
                                           system01.dbf'
                                          contains one or more
                                          corrupt blocks
```

ADVISE FAILURE

Use the ADVISE FAILURE command to display repair options for the specified failures. This command prints a summary of the failures identified by the Data Recovery Advisor and implicitly closes all open failures that are already fixed. The ADVISE FAILURE command indicates the repair strategy that Data Recovery Advisor considers optimal for a given set of failures. Data Recovery Advisor verifies repair feasibility before proposing a repair strategy. For example, it will check that all backups and archived redo log files needed for media recovery are available. It can generate both manual and automated repair options.

The ADVISE command maps a set of failures to the set of repair steps that Data Recovery Advisor considers to be optimal. When possible, Data Recovery Advisor consolidates multiple repair steps into a single repair. For example, if the database has corrupted datafile, missing control file, and lost current redo log group, then Data Recovery Advisor would recommend a single, consolidated repair plan to restore the database and perform point-in-time recovery.

```
RMAN> ADVISE FAILURE;
List of Database Failures
=========================
Failure ID Priority Status  Time Detected Summary
---------- -------- ------- ----
274        HIGH     OPEN    21-FEB-14     One or more non-system
                                          datafiles are missing
329        HIGH     OPEN    21-FEB-14     Datafile 1:
                                          '/u01/oradata/prod/
                                           system01.dbf'
                                          contains one or more
                                          corrupt blocks

analyzing automatic repair options; this may take some time
using channel ORA_DISK_1
analyzing automatic repair options complete

Mandatory Manual Actions
=========================
no manual actions available

Optional Manual Actions
=========================
1. If file /u01/oradata/prod/data01.dbf was unintentionally renamed
or moved, restore it

Automated Repair Options
=========================
Option Repair Description
--- ---------
Restore and recover datafile 31; Perform block
    media recovery of block 43481 in file 1

Strategy: The repair includes complete media recovery with no data
loss
Repair script:
/u01/oracle/log/diag/rdbms/prod/prod/hm/reco_740113269.hm
```

CHANGE FAILURE

The CHANGE FAILURE command allows you to change the failure priority from HIGH to LOW or the reverse, or to close it. You cannot change to or from CRITICAL priority.

```
RMAN> CHANGE FAILURE 3 PRIORITY LOW;
```

REPAIR FAILURE

The REPAIR FAILURE command is used to repair database failures identified by the Data Recovery Advisor. The target database instance must be started, it must be a single-instance database and cannot be a physical standby database. It is important that at most one RMAN session is running the REPAIR FAILURE command. The only exception is REPAIR FAILURE ... PREVIEW, which is permitted in concurrent RMAN sessions. To perform an automated repair, the Data Recovery Advisor may require specific backups and archived redo logs. If the files are not available, then the recovery will not be possible. Data Recovery Advisor consolidates repairs whenever possible so that a single repair can fix multiple failures. If one has not yet been issued in the current RMAN session, REPAIR FAILURE performs an implicit ADVISE FAILURE. RMAN always verifies that failures are still relevant and automatically closes failures that have already been repaired. After executing a repair, RMAN reevaluates all open failures on the chance that some of them may also have been fixed.

Duplicate PDBs using RMAN

The DUPLICATE command of RMAN can be used to duplicate PDBs. It is possible to duplicate a single PDB, a set of PDBs, or a set of tablespaces within a PDB. This action must be performed while logged in to the root of the CDB as a user either the SYSDBA or SYSBACKUP privilege. In order to duplicate PDBs, it is required to create the auxiliary instance as a CDB by starting the instance with the declaration enable_pluggable_database=TRUE in the initialization parameter file.

When one or more PDBs is duplicated, RMAN will also duplicate the root (CDB$ROOT) and the seed database (PDB$SEED). The result after the duplication operation is a separate database that is a fully functional CDB. The options that can be used when duplicating PDBs or tablespaces within PDBs are:

- **PLUGGABLE DATABASE pdb_name** -- Duplicates the specified PDBs in the CDB. Use a comma-delimited list to duplicate multiple PDBs.
- **SKIP PLUGGABLE DATABASE pdb_name** -- Duplicates all the PDBs in the CDB, except the PDBs specified by pdb_name. Use a comma-delimited list to specify multiple PDBs that must be excluded.
- **TABLESPACE pdb_name:tablespace_name** -- Duplicates specified tablespaces within a PDB. The tablespace name must be prefixed with the name of the PDB that contains the tablespace. If you omit the name of the PDB, root is taken as the default.
- **SKIP TABLESPACE pdb_name:tablespace_name** -- Duplicates all tablespaces in the CDB except the specified tablespaces in the specified PDB.

The steps to duplicate a PDB are:

1. Start RMAN and connect to the necessary database instances.
2. If the source database instance is not mounted or open, then mount or open it. To perform duplication of an open database, it must have archiving enabled.
3. Configure RMAN channels (if necessary).
4. Run the DUPLICATE command with either the PLUGGABLE DATABASE or SKIP PLUGGABLE DATABASE option. Some examples include:
   - Duplicate the PDB pdb1 to the CDB cdb1::

     ```
     DUPLICATE DATABASE TO cdb1
        PLUGGABLE DATABASE pdb1;
     ```

   - Duplicate the PDBs pdb1, pdb3, and pdb4 to the database cdb1:

     ```
     DUPLICATE DATABASE TO cdb1
        PLUGGABLE DATABASE pdb1,pdb3,pdb4;
     ```

   - Duplicate all the databases in the CDB, except the PDB pdb3:

     ```
     DUPLICATE DATABASE TO cdb1
        SKIP PLUGGABLE DATABASE pdb3;
     ```

The steps to duplicate tablespaces within a PDB are:

1. Start RMAN and connect to the necessary database instances.
2. If the source database instance is not mounted or open, then mount or open it. To perform duplication of an open database, it must have archiving enabled.
3. Configure RMAN channels (if necessary).
4. Run the DUPLICATE command with the TABLESPACE option. Some examples of duplicating tablespaces contained in PDBs are:
   o Duplicate the users tablespace that is part of PDB pdb1:

   ```
   DUPLICATE DATABASE TO cdb1
      TABLESPACE pdb1:users;
   ```

   o Duplicate the PDB pdb1 and the users tablespace in PDB pdb2:

   ```
   DUPLICATE DATABASE TO cdb1
      PLUGGABLE DATABASE pdb1
      TABLESPACE pdb2:users;
   ```

Perform Flashback for a CDB

It is possible to perform Flashback Database Operations on a CDB as you would on a non-CDB. One exception is performing a flashback when one or more of the PDBs were recovered using Point-In-Time-Recovery. In order to maintain backward compatibility, Flashback Database operations on a CDB may not be permitted if point-in-time recovery has been performed on any of its PDBs. When this has occurred, it is not possible to directly rewind the CDB to a point <u>earlier</u> than where the DBPITR was performed for the PDB. Attempting to flashback to an earlier point will generate the following error:

```
ORA-39866: Data files for pluggable database <PDB_name> must be
offline to flashback across a PDB point-in-time recovery
```

If it is necessary to flashback the CDB to a point earlier than the DBPITR of the PDB, you must perform the following steps:

- Start RMAN and connect to the root as a user with the SYSBACKUP or SYSDBA privilege.
- Determine the target time to which the CDB must be recovered.
- Take all files that correspond to the PDB for which PITR was performed offline.
- Rewind the CDB to the desired target time. The PDB whose files are offline will not be affected.
- Recover the PDB for which PITR was performed using the RESTORE PLUGGABLE DATABASE and RECOVER PLUGGABLE DATABASE commands.

Managing Performance

Monitor operations and performance in a CDB and PDBs

There are a significant number of tools and techniques for identifying performance issues. One of the easiest in recent releases of Oracle has been to use Enterprise Manager. In 12c, there is Enterprise Manager Cloud Control, Oracle's enterprise information technology management product. EM Cloud Control is designed to manage entire IT environments, including databases, server, middleware products and more. The kid brother of EM Cloud Control is EM Express.

EM Express is a web-based tool for managing Oracle Database 12c that is built into the database server. It is a lightweight tool designed to incur minimal overhead on the database server and provides the ability to perform basic administrative tasks as well as the ability to diagnose performance issues and tune the database. There are no background tasks or information-collecting processes associated with EM Express. The tool makes use of data that is already collected by the Oracle database. The Performance Hub of EM Express is going to be the 'go to' spot for many administrators in 12c for diagnosing performance issues. The image below shows the main page of the EM Express Performance Hub.

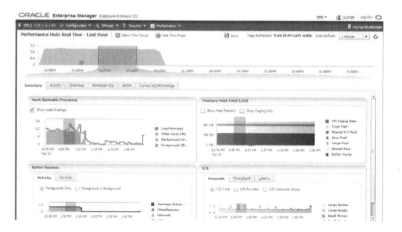

The Performance Hub provides a consolidated view of all performance data for a given time range. The performance data shown includes ASH Analytics, SQL Monitor, ADDM, as well as metrics that describe workload characteristics and database resource usage.

The Performance Hub can be used to view both historical and real-time data. A time range can be selected using a time picker at the top of the page, and the detail tabs will display the available performance data for the selected time range. The time picker displays average active sessions over time. When there are peaks in the time picker, the selected time range can be moved to the period of interest to gain more information.

When functioning in real-time mode, performance data is retrieved from in-memory views. The time picker shows data for the past hour and the user can select any time range from within this period. The default selection is the past 5 minutes. When functioning in historical mode, data is retrieved from the Automatic Workload Repository (AWR). The user can select any time period, provided there is sufficient data in AWR. The Performance Hub can also be saved as a Composite Active Report.

The Performance Hub organizes performance data by dividing it into different tabs that address a specific aspect of database performance. The tabs available in the Performance Hub are:

- **Summary** -- In real-time mode, this tab shows metrics data that gives an overview of system performance in terms of Host Resource Consumption (CPU, I/O and Memory), and Average Active Sessions. In historical mode, the tab displays system performance in terms of resource consumption, average active sessions, and load profile information.
- **Activity** -- Displays ASH Analytics in both real-time and historical mode.
- **Workload** -- Displays metric information about the workload profile, such as call rates, logon rate and the number of sessions. In addition, the tab also displays the Top SQL for the selected time range. In real-time mode, the tab displays Top SQL only by DB

time. In historical mode, the user can also display Top SQL by other metrics, such as CPU time or Executions.

- **RAC** -- Displays RAC-specific metrics such as the number of global cache blocks received, and the average block latency when the database is in a RAC configuration.
- **Monitored SQL** -- Displays Monitored Executions of SQL, PL/SQL and Database Operations in both real-time and historical mode.
- **ADDM** -- Displays ADDM and Automatic Real Time ADDM reports in both real-time and historical mode.
- **Current ADDM Findings** -- Displays a real-time analysis of system performance for the past 5 minutes. The tab is available only in real-time mode and the contents of this tab are populated only if the time selector includes the current time.

Manage allocation of resources between PDBs and within a PDB

The Oracle Database Resource Manager (DRM) is designed to optimize resource allocation among concurrent database sessions. It attempts to prevent problems that can happen if the operating system makes resource decisions when presented with high overhead without having awareness of the database needs. DRM helps to overcome these problems by giving the database more control over how hardware resources are allocated. DRM enables you to classify sessions into groups based on session attributes, and then allocate resources to those groups in a way that optimizes hardware utilization for your application environment. The information that performs the functions of classifying sessions and assigning resources is called a resource plan. Oracle 12c comes with several predefined resource plans that provide resource management directives that should provide immediate benefits for the majority of database installations:

- **DEFAULT_MAINTENANCE_PLAN** -- Default plan for maintenance windows.
- **DEFAULT_PLAN** -- Basic default plan that prioritizes SYS_GROUP operations and allocates minimal resources for automated maintenance and diagnostics operations.
- **DSS_PLAN** -- Example plan for a data warehouse that prioritizes critical DSS queries over non-critical DSS queries and ETL operations.
- **ETL_CRITICAL_PLAN** -- Example plan for a data warehouse that prioritizes ETL operations over DSS queries.
- **INTERNAL_QUIESCE** -- For quiescing the database. This plan cannot be activated directly. To activate, use the QUIESCE command.
- **MIXED_WORKLOAD_PLAN** -- Example plan for a mixed workload that prioritizes interactive operations over batch operations.

There are three elements of DRM:

- **Resource consumer group**: A group of sessions that are grouped together based on resource requirements.
- **Resource plan**: A container for directives that specify how resources are allocated to resource consumer groups.
- **Resource plan directive**: Associates a resource consumer group with a particular plan and specifies how resources are to be allocated to that resource consumer group.

Resource Plan Directives

A resource plan directive for a consumer group can specify limits for CPU and I/O resource consumption for sessions in that group. This is done by specifying the action to be taken if a call within a session exceeds one of the specified limits. These actions, called switches, occur only for sessions that are running and consuming resources, not waiting for user input or for CPU cycles. The possible actions are the following:

- The session is switched to a consumer group with lower resource allocations.
- The session is killed (terminated).
- The session's current SQL statement is aborted.

The resource plan directive attribute that determines which of the above three actions will be taken is SWITCH_GROUP. This attribute specifies the consumer group to which a session is switched if the specified criteria are met. If the value of this parameter is a consumer group, the session will be switched to that group. If the group name is 'CANCEL_SQL', the current call for that session is canceled. Finally, if the group name is 'KILL_SESSION', then the session is killed.

Per session I/O or CPU Limits

The resource plan directive attributes that can be used in specifying the criteria to use in making switch determinations follow. If not set, all default to UNLIMITED.

- **SWITCH_TIME**: Specifies the time (in CPU seconds) that a call can execute before an action is taken.
- **SWITCH_IO_MEGABYTES**: Specifies the number of megabytes of I/O that a session can transfer (read and write) before being switched.
- **SWITCH_IO_REQS**: Specifies the number of I/O requests that a session can execute before an action is taken.

There are two resource plan attributes that can be used to modify the behavior of resource plan switching:

- **SWITCH_ESTIMATE**: If TRUE, the database estimates the execution time of each call. If the estimated execution time exceeds SWITCH_TIME, the session is moved to the SWITCH_GROUP before beginning the call. The default is FALSE.

- **SWITCH_FOR_CALL**: If TRUE, a session that was automatically switched to another consumer group is returned to its original consumer group when the top level call completes. The default is NULL.

Resource Manager and CDBs

Competing workloads are complex enough in an Oracle database that is not using the multitenant architecture. Resource management in a CDB becomes much more complex as resources are now being shared among multiple PDBs competing for system and CDB resources. Resource Manager works on two basic levels in a CDB environment:

- **CDB level** - It manages the workloads for multiple PDBs that are competing for resources. It is possible to specify how resources should be allocated among various PDBs, and limits can be set for specific PDBs.
- **PDB level** - Workloads within each PDB can be managed.

Resources are allocated in a two-step process:

- Each PDB is allocated a portion of the total system resources in the CDB.
- Within each specific PDB, the resources obtained in the first step are allocated among the connected sessions.

The Resource Manager allows administrators to perform the following:

- Specify that different PDBs should receive varying shares of the system resources based on the relative importance of each PDB.
- Limit the CPU usage of a particular PDB
- Limit the number of parallel execution servers that a particular PDB can use
- Limit the resource usage of different sessions connected to a single PDB

- Monitor the resource usage of PDBs

Perform Database Replay

Before making significant hardware or software upgrades to a production Oracle database, ideally administrators should perform extensive testing to ensure the changes will not adversely affect the system. However, making such testing close enough to reality to provide a valid test is very difficult. Often problems are encountered after the upgrade that were not located during the testing period. There are various third-party tools on the market to provide load testing for Oracle by simulating the workload from multiple users. However, the workloads generated are not as complex and interactive as that generated by a real production system. The Database Replay feature enables system administrators to perform real-world testing by capturing the production database workload and replaying it on another database. In addition, it provides analysis and reporting of potential problems and recommend ways to resolve these problems.

Oracle Database Replay captures all external database calls made to the system during the workload capture period. The capture includes all relevant information about the client request, such as SQL text, bind values, and transaction information. Background activities of the database and scheduler jobs are not captured. In addition, the following types of client requests are not captured in a workload:

- Direct path load of data from external files using utilities such as SQL*Loader
- Shared server requests (Oracle MTS)
- Oracle Streams
- Advanced replication streams
- Non-PL/SQL based Advanced Queuing (AQ)
- Flashback queries
- Oracle Call Interface (OCI) based object navigations
- Non SQL-based object access

- Distributed transactions

It is a best practice to restart the database before capturing the production workload. This ensures that ongoing and dependent transactions are allowed to be completed or rolled back before the capture begins. If the database is not restarted before the capture, transactions that are in progress or have yet to be committed will be only partially captured in the workload.

By default, all activities from all user sessions are recorded during workload capture. Workload filters can be used to include or exclude specific user sessions during the workload capture. You can use either inclusion filters or exclusion filters in a workload capture, but not both simultaneously. Inclusion filters specify user sessions that will be captured in the workload. Exclusion filters enable you to specify user sessions that will not be captured in the workload. To add filters to a workload capture, you use the DBMS_WORKLOAD_CAPTURE.ADD_FILTER procedure. To remove an existing filter, you use the DBMS_WORKLOAD_CAPTURE.DELETE_FILTER procedure.

Before starting the workload capture, you must decide on the directory where the captured workload will be stored. Before starting the capture, verify that the directory is empty and has enough space for the workload. If the directory runs out of disk space during a workload capture, the capture will stop. You should have a well-defined starting point for the workload so that the database being used to replay the workload can be restored to the same point before starting the captured workload. It is best not to have any active user sessions when starting a workload capture. Active sessions may have ongoing transactions which will not be replayed completely. Consider restarting the database in RESTRICTED mode prior to starting the workload capture. When the workload capture begins, the database will automatically switch to UNRESTRICTED mode and normal operations can continue while the workload is being captured. You begin a workload capture using the procedure DBMS_WORKLOAD_CAPTURE.START_CAPTURE. To stop a workload capture in progress, you use the FINISH_CAPTURE procedure of the DBMS_WORKLOAD_CAPTURE package.

You can export AWR data from the production machine in order to enable detailed analysis of the workload on both systems. This data is required if you plan to run the AWR Compare Period report on a pair of workload captures or replays. To export AWR data, you use the DBMS_WORKLOAD_CAPTURE.EXPORT_AWR procedure.

The following views allow you to monitor a workload capture. You can also use Oracle Enterprise Manager to monitor a workload capture:

- **DBA_WORKLOAD_CAPTURES** -- Lists all the workload captures that have been created in the current database.
- **DBA_WORKLOAD_FILTERS** -- Lists all workload filters used for workload captures defined in the current database.

Replay

After the workload has been captured, it's necessary to preprocess the capture files prior to using them in a replay. Preprocessing converts the captured data into replay files and creates the required metadata needed to replay the workload. After preprocessing the captured workload, it can be replayed multiple times on any replay system running the same version of Oracle. As a general rule, it's recommended to move the capture files to another system for preprocessing. While the capture itself has a minimal overhead, workload preprocessing can be time consuming and resource intensive. It is better that this step be performed on the test system where the workload will be replayed rather than on the production database. Capture files are processed using the PROCESS_CAPTURE procedure of the DBMS_WORKLOAD_REPLAY package.

After you have preprocessed a captured workload, it can be replayed on the test system. In the workload replay, Oracle will perform the actions recorded during the workload capture. It will re-create all captured external client requests with the same timing, concurrency, and transaction dependencies that occurred on the production system. Database Replay uses a program called the replay client to re-create the external client requests. You may need to use multiple replay clients depending on the scope of the captured workload. The replay client has an imbedded calibration tool to help determine the number of replay clients required for a given workload. The entire workload from the production database is replayed. This includes DML and SQL queries, so the data in the replay system must be as logically similar to the data in the capture system as possible. Ensuring the systems are as identical as possible will minimize data divergence and enable a more reliable analysis of the replay. Replaying a database workload requires the following steps:

The captured workload must have been preprocessed and copied to the replay system. An Oracle directory object for the directory to which the preprocessed workload has been copied must exist in the replay system.

A captured workload may contain references to external systems, such as database links or external tables. These should be reconfigured to avoid impacting production systems during replay. External references that need to be resolved before replaying a workload include: Database links, external tables, directory objects, URLs, and e-mail addresses. If these external connections are not changed before starting the replay, you could end up changing data in production systems, sending emails to users, and other undesirable actions.

Connection strings used to connect to the production system are captured in the workload. You must remap these connection strings to the replay system for the replay to succeed. The clients can then connect to the replay system using the remapped connections. For Oracle Real Application Cluster databases, you can map all connection strings to a load balancing connection string.

There are several options that determine the behavior of the database replay.

- **synchronization** -- determines whether the COMMIT order will be preserved during replay. By default, synchronization is enabled. All transactions will be executed only after all dependent transactions have been committed. If you disable this option, the replay will likely have significant data divergence. This may be not be a problem if the workload consists primarily of independent transactions. Not preserving the commit order can also lead to a faster replay, if 'stress testing' of the replay system is desirable.
- **connect_time_scale** -- enables you to scale the elapsed time between the time when the sessions connected to the database during the workload capture began and when each session connects during the replay. This option allows you to manipulate the session connect time during replay with a given percentage value. By default, the value is 100, which will attempt to connect all sessions as captured. Setting this parameter to 0 will attempt to connect all sessions immediately.
- **think_time_scale** -- allows you to scale user think time during replay. User think time is the elapsed time while the replayed user waits between issuing calls within a single session. A value of 100 means that time between calls will be the same as they were during the capture. A value of zero will eliminate all wait time between calls.
- **think_time_auto_correct** -- If user calls are being executed slower during replay than during capture, you can make the database replay attempt to catch up by setting this parameter to TRUE. When set to true, it will make the replay client shorten the think time between calls, so that the overall elapsed time of the replay will more closely match the captured elapsed time.

The replay client is a multithreaded program where each thread submits a workload from a captured session. It is an executable file named wrc located in the $ORACLE_HOME/bin directory. The replay user that wrc logs in as needs the DBA role and cannot be SYS. The wrc executable uses the following syntax:

```
wrc [user/pword[@server]] MODE=[value] [keyword=[value]]
```

The mode parameter specifies the action to be taken when the wrc executable is run. Possible values include replay (the default), calibrate, and list_hosts. The parameter keyword specifies the options to use for the execution and is dependent on the mode selected. To display the possible keywords and their corresponding values, run the wrc executable without any arguments. The modes that you can select when running the wrc executable and their corresponding keywords are:

- **replay (the default)** -- runs a captured workload. In replay mode, the wrc executable accepts the following keywords:
    - o **userid and password** -- specify the user ID and password of a replay user for the replay client. If unspecified, the user ID defaults to the SYSTEM user.
    - o **server** -- specifies the connection string that is used to connect to the replay system. If unspecified, the value defaults to an empty string.
    - o **replaydir** -- specifies the directory that contains the preprocessed workload capture you want to replay. If unspecified, it defaults to the current directory.
    - o **debug** -- specifies whether debug data will be created.
    - o **workdir** -- specifies the directory where the client logs will be written. This parameter is only used in conjunction with the debug parameter.
    - o **connection_override** -- specifies whether to override the connection mappings stored in the DBA_WORKLOAD_CONNECTION_MAP view.
- **calibrate** -- causes wrc to return an estimate of the number of replay clients and hosts that are required to replay a particular workload. In calibration mode, wrc accepts the following keywords:
    - o **replaydir** -- specifies the directory that contains the preprocessed workload capture. It defaults to the current directory.
    - o **process_per_cpu** -- specifies the maximum number of client processes that can run per CPU. The default value is 4.

- ○ **threads_per_process** -- specifies the maximum number of threads that can run within a client process. The default value is 50.
- **list_hosts** -- Displays the hosts that participated in a workload capture and workload replay. In list_hosts mode, the wrc executable accepts only one keyword:
  - ○ replaydir -- specifies the directory that contains the preprocessed workload capture you want to replay. If unspecified, it defaults to the current directory

Once the workload replay has completed, in-depth reporting is available so that you can perform detailed analysis of both the workload capture and the replay operation. The summary report provides basic information such as errors encountered during replay and data divergence in rows returned by DML or SQL queries. A comparison of several statistics between the source and replay servers is also provided. You can use Automatic Workload Repository reports for advanced analysis of the workload processing between the two servers.

Moving Data, Performing Security Operations, and Interacting with Other Oracle Products

Use Data Pump

The Oracle Data Pump utility is designed to provide high-speed movement of data and metadata from one database to another. It replaces the export/import functionality that existed in earlier releases of Oracle. Data Pump is made up of three distinct parts:

- **expdp and impdp** – These are command-line clients that use the procedures provided in the DBMS_DATAPUMP package to execute export and import commands. They accept parameters entered at the command line that enables the exporting and importing of data and metadata for a complete database or for subsets of a database.
- **DBMS_DATAPUMP** – Also known as the Data Pump API, this package provides a high-speed mechanism to move all or part of the data and metadata for a site from one database to another. DBMS_DATAPUMP can be used independently of the impdp and expdp clients.
- **DBMS_METADATA** – Also known as the Metadata API, this package provides a centralized facility for the extraction, manipulation, and re-creation of dictionary metadata. DBMS_METADATA can be used independently of the impdp and expdp clients.

Data Pump jobs use a master table, a master process, and worker processes to perform the work and keep track of progress:

- **Master Table** – A master table is used to track the progress within a job while the data and metadata are being transferred. It is implemented as a user table within the database. A user performing an impdp or expdp must have the CREATE TABLE system privilege for the master table to be created plus sufficient tablespace quota. The master table will have the same name as the job that created it. A Data Pump job cannot have the same name as an existing table or view in that schema. The information in the master table is used to restart a job.

- **Master process** – A master process is created for every Data Pump Export job and Data Pump Import job. It controls the entire job, including communicating with the clients, creating and controlling a pool of worker processes, and performing logging operations.
- **Worker Process** – The master process allocates work to be executed to worker processes that perform the data and metadata processing within an operation. Data Pump can employ multiple worker processes, running in parallel, to increase job performance.

Monitor a Data Pump job

It's possible to use the Data Pump Export and Import utilities to attach to a running job. When attached in logging mode, status about the job is automatically displayed during execution in real-time. When attached using interactive-command mode, it's possible to request the job status.

Optionally, a log file can be written during the execution of a job. It summarizes the progress of the job, lists any errors, and records the completion status. You can also determine job status or to get other information about Data Pump jobs, through the Data Pump views:

- **DBA_DATAPUMP_JOBS** – Identifies all active Data Pump jobs in the database, regardless of their state, on an instance (or on all instances for RAC). It also shows all Data Pump master tables not currently associated with an active job.
- **DBA_DATAPUMP_SESSIONS** – Identifies the user sessions that are attached to a Data Pump job. The information in this view is useful for determining why a stopped Data Pump operation has not gone away.
- **V$SESSION_LONGOPS** – Data Pump operations that transfer table data (export and import) maintain an entry indicating the job progress. The entry contains the estimated transfer size and is periodically updated to reflect the actual amount of data transferred.

The V$SESSION_LONGOPS columns that are relevant to a Data Pump job are as follows:

- **USERNAME** - job owner
- **OPNAME** - job name
- **TARGET_DESC** - job operation
- **SOFAR** - megabytes transferred thus far during the job
- **TOTALWORK** - estimated number of megabytes in the job
- **UNITS** - megabytes (MB)
- **MESSAGE** - a formatted status message of the form: 'job_name: operation_name : nnn out of mmm MB done'

The Data Pump Export utility is invoked using the expdp command. The actions performed by the export operation are defined by the parameters you specify. They can be supplied either on the command line or in a parameter file. Data Pump Export can be controlled using a command line, a parameter file, or an interactive-command mode.

- **Command-Line** – Enables you to specify most of the export parameters from the command line.
- **Parameter File** – Allows you to specify command-line parameters in a parameter file. The PARFILE parameter cannot be used in a parameter file, because parameter files cannot be nested.
- **Interactive-Command** – Displays an export prompt from which you can enter various commands. Some commands are specific to interactive-command mode.

Data Pump jobs manage the following types of files:

- **Dump files** – Contain the data and metadata being moved.
- **Log files** – Record the messages associated with an operation.
- **SQL files** – Record the output of a SQLFILE operation.
- **Data Files** – Files specified by the DATA_FILES parameter during a transportable import.

There are different expdp modes for unloading different portions of the database. The mode is specified using the appropriate parameter. The available modes are:

- **Full** – In a full database export, the entire database is unloaded. This mode requires the user performing the export to have the DATAPUMP_EXP_FULL_DATABASE role. Specified using the FULL parameter.
- **Schema** – This is the default export mode. If you have the DATAPUMP_EXP_FULL_DATABASE role, then you can provide a list of schemas to export. Otherwise you can export only your own schema. Specified using the SCHEMAS parameter.
- **Table** – In table mode, only a specified set of tables, partitions, and their dependent objects are unloaded. You must have the DATAPUMP_EXP_FULL_DATABASE role to export tables that are not in your own schema. Specified using the TABLES parameter.
- **Tablespace** – In tablespace mode, only the tables contained in a specified set of tablespaces are unloaded. If a table is unloaded, then its dependent objects are also unloaded. Privileged users get all tables. Unprivileged users get only the tables in their own schemas. Specified using the TABLESPACES parameter.
- **Transportable Tablespace** – In transportable tablespace mode, only the metadata for the tables (and their dependent objects) within a specified set of tablespaces is exported. The tablespace data files are copied in a separate operation. Specified using the TRANSPORT_TABLESPACES parameter.

expdp Parameters

The following parameters are applicable to expdp:

- **ATTACH** – Attaches the client session to an existing export job and automatically places you in the interactive-command interface.
- **CONTENT** – Enables you to filter what Export unloads: data only, metadata only, or both.
- **DIRECTORY** – Specifies the default location to which Export can write the dump file set and the log file.

- **DUMPFILE** – Specifies the names, and optionally, the directory objects of dump files for an export job.
- **ESTIMATE** – Specifies the method that Export will use to estimate how much disk space each table in the export job will consume (in bytes).
- **ESTIMATE_ONLY** – Instructs Export to estimate the space that a job would consume, without actually performing the export operation.
- **EXCLUDE** – Enables you to filter the metadata that is exported by specifying objects and object types to be excluded from the export operation.
- **FILESIZE** – Specifies the maximum size of each dump file.
- **FULL** – Specifies that you want to perform a full database mode export.
- **INCLUDE** – Enables you to filter the metadata that is exported by specifying objects and object types for the current export mode.
- **JOB_NAME** – Used to identify the export job in subsequent actions.
- **LOGFILE** – Specifies the name, and optionally, a directory, for the log file of the export job.
- **PARFILE** – Specifies the name of an export parameter file.
- **QUERY** – Allows you to specify a query clause that is used to filter the data that gets exported.
- **SCHEMAS** – Specifies that you want to perform a schema-mode export.
- **TABLES** – Specifies that you want to perform a table-mode export.
- **TABLESPACES** – Specifies a list of tablespace names to be exported in tablespace mode.
- **TRANSPORT_TABLESPACES** -- Specifies that you want to perform an export in transportable-tablespace mode. This parameter is used to specify a list of tablespace names for which object metadata will be exported from the source database into the target database.

impdp Parameters

Many of the above parameters are also applicable to impdp. In addition, several of the more common impdp parameters are:

- **REUSE_DATAFILES** – Specifies whether the import job should reuse existing data files for tablespace creation.
- **SQLFILE** – Specifies a file into which all of the SQL DDL that Import would have executed, based on other parameters, is written.
- **STATUS** – Specifies the frequency at which the job status display is updated.
- **TABLE_EXISTS_ACTION** – Tells import what to do if the table it is trying to create already exists.
- **REMAP_DATAFILE** – Changes the name of the source data file to the target data file name in all SQL statements where the source data file is referenced.
- **REMAP_SCHEMA** – Loads all objects from the source schema into a target schema.
- **REMAP_TABLE** – Allows you to rename tables during an import operation.
- **REMAP_TABLESPACE** – Remaps all objects selected for import with persistent data in the source tablespace to be created in the target tablespace.

The following commands are applicable when using Interactive mode:

- **ADD_FILE** – Add additional dump files.
- **CONTINUE_CLIENT** – Exit interactive mode and enter logging mode.
- **EXIT_CLIENT** – Stop the import or export client session, but leave the job running.
- **KILL_JOB** – Detach all currently attached client sessions and terminate the current job.
- **PARALLEL** – Increase or decrease the number of active worker processes for the current job.
- **START_JOB** – Restart a stopped job to which you are attached.
- **STATUS** – Display detailed status for the current job and/or set status interval.

- **STOP_JOB** – Stop the current job for later restart.

Network-based Data Pump operations

When the NETWORK_LINK parameter is used with impdp as part of an import operation, data is moved directly using SQL. A SELECT clause retrieves the data from the remote database using the network link supplied with the parameter. A corresponding INSERT clause inserts the data into the target database. No dump files are involved in the operation. When the NETWORK_LINK parameter is used with expdp as part of an export operation, data from the remote database is written to dump files on the target database. A 'Current User' database link is not supported for use with Data Pump. Only the following types of database links are supported:

- Public (both public and shared)
- Fixed user
- Connected user

There are some restrictions for operations performed using the NETWORK Link parameter:

- When using full transportable export, tables with LONG or LONG RAW columns that reside in administrative tablespaces (such as SYSTEM or SYSAUX) are not supported.
- When transporting a database over the network using full transportable export, auditing cannot be enabled for tables stored in an administrative tablespace (such as SYSTEM and SYSAUX) if the audit trail information itself is stored in a user-defined tablespace.
- The source and target databases can differ by no more than two versions. For example, if one database is Oracle Database 12c, then the other database must be 12c, 11g, or 10g.

Oracle 12c Enhancements

When performing a full database export, Data Pump has a new full transportable export option. A full transportable export is performed when the TRANSPORTABLE=ALWAYS parameter is specified along with the FULL parameter. This functionality exports all objects and data required to create a complete copy of the database. Two data movement methods are performed by Data Pump depending on whether the tablespaces are transportable or not:

- **Non-transportable tablespaces** -- Tablespaces like SYSTEM and SYSAUX that cannot be transported have both their metadata and data unloaded into the dump file set, using direct path unload and external tables.
- **Transportable tablespaces** -- For transportable tablespaces, only metadata unloaded into the dump file set. The contents of the tablespaces are moved when you the data files are copied to the target database.

There are several restrictions for performing a full transportable export, including:

- The DATAPUMP_EXP_FULL_DATABASE privilege is required to perform this operation.
- The default tablespace of the user performing the export must not be set to one of the tablespaces being transported.
- If the database being exported contains either encrypted tablespaces or tables with encrypted columns, the ENCRYPTION_PASSWORD parameter must be supplied.
- If there are encrypted tablespaces in the source database, the source and target databases must be on platforms with the same endianness.
- If the source platform and the target platform are of different endianness, then you must convert the data being transported so that it is in the format of the target platform.
- A full transportable export is not restartable.
- All objects with storage that are selected for export must have all of their storage segments either entirely within administrative,

non-transportable tablespaces (SYSTEM / SYSAUX) or entirely within user-defined, transportable tablespaces. Storage for a single object cannot straddle the two kinds of tablespaces.

The new functionality can be used to move a non-CDB into a pluggable database (PDB) or to move a PDB into another PDB. Full transportable operations can reduce both the export time and import times required for a full export. When this option is used, table data does not need to be unloaded and reloaded and index structures in user tablespaces do not need to be re-created. The full transportable feature is ideal for moving a database to a new computer system or upgrading to a new release of Oracle.

There are two enhancements to the way Data Pump works with compression.

- **Compression on import** -- A new option has been added to impdp and to the DBMS_DATAPUMP package that allows the compression options for a table to be changed during the import operation. The TRANSFORM parameter of impdp has a new TABLE_COMPRESSION_CLAUSE. If NONE is specified, the table gets the default compression for the tablespace. When the value is a valid table compression clause (for example, NOCOMPRESS), tables are created with the specified compression. Specifying this transform changes the type of compression for all tables in the job.
- **Compression on export** -- A new option has been added expdp and the DBMS_DATAPUMP package to control the degree of compression used when creating an Oracle Data Pump dump file. The COMPRESSION parameter can be used to compress the entire operation, the data only, the metadata only, or perform no compression. By default, only the metadata is compressed. The new parameter allows the DBA more control over the resources used during an export operation.

Other enhancements to Data Pump include:

- **Export View As a Table** -- A new expdp command-line option will cause Data Pump to export a view as a table. Rather than exporting the view definition, Data Pump will export a table definition and unload data from the view as if it were a table. When the dump file is imported, impdp will create a table using the table definition and insert the data
- **LOGTIME** -- The new LOGTIME command-line parameter will cause messages displayed during export and import operations be timestamped. The option is available in impdp, expdp, and the DBMS_DATAPUMP.SET_PARAMETER procedure. The valid values are:
  - **NONE** -- No timestamps on status or log file messages (the default)
  - **STATUS** -- timestamps on status messages only
  - **LOGTIME** -- timestamps on log file messages only
  - **ALL** -- timestamps on both status and log file messages
- **Audit Commands** -- Oracle Data Pump commands can now be audited.
- **No Logging Option** -- A new DISABLE_ARCHIVE_LOGGING option has been added to the TRANSFORM parameter of impdp and the DBMS_DATAPUMP package. When utilized, it will disable redo logging when loading data into tables and when creating indexes. When the option is used, the disk space required for redo logs during an Oracle Data Pump import will be smaller. After performing the import operation, the DBA should perform an RMAN backup. Other operations still generate redo, including CREATE and ALTER statements (except CREATE INDEX) and operations against the master table used by Oracle Data Pump.
- **Security** -- The ENCRYPTION_PWD_PROMPT parameter has been added to the expdp and impdp command line. The parameter is used to indicate whether the Oracle Data Pump client should prompt for passwords or whether it should retrieve the value from the command line.
- **SecureFiles LOB as Default** – A new option for impdp and the DBMS_DATAPUMP package forces Oracle Data Pump to create all LOBs as SecureFiles LOBs. By default, Data Pump re-creates tables exactly as they existed in the exported database, so if a LOB column was a BasicFile LOB in the exported database, Data Pump

attempts to re-create it as a BasicFile LOB in the imported database.

Use SQL*Loader

SQL*Loader is useful for loading data from non-Oracle databases. It has a very flexible data parsing engine that can handle a wide range of flat file formats when loading data. Essentially any database has the ability to export data to a flat file format. SQL*Load can then make use of these files to import the data into tables in an Oracle database. SQL*Loader can perform the following functions:

- Load data across a network if your data files are on a different system than the database.
- Load data from multiple data files during the same load session.
- Load data into multiple tables during the same load session.
- Specify the character set of the data.
- Selectively load data based on the record values.
- Manipulate data before loading it, using SQL functions.
- Generate unique sequential key values in specified columns.
- Use the operating system's file system to access the data files.
- Load data from disk, tape, or named pipe.
- Generate sophisticated error reports.
- Load arbitrarily complex object-relational data.
- Use secondary data files for loading LOBs and collections.
- Use conventional, direct path, or external table loads.

SQL*Loader can be used with or without a control file. Using a control file provides more control over the load operation. Simple load operations can be performed without specifying a control file. This is referred to as SQL*Loader express mode. SQL*Loader sessions make use of the following files:

- **Control** – Defines the format of the data file and controls the behavior of SQL*Loader.
- **Data** – One or more data files will contain the information to be loaded.
- **Log** – Contains a log of the actions performed by SQL*Loader and errors encountered.
- **Bad** – Contains all records that could not be loaded due to errors.
- **Discard** – Contains all records that the control file identified to be bypassed.

The sqlldr executable is used to invoke SQL*Loader. It is optionally followed by parameters that establish session characteristics. Parameters can also be specified using the following methods instead of the command line:

- Parameters can be added to a parameter file. To use a parameter file, the name of the file can be supplied in the command line using the PARFILE parameter.
- Some parameters can be specified within the SQL*Loader control file using the OPTIONS clause.

If the same parameter is specified on the command line and in a parameter file or OPTIONS clause, the value in the command line is used.

The SQL*Loader control file is a text file that tells SQL*Loader where to find the data file, the format to use in parsing the data, what table(s) to insert the data in to, and more. A control file has three loosely-defined sections:

- The first section contains session-wide information such as global options, the input data file location, and the data to be loaded.
- The second section consists of one or more INTO TABLE blocks. The blocks hold information about the destination table.
- The third section is optional and, if present, contains input data.

SQL*Loader has two methods of inserting data into Oracle tables, Conventional Path and Direct Load options. In conventional path, SQL*Loader effectively creates INSERT statements for the records in the file to be loaded and passes them to the Oracle SQL Parser to be handled. When using Direct Path, SQL*Loader bypasses SQL and the parser and loads data directly into the target table(s). Direct Path load is much faster, but Conventional Path is more flexible. Some restrictions of the Direct Path load are:

- It cannot run concurrently with other transactions against the target table.
- Triggers on the table do not fire.
- Data is written above the high-water mark of the table even if there is space below.
- Clustered tables are not supported.
- Foreign Key constraints are disabled during the load.

Express Mode

The new SQL*Loader express mode makes it possible to load data from a flat file by specifying only a table name. For the functionality to succeed, the file must contain only delimited data and the table columns must be all character, number, or datetime types. When running in express mode, no control file is used. SQL*Loader uses the table column definitions to determine the input field order and data types in the file. For other settings, it makes use of default values unless overridden with command-line parameters. The following example performs a basic load into the EMPLOYEES table:

```
sqlldr username TABLE=employees
```

By default, SQL*Loader express mode assumes the following values unless specified otherwise:

- **Data file** -- When none is specified, SQL*Loader looks for a file named [table_name].dat in the current directory.
- **Load method** -- By default external tables is used. For some errors, SQL*Loader express mode will automatically switched to direct path load.
- **Fields** -- The fields use the names, column types, and order from the destination table. Records are delimited by a comma, separated by a newline, have no enclosure and use left-right trimming.
- **DOP** -- The DEGREE_OF_PARALLELISM parameter is set to AUTO.
- **Date Format** -- The NLS settings are used.
- **Character Set** -- The NLS settings are used.
- **Append mode --** New data is to be appended to the table if it already has data in it.
- **File Names** -- When a data file is not specified, the data, log, and bad files take the following default names. (The %p is replaced with the process ID of the Oracle Database slave process.):
  - **Data File** -- table-name.dat
  - **SQL*Loader Log File** -- table-name.log
  - **Oracle Database Log Files** -- table-name_%p.log_xt
  - **Bad File** -- table-name_%p.bad

Use other products with a CDB and PDBs: Database Vault, Data Guard, LogMiner

Database Vault

In order to use Oracle Database Vault in a multitenant environment, you must register it in the root first. Once Oracle Database Vault has been registered in the root, it can be registered in the PDBs. An attempt to register it in a PDB first will result in the error "ORA-47503: Database Vault is not enabled on CDB$ROOT.

The first step in registering Database Vault is to log into the root of the database instance as a user who has privileges to create users and grant the CREATE SESSION and SET CONTAINER privileges. Ideally you should create two accounts to be used for Database Vault accounts and grant both the CREATE SESSION and SET CONTAINER privileges. The first account will be for the Database Vault Owner user. The second is optional, but recommended. If created, it will be the Database Vault Account Manager account. Both accounts should have at minimum the CREATE SESSION privilege. If a Database Vault Account Manager account is not created, the owner account will have the Database Vault Account Manager privileges. Oracle recommends creating both accounts for better separation of duties. Since both accounts will be common users, their names should be prefixed with c## or C##. For example:

```
GRANT CREATE SESSION, SET CONTAINER TO c##dbv_owner_root
   IDENTIFIED BY password CONTAINER = ALL;
GRANT CREATE SESSION, SET CONTAINER TO c##dbv_acctmgr_root
   IDENTIFIED BY password CONTAINER = ALL;
```

Once the account(s) have been created, you must connect to the root as SYS with the SYSDBA administrative privilege and execute the DVSYS.CONFIGURE_DV procedure:

```
BEGIN
 DVSYS.CONFIGURE_DV (
   dvowner_uname          => 'c##dbv_owner_root',
   dvacctmgr_uname        => 'c##dbv_acctmgr_root');
 END;
```

Once the procedure completes, execute the utlrp.sql script to recompile invalidated objects in the root. After the objects are recompiled, connect to the root using the Database Vault Owner account that was just configured. Execute the DBMS_MACADM.ENABLE_DV procedure to enable Database Vault. Then connect to the root with SYSDBA privileges and restart the database:

```
BEGIN
  DBMS_MACADM.ENABLE_DV;
END;
```

Once Database Vault has been configured in the root, it is possible to register the common users in specific PDBs or in every PDB in the CDB. To register the users in specific PDBs, you must connect to each PDB individually and grant the CREATE SESSION and SET CONTAINER privileges to the users.

```
GRANT CREATE SESSION, SET CONTAINER TO c##dbv_owner_root;
GRANT CREATE SESSION, SET CONTAINER TO c##dbv_acctmgr_root;
```

To grant them access to all PDBs in the CDB, you would instead use the following syntax:

```
GRANT CREATE SESSION, SET CONTAINER TO c##dbv_owner_root
    IDENTIFIED BY password CONTAINER = ALL;
GRANT CREATE SESSION, SET CONTAINER TO c##dbv_acctmgr_root
    IDENTIFIED BY password CONTAINER = ALL;
```

Regardless which of the two methods are used, you must go into each PDB that is to be registered with database vault and perform the following steps (which are the same as the root example above except for the container they are run in):

1. Execute the DVSYS.CONFIGURE_DV procedure
2. Run the utlrp.sql script
3. Execute the DBMS_MACADM.ENABLE_DV
4. Restart the PDB

Data Guard

Oracle's Data Guard has full support for the Multitenant database architecture. It is possible to create a physical standby of a container database in the same fashion as a regular primary database. There are some differences that must be considered when a administering the physical standby for a CDB, including the following:

- The database role is defined at the CDB level, not by individual container.
- If a switchover or failover operation is performed, it affected the entire CDB.
- DDL related to role changes and recovery must be executed in the root container.
- To administer a multitenant environment, you must have the CDB_DBA role.
- Oracle recommends that the standby database have its own keystore.
- The redo must be shipped to the root container of the standby database.

LogMiner

It is possible to use LogMiner in a multitenant container database. However, there are several differences to be aware of when using LogMiner in a CDB. When used in a container database, several views used by LogMiner contain an additional column named CON_ID. The CON_ID column identifies the container ID that is associated with the session for which information is being displayed. When any of the views is queried from a pluggable database (PDB), only rows from that PDB will be displayed. The views affected by this change include:

- V$LOGMNR_DICTIONARY_LOAD
- V$LOGMNR_LATCH
- V$LOGMNR_PROCESS

- V$LOGMNR_SESSION
- V$LOGMNR_STATS

There are also a number of new views available that are equivalent to legacy DBA_ views. The DBA views show information for sessions defined in the container from which they are queried. The new CDB views contain a CON_ID column and show information for all containers when queried from the root. The views affected by this and the new CDB view include:

- DBA_LOGMNR_LOG -> CDB_LOGMNR_LOG
- DBA_LOGMNR_PURGED_LOG -> CDB_LOGMNR_PURGED_LOG
- DBA_LOGMNR_SESSION -> CDB_LOGMNR_SESSION

The V$LOGMNR_CONTENTS view and its associated functions are restricted to the root container in a CDB. The view has had several new columns added:

- **CON_ID** -- This column contains the ID associated with the container from which the query is executed.
- **SRC_CON_NAME** -- When mining is performed with a current LogMiner dictionary, this column contains the PDB name.
- **SRC_CON_ID** -- This column contains the container ID of the PDB that generated the redo record.
- **SRC_CON_DBID** -- When mining is performed with a current LogMiner dictionary, this column contains the PDB identifier.
- **SRC_CON_GUID** - When mining is performed with a current LogMiner dictionary, this column contains the GUID associated with the PDB.

The syntax for enabling and disabling database-wide supplemental logging is the same as in a non-CDB database. However, in a CDB, minimal supplemental logging affects the entire CDB. All other levels of supplemental logging can be controlled at the PDB level. You must be connected to the PDB to issue the commands. Supplemental logging operations that are started with CREATE TABLE or ALTER TABLE statements can be executed from either the root or a PDB. They will affect only the table to which they are applied.

It is not possible to take a dictionary snapshot for an entire CDB in a single flat file. A snapshot can be taken of a single PDB in a flat file when connected to it. It is only possible to mine the redo logs for the changes associated with the PDB whose data dictionary is contained within the flat file.

Database Administration

Installing and Upgrading to Oracle Database 12c

Install Oracle Grid Infrastructure for a stand-alone server

Oracle Grid Infrastructure provides system support for a single-instance Oracle Database. It includes volume management, a file system, and automatic restart capabilities. For databases that will make use of ASM, Oracle Restart must be installed before the database can be. Oracle Grid Infrastructure for a standalone server includes both Oracle Restart and Oracle Automatic Storage Management. The two infrastructure products have been combined into a single set of binaries that is installed into an Oracle Restart home. Oracle Restart is designed to improve the availability of an Oracle database by providing the following services:

- In the event of a hardware or software failure, it will automatically start all Oracle components, including the Oracle database instance, Oracle Net Listener, database services, and Oracle ASM.
- Components are always started in the proper order when the database host is restarted.
- It runs periodic checks to monitor the status of Oracle components. Any time that a check operation fails for a component, the component will be automatically shut down and restarted.

Installing Oracle Restart requires at least 5.5 GB of disk space for the software and 1 GB of space in the /tmp directory. A software-only installation of the Oracle Grid Infrastructure will copy the binaries to the specified location. After the installation, there are several configuration steps that must be performed to enable Oracle Restart.

- Execute the runInstaller command from the relevant directory on the Oracle Database 12c installation media or download directory.
- Complete a software-only installation of Oracle Grid Infrastructure for a standalone server.
- Verify that the server meets the installation requirements using the command:

```
runcluvfy.sh stage -pre hacfg.
```

The following steps are required to configure and activate a software-only Oracle Grid Infrastructure for a standalone server installation:

- Login as the root user and run the roothas.pl script from Grid_home using the following syntax:

```
Grid_home/perl/bin/perl -I Grid_home/perl/lib -I
Grid_home/crs/install
Grid_home/crs/install/roothas.pl
```

- Change the directory to Grid_home/oui/bin, where Grid_home is the path of the Oracle Grid Infrastructure for a standalone server home.
- Login as the Oracle Restart software owner user and enter the following command:

```
./runInstaller -updateNodeList ORACLE_HOME=Grid_home
    -defaultHomeName CLUSTER_NODES= CRS=TRUE
```

- Use the SRVCTL utility along with Oracle Network Configuration Assistant and Oracle ASMCA to add the listener, the Oracle ASM instance, and all Oracle ASM disk groups to the Oracle Restart configuration.

Install Oracle Database software

There are a number of operating system environment variables that are utilized by Oracle and the Oracle Installer. The OS environment must be properly set prior to running the installer in order for the installation to function correctly. OUI is normally run from the oracle account of the operating system. You must configure the environment of the oracle user prior to initiating the install. Some environment variables must be set before starting the installation. Others are optional, but setting them prior to the install can avoid difficulties later. You should view the appropriate installation guide for the operating system under which you will be performing the install for details on setting environment variables.

Under Linux, the following environment variables must be set:

- The default file mode creation mask (umask) must be set to 022
- The XWindows DISPLAY variable must be set properly.
- The TMP and TMPDIR environment variables must be pointing to the tmp mount point.

The following Oracle environment variables don't have to be set, but ideally should be.

- ORACLE_BASE – sets the base of the directory structure use for OFA.
- ORACLE_SID – Sets the initial instance name used by the OS account.
- ORACLE_HOME – Specifies the directory where the Oracle software is installed.
- NLS_LANG – Specifies language, territory and character set settings.
- LD_LIBRARY_PATH – Specifies the path to Oracle-installed libraries for Linux.

Installing the database software

Once it has been determined that a system can host Oracle 12c, there are a number of pre-installation tasks that must be performed on a Linux server before running the Oracle installer. The complete list is in the Oracle installation manual for Linux. However, if you are running Oracle Linux 6, there is an Oracle RDBMS Server pre-install RPM package available. This package makes it much easier to install the Oracle Database. The pre-install RPM will perform most of the pre-install configuration tasks automatically. Among other things, the package creates the 'oracle' user and the groups needed for Oracle Database installation. It also modifies kernel parameters in /etc/sysctl.conf and resource limits in /etc/security/limits.conf. It also ensures that several packages required by Oracle are installed on the system. This significantly reduces the amount of time required to prepare the server before installing Oracle. The following command will install the pre-installer and prepare your OL6 system for the Oracle install:

```
yum install oracle-rdbms-server-12cR1-preinstall
```

Download the installation files from Oracle. For 64-bit Linux, there are two files, linuxamd64_12c_database_1of2 and linuxamd64_12c_database_2of2. These should be placed into the /tmp directory of your Linux server and then extracted in place as the oracle user with the unzip command:

```
[oracle@ocp tmp]unzip linuxamd64_12c_database_1of2.zip
...
[oracle@ocp tmp]unzip linuxamd64_12c_database_2of2.zip
...
```

Once the files are unzipped, change to the /tmp/database directory and run the Oracle installer:

```
[oracle@ocp database] ./runInstaller
```

The installation of the Oracle Database is a reasonably involved process and until you have done it a few times, the best bet is to have the installation manual for the proper OS open in your browser and to follow it step-by-step as you work. This chapter will cover some of the highlights of installing Oracle 12c on Oracle Linux 6. Before making any changes to the destination system, first check to ensure it meets the minimum requirements for installing Oracle 12c:

The disk space requirements for the software files (*not* the database files) on Linux x86-64 are:

- Enterprise Edition: 6.4 GB
- Standard Edition: 6.1 GB
- Standard Edition One: 6.1 GB

The memory requirements for installing Oracle Database 12c under Linux is 1 GB but 2 or more GB is recommended. The amount of swap space recommended depends on the amount or RAM in the system.

- For systems with 1-2 GB of ram, swap space should be 150% of the RAM.
- For systems with 2-16 GB of ram, swap space should be equal to the RAM.
- For systems with >16 GB of ram, swap space should be 16GB.

Once it has been determined that a system can host Oracle 12c, there are a number of pre-installation tasks that must be performed on a Linux server before running the Oracle installer. The complete list is in the Oracle installation manual for Linux. However, if you are running Oracle Linux 6, there is an Oracle RDBMS Server pre-install RPM package available. This package makes it <u>much</u> easier to install the Oracle Database. The pre-install RPM will perform most of the pre-install configuration tasks automatically. Among other things, the package creates the 'oracle' user and the groups needed for Oracle Database installation. It also modifies kernel parameters in /etc/sysctl.conf and resource limits in /etc/security/limits.conf. It ensures that several packages required by Oracle are installed on the system. This significantly reduces the amount of time required to prepare the server before installing the Oracle software. The following command will install the 12c pre-installer and prepare your OL6 system for the Oracle install:

```
yum install oracle-rdbms-server-12cR1-preinstall
```

Download the installation files from Oracle. For 64-bit Linux, there are two files, linuxamd64_12c_database_1of2 and linuxamd64_12c_database_2of2. These should be placed into the /tmp directory of your Linux server and then extracted in place as the oracle user with the unzip command:

```
[oracle@ocp tmp]unzip linuxamd64_12c_database_1of2.zip
...
[oracle@ocp tmp]unzip linuxamd64_12c_database_2of2.zip
...
```

Once the files are unzipped, change to the /tmp/database directory and run the Oracle installer:

```
[oracle@ocp database] ./runInstaller
```

If everything has been configured correctly, executing the installer should get you to the 'Configure Security Updates' screen of the Oracle 12c installation.

Step 1: Configure Security Updates -- In this screen, you will provide an email address where Oracle can inform you of security issues with the database. Optionally, you can opt to receive security updates via My Oracle Support.

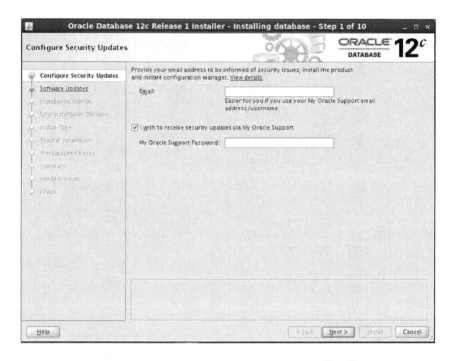

Step 2: Download Software Updates -- You can opt to download software updates via My Oracle Support if you have an account. Optionally, you can choose to use pre-downloaded updates or skip the software updates entirely.

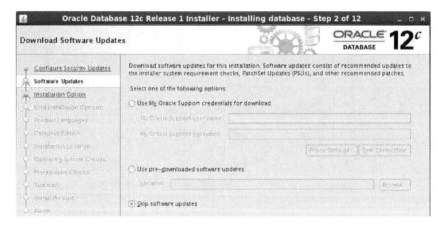

Step 3: Installation Option -- In this step you can choose to install the Oracle software and create a database, just install the software, or upgrade an existing software installation.

Step 4: Grid Installation Options -- This screen allows you to select between a single instance database installation, Oracle Real Application Clusters database installation, or Oracle RAC One Node database installation.

Step 5: Product Language -- In this screen you can add additional languages to the Oracle database installation.

Step 6: Database Edition -- In this screen, you must select between installation the Oracle Enterprise, Standard Edition, or Standard Edition One product versions.

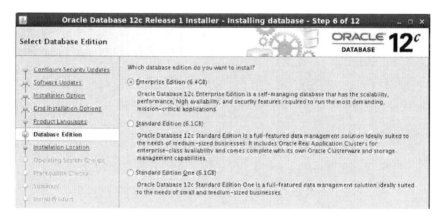

Step 7: Installation Location -- You can alter the default installation location of the software from this screen.

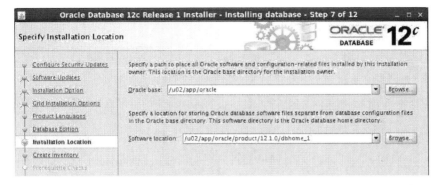

Step 8: Create Inventory -- This screen determines the locations to store the installation metadata files.

Step 9: Operating System Groups -- In this screen, operating system groups are mapped to database privileges.

Step 10: Prerequisite Checks -- The installer verifies that all of the prerequisites for an Oracle installation have been met. If any checks fail, they are listed in the screen. In this case, the swap space on the system is slightly below the expected value. I have clicked to ignore the warning and move on with the install.

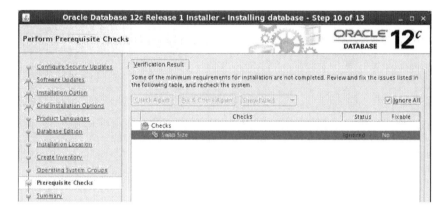

Step 11: Summary -- The installer displays a summary of the options chosen to this point in the install. You can choose to edit many of them from this screen.

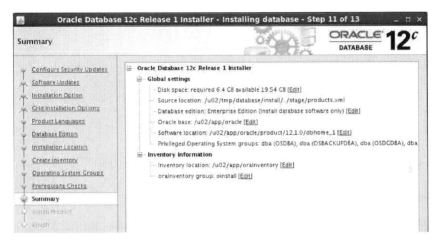

Step 12: Install Product -- In this screen, the installer performs the file copy and other installation tasks.

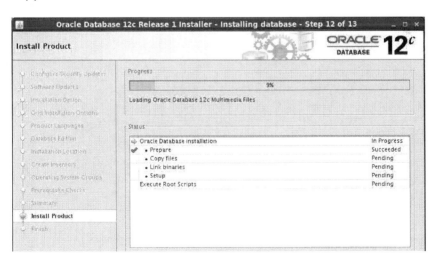

Step 12a: Root Scripts -- The final step of the installation requires two scripts to be run as the root user.

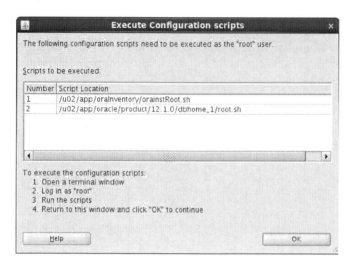

Step 13: Finish -- This is the screen you really want to see.

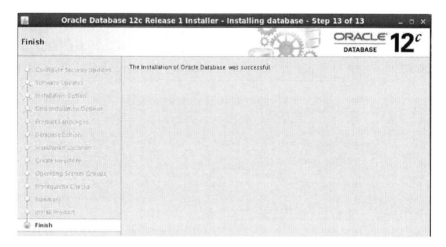

Use Oracle Restart

Any time that a database has Oracle Restart in use, the SRVCTL utility is the only method that should be used to stop and start components. The reasons for this include:

- When SRVCTL is used to start a component, Oracle Restart can first start any components on which it depends. Likewise, when SRVCTL is used to stop a component, dependent components are stopped first.
- SRVCTL will always start a component according to its Oracle Restart configuration, which may not happen when other means are utilized.
- When SRVCTL is used to start a component, all environment variables stored in the Oracle Restart configuration for the component are set automatically.

SRVCTL can be used to start and stop any component managed by Oracle Restart. To start a component, enter the following command:

```
srvctl start object [options]
```

To stop a component, enter the following command:

```
srvctl stop object [options]
```

Some examples of shutting down components with SRVCTL include:

- Starting a Database

  ```
  srvctl start database -db ocpdb
  ```

- Starting a Database NOMOUNT

  ```
  srvctl start database -db ocpdb -startoption nomount
  ```

- Starting the Default Listener

  ```
  srvctl start listener
  ```

Some examples of starting components with SRVCTL include:

- Shutting Down a Database

  ```
  srvctl stop database -db ocpdb
  ```

- Shutting Down a Database with the ABORT option

  ```
  srvctl stop database -db ocpdb -stopoption abort
  ```

Upgrade to Oracle Database 12c

There are several potential methods for upgrading to Oracle 12c. The actions performed by each vary widely, but they all are targeted at the same basic end goal. The final result of an upgrade should be that data and objects which existed in an earlier release of Oracle end up in a 12c database. Oracle supports any of the following methods for upgrading a database to the current release:

- **Database Upgrade Assistant (DBUA)** -- This utility guides you through the upgrade of a database using a graphical user interface. It is possible to launch DBUA during installation from the Oracle Universal Installer. Alternately, DBUA can be run as a standalone tool at any time after the software has been installed.
- **Manual upgrade using SQL scripts and utilities** -- The database can be upgraded from the command line using SQL scripts and utilities.
- **Oracle Data Pump** -- A new 12c database can be created. Data from the legacy database can be exported using Oracle Data Pump with either a full or partial export. The resulting dump file can then be imported into the Oracle Database created with 12c. Using Oracle Data Pump to perform the upgrade allows for a subset of the data in the old database to be pulled to the new release and also leaves the original database unchanged.

- **CREATE TABLE AS SQL statement** -- Similar to the Data Pump option, using SQL queries to transfer the information allows for data to be copied directly from the legacy database into the new Oracle 12c database. Data copying can copy a subset of the data and leave the source database unchanged.

Oracle recommends a six-step process when upgrading a database to the current release. A summary of the major procedures performed during the upgrade process includes:

- Step 1: Prepare to Upgrade Oracle Database
  - Become familiar with the features of the new release of Oracle Database.
  - Determine the upgrade path to the new release.
  - Choose an upgrade method.
  - Choose an Oracle home directory for the new release.
  - Develop a testing plan.
  - Prepare a backup strategy.
- Step 2: Test the Upgrade Process for Oracle Database
  - Perform a test upgrade using a test database. The test upgrade should be conducted in an environment that does not interfere with the production database.
- Step 3: Test the Upgraded Test Oracle Database
  - Perform the tests planned in Step 1 on the test database that was upgraded to the current release.
  - Review the results, noting anomalies in the tests.
  - Investigate ways to correct any anomalies and implement the corrections.
  - Repeat Step 1, Step 2, and the first parts of Step 3, as necessary, until the test upgrade is successful and works with any required applications.
- Step 4: Prepare and Preserve the Production Oracle Database
  - Prepare the current production database to ensure that the upgrade to the new release is successful.
  - Schedule the downtime required for backing up and upgrading the production database.
  - Back up the current production database.

- Step 5: Upgrade the Production Oracle Database
  - Upgrade the production database to the new release of Oracle Database.
  - After the upgrade, perform a full backup of the production database and perform other post-upgrade tasks.
- Step 6: Tune and Adjust the New Production Oracle Database
  - Tune the new production database for Oracle Database 12c. The new production database should perform to the same standards, or better, than the database before the upgrade.
  - Determine which features of Oracle Database 12c to use, and update your applications accordingly.
  - Develop new database administration procedures as needed.
  - Do not upgrade production users to the new release until all applications have been tested and operate properly.

Using Enterprise Manager and Other Tools

Use EM Express

The EM Express utility is a web-based interface that allows you to manage the Oracle database from a graphical user environment. The utility is built into the Oracle database and allows you to monitor and manage performance of the database and do perform some of the most common administration functions. From the web interface, you can view, create, and alter the various storage structures of the database. When you first log into EM Express, you will be presented with a page similar to the below:

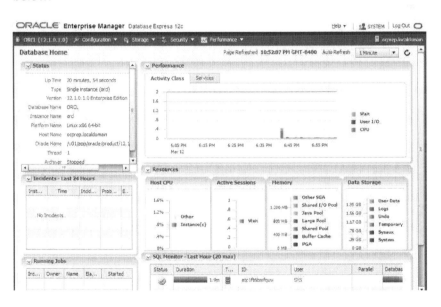

EM Express is specifically designed to be a lightweight interface that imposes negligible overhead on the database server itself. There are no background processes or tasks associated with the utility. It operates using only internal infrastructure components of the Oracle database, such as such as XDB and SQL*Net and utilizes data that is collected by existing Oracle database processes. EM Express data requests to the server are triggered when the user interacts with the web interface. The requested information is processed within the browser to minimize the load against the database server. Because it makes use of the database for its functionality, EM Express cannot perform actions outside the database. In addition, because EM Express makes use of Shockwave Flash (SWF) files, the web browser used must have the Flash plug-in installed.

Immediately upon logging in, you will be at the home page of EM Express. This page displays an overall view of the database instance status and activity. The administrative tasks available via EM Express can be accessed via four menus at the top of the page:

- **Configuration** -- The EM Express Configuration menu allows you to administer initialization parameters for one or more instances of the database. It displays the current memory configuration and the top processes consuming memory within the database. Administrators can also determine the usage of database features and database properties.
- **Storage** -- The storage administration functions allow DBAs to manage redo logs, archive logs, and tablespaces. It allows access to the Undo Advisor and undo statistics. EM Express also displays information regarding the contents of the control file.
- **Security** -- The security menu of EM Express allows DBAs to create and alter users, roles, and profiles as well as granting and revoking privileges.
- **Performance** -- The Performance Hub of EM Express displays performance data for a given time period. The information shown includes SQL Monitor, ASH Analytics, and ADDM. The hub also includes metrics that describe workload characteristics and database resource usage.

EM Express can be accessed via the EM Express URL provided by DBCA during the database configuration process. If you do not know which port EM Express was set to (the default is 5500), it is possible to determine the port with the following SQL statement:

```
SELECT DBMS_XDB_CONFIG.GETHTTPSPORT() FROM dual;
```

The EM Express URL will be in the following format:

```
https://database-hostname:portnumber/em/
```

For example:

```
https://dbhost.company.com:5500/em/
```

If the database instance is running, then the EM Express Login page should appear. If it is not running, you must start the instance prior to accessing EM Express. Provide the credentials of a user account that is authorized to access EM Express. A user that has been granted either the EM_EXPRESS_BASIC or EM_EXPRESS_ALL roles can log in to EM Express. Initially, that user could be either SYS or SYSTEM. However, using the SYS account is highly discouraged and it is recommended that you create a named user account for administering the database in lieu of the SYSTEM account.

Configuring the HTTPS Port for EM Express

The port on which EM Express is accessed can be set or changed at need. Each database instance on a given host must use a unique port. If a port has not been configured for an instance, it is not possible to access EM Express. The steps to manually configure the port follow:

1. The Oracle Net Listener must have already been configured and started before a port can be set. The lsnrctl utility is used to start, stop, and view the status of the listener.

2. If the listener is not running on the default port of 1521, the init.ora file for the database to be managed with EM Express must contain a local_listener entry. The local_listener entry references a TNSNAMES entry that points to the correct listener. For example, the entry

local_listener=orcl1 would be required for an instance defined in the TNSNAMES.ORA file with a non-standard port of 1522 as follows:

```
orcl1= (DESCRIPTION=
        (ADDRESS=
         (PROTOCOL=tcp)(HOST=host_name)(PORT=1522)
        )
        (CONNECT_DATA=
         (SERVICE_NAME=service_name)(SERVER=DEDICATED)
        )
       )
```

3. The TCP dispatcher must be enabled by adding the following entry to the init.ora file for the database you want to manage using EM Express:

```
dispatchers="(PROTOCOL=TCP)(SERVICE=<sid>XDB)"
```

4. The database must be restarted in order for the changes made in the init.ora file to take effect.

5. The PL/SQL procedure DBMS_XDB_CONFIG.SETHTTPSPORT can then be used to set the HTTPS port for EM Express. This procedure will change the HTTPS port in the xdbconfig.xml file in the Oracle XML DB Repository. You must be connected with SYSDBA privileges in order to run the procedure. The following example sets the port to 5600:

```
exec DBMS_XDB_CONFIG.SETHTTPSPORT(5600);
```

The Oracle Database 2 Day DBA documentation for 12c covers the EM Express interface in greater detail. Ideally, you should install Oracle 12c and become familiar with the utility by accessing the various screens.

Use DBCA to create and manage databases

In the bad old days, creating a database meant building a CREATE DATABASE statement that did everything you wanted it to. No one misses those days. Oracle's Database Configuration Assistant (DBCA) is a much simpler means of creating a database. In addition, once DBCA has completed, the database is immediately ready to use. By contrast, a database generated with the CREATE DATABASE statement still requires several scripts to be run before the database can be used. DBCA can be launched directly from the Oracle Installer, or it can be launched as a standalone tool at any point after the Oracle software has been installed.

DBCA has two modes of operation: interactive mode or noninteractive/silent mode. The interactive mode makes use of a graphical user interface and guides you through creating and configuring a database. The noninteractive mode allows you to create the database via a script. DBCA is run in noninteractive mode by specifying command-line arguments, a response file, or both. This chapter will cover only the interactive mode.

To start DBCA, log on to your computer as a member of the group that is authorized to install Oracle and to create and run the database. To start DBCA on UNIX or Linux, or at the command-line prompt in Microsoft Windows, enter the following command: dbca. The dbca executable is located in the ORACLE_HOME/bin directory. Once started, the DBCA user interface guides you through a step-by-step process to create a database.

Step 1: Database Operation -- This screen allows you to create a database, configure or delete a database (both grayed out in the screenshot below because no databases exist yet), manager templates for database creation, or manage pluggable databases (again grayed out because no CDB exists).

Step 2: Creation Mode -- In this step, you must choose the database name, storage type, location of the data files and fast recovery area, character set and the admin password. When using Oracle Enterprise Edition, you can also opt to create this as a container database. If you click the Advanced Mode radio button, you can customize many of the database parameters.

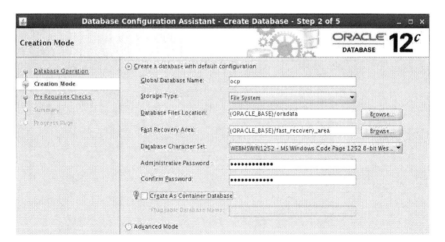

Step 3: Pre Requisite Checks -- DBCA verifies that all prerequisites have been met to create the database.

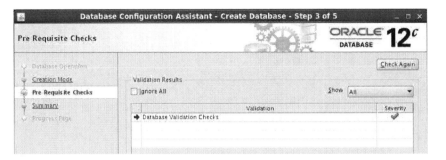

Step 4: Summary -- This screen shows details about how the database is going to be configured if you choose to complete the process at this point.

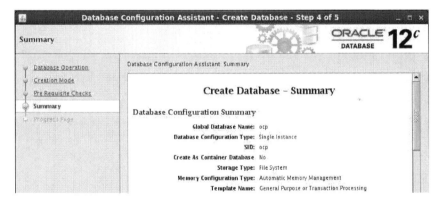

Step 5: Progress Page -- This screen allows you to follow the progress of DBCA as it builds the database.

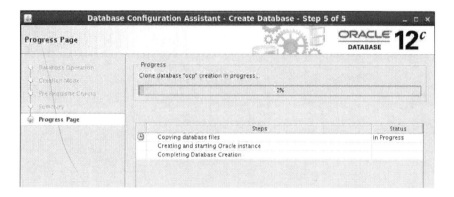

Once DBCA completes, the new database is started and ready to be used. You can connect to the database and begin creating users and objects immediately.

Ideally, you should run the utlrp.sql script after creating or upgrading a database. The script will recompile all PL/SQL modules that might be in an invalid state, including packages, procedures, and types. By default it will recompile the objects in parallel based on the CPU_COUNT of the system it is run on. This step is optional, but Oracle recommends that you do it during installation and not at a later date.

Use Oracle Database Migration Assistant for Unicode

The Database Migration Assistant for Unicode (DMU) ships with Oracle Database 12c Release 1 (12.1) and is now the officially supported method for migration to the Unicode character set. The legacy Database Character Set Scanner (CSSCAN) and CSALTER utilities have been removed from the database installation and are de-supported.

DMU guides the DBA through the entire migration process and automates many of the migration tasks. For post-migration and existing databases already using the Unicode character set, the DMU has a validation mode. The validation mode identifies data not correctly encoded in Unicode to identify potential issues with implementation of Unicode in database applications.

A database must meet certain requirements to be supported by the DMU, including:

- The release of Oracle Database must be 10.2.0.4, 10.2.0.5, 11.1.0.7, 11.2.0.1, or later.
- The database character set must be ASCII-based.
- The SYS.DBMS_DUMA_INTERNAL package must be installed in the database.
- Oracle Database Vault must be disabled before starting the migration process.
- The database cannot be a 12c Pluggable Database (PDB).
- The database must be opened in read/write mode.

Some of the features of the DMU include:

- **Selective Conversion** -- The DMU has the ability to process only the data that must be converted, at the table, column, and row level.
- **Monitoring** -- DMU includes a GUI to visualize the conversion progress.
- **Inline Conversion** -- Oracle Database supports inline conversion of database contents using the DMU.
- **Scheduling** -- Cleansing actions can be scheduled for later execution during the conversion step.

Before it is possible to convert a database to Unicode, DMU must analyze the character data in VARCHAR2, CHAR, LONG, and CLOB table columns. This process will determine if any issues exist that would cause the conversion to corrupt data. The DMU converts character column values in the database from their declared character set to the target Unicode character set. It then checks each value for the following problems:

- The conversion result differs from the original value.
- The conversion result fits into the length limit of its column.
- The conversion result fits into its data type.
- The conversion result does not contain any replacement characters, that is, each converted source character code is valid in the declared character set of the column.

[handwritten: ~~Not~~ COMPATIBLE WITH LINUX HugePages ↑]

Monitoring and Managing Memory

Implement Automatic Shared Memory Management

Automatic Shared Memory Management (ASMM) was the precursor to Automatic Memory Management (AMM). If you want to use ASMM instead of AMM, the total amount of SGA memory available to an instance is specified using the SGA_TARGET initialization parameter. Oracle will automatically distribute this memory among the various SGA components. When using ASMM, a few components of the SGA are still manually sized, including:

- **LOG_BUFFER** -- The log buffer.
- **DB_KEEP_CACHE_SIZE** -- The keep buffer cache.
- **DB_RECYCLE_CACHE_SIZE** -- The recycle buffer cache.
- **DB_nK_CACHE_SIZE** -- Nonstandard block size buffer caches

Any memory allocated to the manually-sized components is subtracted from the SGA_TARGET value and the remainder is allocated among the automatically Sized SGA Components:

- **SHARED_POOL_SIZE** -- The shared pool.
- **LARGE_POOL_SIZE** -- The large pool
- **JAVA_POOL_SIZE** -- The Java pool
- **DB_CACHE_SIZE** -- The buffer cache
- **STREAMS_POOL_SIZE** -- The Streams pool

The dynamic memory allocation functionality of both Automatic Memory Management and Automatic Shared Memory Management make use of statistics gathered for the database in allocating memory. For this reason, neither option can be used if the initialization parameter STATISTICS_LEVEL is set to BASIC.

[handwritten: AMM not compatible with Linux HugePages]

Manually configure SGA parameters for various memory components in the SGA

The only case where it is required to manually configure the sizes of the following SGA components is if the system is not using automatic memory management or automatic shared memory management. Since the vast majority of Oracle database administrators use either AMM or ASMM, having this section in the 1Z0-067 test is fairly pointless. That aside, if you decide for some reason to spend your time as a DBA tuning the SGA, you must manually configure the following memory components:

- **Database buffer cache** -- The database buffer cache is sized using the DB_CACHE_SIZE initialization parameter. To properly size the cache, you must make use of information in the V$DB_CACHE_ADVICE view. You must also understand the Buffer Cache Hit Ratio and how changing the size of the buffer cache will impact it.

- **Shared pool** -- The shared pool is sized using the SHARED_POOL_SIZE initialization parameter. In order to properly size the shared pool, a DBA must make use of Library Cache Statistics (using the V$LIBRARYCACHE view), Dictionary Cache Statistics (using the V$ROWCACHE view), and Shared Pool Advisory Statistics (using the V$SHARED_POOL_ADVICE, V$LIBRARY_CACHE_MEMORY, V$JAVA_POOL_ADVICE, and V$JAVA_LIBRARY_CACHE_MEMORY views).

- **Large pool** -- The large pool is sized using the LARGE_POOL_SIZE initialization parameter. Memory in the large pool is used by the shared server architecture, parallel queries, and Recovery Manager. The V$SGASTAT view can be used to determine the pool in which the memory for an object resides.

- **Java pool** -- The Java pool is sized using the JAVA_POOL_SIZE initialization parameter. The V$JAVA_POOL_ADVICE can be used to help determine an appropriate size.

- **Streams pool** -- The Streams pool is sized using the STREAMS_POOL_SIZE initialization parameter.

All of the steps used for calculating the sizes of these various pools make use of statistics gathered by Oracle and then performing calculations based on those statistics. Since that is exactly what AMM and ASMM do automatically, there is absolutely no reason for a DBA to perform these calculations and memory adjustments manually.

Use Automatic PGA Memory Management

Oracle will automatically manage the amount of memory allocated to the instance PGA by default. The initialization parameter PGA_AGGREGATE_TARGET can be utilized to explicitly control this value. When set, the database will attempt to keep the total amount of PGA memory allocated below this target. When creating a database using the DBCA utility, it is possible to specify a value for the total instance PGA. If a value is specified, DBCA will use this value in the PGA_AGGREGATE_TARGET initialization parameter in the server parameter file. When a value is not specified, DBCA will use a reasonable default. When a database is created using the CREATE DATABASE SQL statement and a text initialization parameter file, it is possible to provide a value for PGA_AGGREGATE_TARGET. If the parameter is omitted, the database will choose a default value.

The following dynamic performance views provide statistics on allocation and use of work area memory:

- V$SYSSTAT
- V$SESSTAT
- V$PGASTAT
- V$SQL_WORKAREA
- V$SQL_WORKAREA_ACTIVE

The V$PROCESS view contains three columns that report the PGA memory allocated and used by an Oracle Database process:

- PGA_USED_MEM
- PGA_ALLOCATED_MEM
- PGA_MAX_MEM

Implement Automatic Memory Management

Since Oracle 11g it has been possible to allow the database instance to automatically manage all of the memory pools. When the MEMORY_TARGET parameter is to a target memory size, the Oracle instance will grab this much memory on startup, allocate it automatically to the various pools, and adjust the amount available to each over time.

Optionally you can also specify a maximum memory size with the MEMORY_MAX_TARGET initialization parameter. The MEMORY_TARGET initialization parameter is dynamic and can be changed without restarting the database. The MEMORY_MAX_TARGET is not dynamic and requires a shutdown to change. It serves as an upper limit on the value that can be assigned to the MEMORY_TARGET parameter so that you cannot accidentally set it too high.

When using Automatic memory management, the instance distributes memory between the SGA and PGA automatically. The instance dynamically redistributes memory between the two as memory requirements change. Databases created with DBCA using the basic installation option will have automatic memory management enabled by default. If a database is not currently using Automatic Memory Management, you can enable it using the following commands:

```
ALTER SYSTEM SET MEMORY_TARGET = nM;
ALTER SYSTEM SET SGA_TARGET = 0;
ALTER SYSTEM SET PGA_AGGREGATE_TARGET = 0;
```

Optionally you can issue the following command:

```
ALTER SYSTEM SET MEMORY_MAX_TARGET = nM SCOPE = SPFILE;
```

The relationships between the four parameters utilized by Automatic Memory Management are:

- **memory_target** – When MEMORY_TARGET is set, the database will allocate this much memory on startup, by default granting 60% to the SGA and 40% to the PGA. Over time, as the database runs, it will redistribute memory as needed between the system global area (SGA) and the instance program global area (instance PGA). If MEMORY_TARGET is not set, automatic memory management is not enabled, even if you have set a value for MEMORY_MAX_TARGET.
- **memory_max_target** – When set, this determines the maximum amount of memory that Oracle will grab from the OS for the SGA and PGA. If this value is not set, it will default to the MEMORY_TARGET value.
- **sga_target** – This value is not required if using automatic memory management. If this value is set and MEMORY_TARGET is also set, then the value of SGA_TARGET becomes the minimum amount of memory allocated to the SGA by automatic memory management.
- **pga_aggregate_target** – This value is not required if using automatic memory management. If this value is set and MEMORY_TARGET is also set, then the value of PGA_AGGREGATE_TARGET becomes the minimum amount of memory allocated to the PGA by automatic memory management.

Storage Management

Create and maintain bigfile tablespaces

Standard tablespaces in Oracle consists of one or more operating system files. By contrast, a bigfile tablespace consists of a single (potentially very large) file. Bigfile tablespaces provide a number of advantages over smallfile tablespaces:

- The datafile for a bigfile tablespace can be huge. A bigfile tablespace with a 32K blocks can have a 128 terabyte datafile. They allow Oracle to hold more data with fewer datafiles. Because the total number of datafiles an Oracle database can have is limited, it also increases the maximum storage capacity of the database.
- Fewer datafiles allows for a lower setting for DB_FILES initialization parameter, which reduces the amount of SGA space required for datafile information.
- The MAXDATAFILES parameter of the CREATE DATABASE and CREATE CONTROLFILE statements can be lowered to reduce the size of the control file.
- Bigfile tablespaces provide datafile transparency. The ALTER TABLESPACE statement allows you perform operations on tablespaces, rather than the underlying individual datafiles.

Bigfile tablespaces are supported only for locally managed tablespaces with automatic segment space management. Undo, temporary, and SYSTEM tablespaces cannot be created using the bigfile option. Bigfile tablespaces should be created on a filesystem controlled by a volume manager that supports striping or RAID.

Bigfile tablespaces are created when the BIGFILE keyword is specified in the CREATE TABLESPACE statement. Oracle will automatically create a locally managed tablespace with automatic segment space management. If the CREATE TABLESPACE statement explicitly specifies EXTENT MANAGEMENT DICTIONARY or SEGMENT SPACE MANAGEMENT

MANUAL, an error will be returned. The remaining syntax of the statement is the same as for the CREATE TABLESPACE statement.

```
CREATE BIGFILE TABLESPACE bf_tbs
DATAFILE '/u02/oracle/data/bftbs01.dbf' SIZE 50G
...
```

The following views contain a BIGFILE column that identifies a tablespace as a bigfile tablespace:

- DBA_TABLESPACES
- USER_TABLESPACES
- V$TABLESPACE

Rename tablespaces

The ALTER TABLESPACE statement can be used to rename a permanent or temporary tablespace if required. When a tablespace is renamed, Oracle updates all references to the tablespace name in the data dictionary, control file, and all online datafile headers. The tablespace ID remains the same. Any users who had the tablespace as their default will continue to do so after the rename operation. Some restrictions to the operation include:

- The COMPATIBLE parameter must be 10.0.0 or higher.
- The SYSTEM and SYSAUX tablespaces cannot be renamed.
- The tablespace and all datafiles must be online.
- If the tablespace is read only, its datafile headers are not updated. A message will be written to the alert log indicating that datafile headers have not been renamed. The data dictionary and control file are updated.

Renaming an undo tablespace has some additional considerations.

- If a server parameter file was used to start the instance and the tablespace name is specified as the UNDO_TABLESPACE for any instance, the tablespace name is changed to the new tablespace name in the server parameter file.
- If the instance was started using a traditional initialization parameter file, a message will be written to the alert log stating that the initialization parameter file must be manually changed.

The syntax for renaming a tablespace is:

```
ALTER TABLESPACE users RENAME TO users_new;
```

Create a default permanent tablespace

It is possible to set a default permanent tablespace to be used for user accounts that have not been explicitly assigned a default tablespace. This feature was added to prevent the nasty alternative, which was newly-created users having their default permanent tablespace become SYSTEM when one was not assigned. Both the CREATE DATABASE and ALTER DATABASE statements have a DEFAULT TABLESPACE clause. The following example sets the default permanent tablespace to USERS:

```
ALTER DATABASE DEFAULT TABLESPACE users;
```

The current settings for the default tablespaces can be determined by querying the database_properties view:

```
SELECT property_name, property_value
FROM   database_properties
WHERE  property_name like '%TABLESPACE';

PROPERTY_NAME                      PROPERTY_VALUE
---------------------------------  --------------
DEFAULT_TEMP_TABLESPACE            TEMP2
DEFAULT_PERMANENT_TABLESPACE       USERS
```

When a default permanent tablespace is set (or changed) all objects created by users who do not have a default tablespace explicitly assigned will be created there unless the create statement explicitly references another tablespace.

Space Management

Manage resumable space allocation

Resumable space allocation allows for large database operations to be suspended and later resumed in the event of a space allocation failure. Prior to this feature, when such an operation ran out of space, it immediately failed and was rolled back. Even with the new capability, a statement executes in a resumable mode only if its session has been enabled for resumable space allocation.

If a resumable statement is suspended, the error causing the suspension is reported in the alert log, and the system issues the Resumable Session Suspended alert. If the user has a trigger on the AFTER SUSPEND system event, it will be executed. If the error condition is resolved before the timeout period expires, the suspended statement resumes automatically and the Resumable Session Suspended alert is cleared. If a statement is suspended for the full timeout interval (the default is two hours), it will wake up and return the exception to the user. It is possible for a resumable statement to be suspended and resumed multiple times during execution.

There are three classes of correctable errors:

- Out of space
- Maximum extents reached
- Space quota exceeded

Enabling and Disabling Resumable Space Allocation

Resumable space allocation is only possible if the session a statement is executed in has resumable mode enabled. Resumable mode can be enabled at the system level with the RESUMABLE_TIMEOUT initialization parameter, or users can enable it at the session level using the ALTER SESSION statement. Users can only do this if they have been granted the RESUMABLE system privilege.

By default, the RESUMABLE_TIMEOUT parameter is set to 0. This disables resumable for all sessions by default. Providing a non-zero value will enable resumable space allocation by default for all sessions with the supplied number of seconds. The parameter can be changed dynamically by issuing an ALTER SYSTEM SET RESUMABLE_TIMEOUT command with the desired value. Within a session, a user can alter the resumable behavior with the ALTER SESSION SET RESUMABLE_TIMEOUT statement.

A user can enable or disable resumable mode for a session with ALTER SESSION:

```
ALTER SESSION ENABLE RESUMABLE;
ALTER SESSION DISABLE RESUMABLE;
```

When resumable mode is enabled for a session, the following statement specifies that resumable transactions will time out and error after 3600 seconds:

```
ALTER SESSION ENABLE RESUMABLE TIMEOUT 3600;
```

When enabling resumable statements, it is possible to give them a name. If a name is not set, a statement name will default to 'User username(userid), Session sessionid, Instance instanceid'.

```
ALTER SESSION ENABLE RESUMABLE TIMEOUT 3600 NAME 'Really Huge Table
Insert';
```

The following views can be queried to obtain information about the status of resumable statements:

- **DBA_RESUMABLE & USER_RESUMABLE** -- Contain rows for all currently executing or suspended resumable statements. They can be used to monitor the progress of, or obtain specific information about, resumable statements.

- **V$SESSION_WAIT** -- When a statement is suspended the session invoking the statement is put into a wait state. A row is inserted into this view for the session with the EVENT column containing "statement suspended, wait error to be cleared".

The DBMS_RESUMABLE package helps control resumable space allocation. The following procedures can be invoked:

- **ABORT(sessionID)** -- This procedure aborts a suspended resumable statement.
- **GET_SESSION_TIMEOUT(sessionID)** -- This function returns the current timeout value of resumable space allocation for the session with sessionID.
- **SET_SESSION_TIMEOUT(sessionID, timeout)** -- This procedure sets the timeout interval of resumable space allocation for the session with sessionID.
- **GET_TIMEOUT()** -- This function returns the current timeout value of resumable space allocation for the current session.
- **SET_TIMEOUT(timeout)** -- This procedure sets a timeout value for resumable space allocation for the current session.

Reclaim wasted space from tables and indexes by using the segment shrink functionality

The online segment shrink capability of Oracle allows you to reclaim fragmented free space below the high watermark in a segment. Shrinking a segment provides the following benefits:

- Compaction of data leads to better cache utilization.
- Compacted data requires fewer blocks to be scanned in full table scans.

Segment shrink is an online, in-place operation that does not interfere with DML operations or queries. Concurrent DML operations are blocked for a short time at the end of the shrink operation, when the space is deallocated. Indexes are maintained during the shrink operation and remain usable after completion. No extra disk space needs to be allocated. Segment shrink reclaims unused space both above and below the high water mark. By default, a shrink operation compacts the segment, adjusts the high water mark, and releases the reclaimed space.

Segment shrink requires that rows be moved to new locations. You must first enable row movement in the object and disable any rowid-based triggers. Shrink operations can be performed only on segments in locally managed tablespaces with automatic segment space management (ASSM). Within an ASSM tablespace, all segment types are eligible for online segment shrink except the following:

- IOT mapping tables
- Tables with rowid based materialized views
- Tables with function-based indexes
- SECUREFILE LOBs
- Compressed tables

Invoking Online Segment Shrink

You can shrink space in a table, index-organized table, index, partition, subpartition, materialized view, or materialized view log. You do this using ALTER TABLE, ALTER INDEX, ALTER MATERIALIZED VIEW, or ALTER MATERIALIZED VIEW LOG statement with the SHRINK SPACE clause. There are two optional clauses that control the behavior of the shrink operation:

- **COMPACT** – This clause divides the shrink segment operation into two phases. When specified, the Database defragments the segment space and compacts the table rows but does not reset the high water mark or deallocate space. You can reissue the SHRINK SPACE clause without the COMPACT clause during off-peak hours to complete the shrink operation.
- **CASCADE** – This clause extends the segment shrink operation to all dependent segments of the object.

Examples

Shrink a table and all of its dependent segments:

```
ALTER TABLE employees SHRINK SPACE CASCADE;
```

Shrink a single partition of a partitioned table:

```
ALTER TABLE customers MODIFY PARTITION cust_P1 SHRINK SPACE;
```

Rebuild indexes online

During an index rebuild, an existing index is used as the data source to build a duplicate. Index rebuilds allow administrators to change storage characteristics or move in index to a new tablespace. During the rebuild, any intra-block fragmentation will be eliminated. The operation will create a new tree, shrinking the height if applicable. An index rebuild operation has better performance when compared to dropping the index and using the CREATE INDEX statement to re-create it.

The following statement rebuilds the existing index ocp_emps:

```
ALTER INDEX ocp_emps REBUILD;
```

It is also possible to rebuild the index online. Rebuilding online allows the base tables to be updated concurrent with the rebuild operation. The following statement rebuilds the ocp_emps index online:

```
ALTER INDEX ocp_emps REBUILD ONLINE;
```

Reduce space-related error conditions by proactively managing tablespace usage

A tablespace that is locally managed uses bitmaps within the tablespace itself to track all extent information. Local management has several benefits over traditional tablespaces where this information is stored in the data dictionary:

- Space allocations and deallocations modify locally managed resources. This makes them fast and concurrent, resulting in enhanced performance.
- Locally managed temporary tablespaces do not generate any undo or redo.
- If the AUTOALLOCATE clause is specified, the database automatically selects the appropriate extent size.
- Reliance on the data dictionary is reduced, reducing contention in times of high activity to tables.
- There is no need to coalesce free extents.

Any tablespace can be locally managed, including SYSTEM and SYSAUX. There are maintenance procedures in the DBMS_SPACE_ADMIN package specific to locally managed tablespaces.

The syntax to create a locally managed tablespace, is the keyword LOCAL in the EXTENT MANAGEMENT clause of the CREATE TABLESPACE statement. The default value for new permanent tablespaces is 'EXTENT MANAGEMENT LOCAL AUTOALLOCATE'. Specifying this clause is optional unless you do not want local management or you want to use the UNIFORM keyword rather than AUTOALLOCATE. When the AUTOALLOCATE keyword is used, the database will manage extents automatically. If you want the tablespace to utilize uniform extents of a specific size, you must specify the UNIFORM keyword. The two commands below will have identical effects:

```
CREATE TABLESPACE ocpts DATAFILE '/u02/oracle/data/ocpts01.dbf' SIZE
50M
EXTENT MANAGEMENT LOCAL AUTOALLOCATE;

CREATE TABLESPACE ocpts DATAFILE '/u02/oracle/data/ocpts01.dbf' SIZE
50M;
```

There are two methods that Oracle Database can use to manage segment space in a locally managed tablespace. Manual space management uses freelists to manage free space in a segment. Automatic segment space management uses bitmaps. Automatic segment space management is more efficient and is the default for all new permanent, locally managed tablespaces. You can explicitly enable it with the SEGMENT SPACE MANAGEMENT AUTO clause:

```
CREATE TABLESPACE ocpts DATAFILE '/u02/oracle/data/ocpts01.dbf' SIZE
50M
EXTENT MANAGEMENT LOCAL AUTOALLOCATE
SEGMENT SPACE MANAGEMENT AUTO;
```

Compression

When you create a tablespace, it's possible to specify that all tables created in it be compressed by default. This is done with the DEFAULT keyword, followed by the compression type to be used. There are four different compression options:

- **DEFAULT COMPRESS [BASIC]** – Basic table compression compresses data inserted by direct path load only and supports limited data types and SQL operations.
- **DEFAULT COMPRESS FOR OLTP** – All tables created in the tablespace will use OLTP compression, unless otherwise specified. OLTP table compression is intended for OLTP applications and compresses data manipulated by any SQL operation.
- **DEFAULT COMPRESS FOR QUERY [LOW|HIGH]** – This compression method can result in high CPU overhead and works best for direct-path load. Rows inserted without using direct-path insert and updated rows go to a block with a less compressed format and have lower compression level.

- **DEFAULT COMPRESS FOR ARCHIVE [LOW|HIGH]** – This compression method can result in high CPU overhead and works best for direct-path load. Rows inserted without using direct-path insert and updated rows go to a block with a less compressed format and have lower compression level.

You can get more information on the compression types from the Oracle Database Administrator's Guide. Tables created in a tablespace with the compression option enabled will default to that method. However, you can create tables uncompressed or using a different method by supplying a compression clause in the CREATE TABLE statement. If you alter the default compression in a tablespace, all new tables created will default to the new method, but existing tables are unchanged.

Use different storage options to improve the performance of queries

SQL Queries access the data stored in tables (obviously). However, the type of queries that will be executed against a table, its eventual size, and its relationship to other tables in the database all have query performance implications. Administrators should consider these when making decisions about the storage options used when creating a table. There are four broad classes of table storage types: Heap organized, Index organized, Clustered, and Partitioned.

Heap-organized tables are the general-purpose tables that make up the majority of table objects created in Oracle databases. Data in these tables is stored in an unorganized fashion. Unless there is a specific reason for using another type of table, data should be stored in heap-organized tables.

Index-organized tables (IOTs) store data in a B-tree index structure sorted by the primary key of the table. The index entries of the B-tree store not only the key columns but all of the nonkey columns of the table as well. Storing the table data in this fashion provides fast random access on the primary key because an index-only scan is sufficient to locate the data. IOTs also provide fast range access on queries that use the primary key.

A clustered table is any table that is part of a cluster. A cluster is created using a group of tables that share common columns and are often used together. When organized as a cluster, these tables will share data blocks for the common columns (known as the cluster key). Storing the related rows of multiple tables together in this fashion provides two primary benefits:

- Disk I/O is reduced and access time improves for joins of clustered tables.
- The cluster key value is stored only once each in the cluster and the cluster index, no matter how many rows of different tables contain the value.

Partitioned tables allow administrators to break the data stored in the table into pieces. These pieces are called partitions or subpartitions. Each partition of a table is separate data dictionary object. Each partition of a single table can have different settings for physical attributes such as compression, storage settings, and tablespace. This allows administrators to fine-tune the physical structure of a table for availability and performance.

The previous section discussed four compression options that can be set as the tablespace default: BASIC, OLTP, COMPRESS FOR QUERY, and COMPRESS FOR ARCHIVE. No matter what the tablespace default is, administrators can chose to create individual tables (or individual partitions) using any of the options (or no compression at all). Compressing data in a table not only saves disk space, it also reduces memory use in the database buffer cache. It can also improve query execution performance during reads. There is a CPU cost for tables using compression during data loading and DML operations. However, the reduced I/O requirements of reading the data back (more rows per block) can make up for this cost.

Use automatic undo retention tuning and temporary undo

Any time that automatic undo management is enabled, there is an undo retention period. This is the minimum amount of time that the database will try to keep old undo information from being overwritten. The undo retention period is based on the undo tablespace size and system activity. It is possible to use the UNDO_RETENTION initialization parameter to specify a minimum undo retention period.

It the undo tablespace is fixed size, the value of UNDO_RETENTION is ignored. The database automatically uses system activity and undo tablespace size to tune the undo retention period for the best possible retention. For an undo tablespace set to AUTOEXTEND, the database will attempt to honor the specified UNDO_RETENTION period. When space is low, the tablespace will auto-extend (up to the MAXSIZE) instead of overwriting unexpired undo information. If the MAXSIZE is reached, the database may not be able to meet the UNDO_RETENTION value. The minimum undo retention period (in seconds) can be set in two ways:

- Set UNDO_RETENTION in the initialization parameter file.

    ```
    UNDO_RETENTION = 2000
    ```

- The UNDO_RETENTION value can be modified dynamically using the ALTER SYSTEM statement.

    ```
    ALTER SYSTEM SET UNDO_RETENTION = 3000;
    ```

The effect of an UNDO_RETENTION parameter change can only be honored if the current undo tablespace has sufficient space.

When using a fixed-size undo tablespace, the Undo Advisor is valuable for estimating the optimum size. It can be accessed through Oracle Enterprise Manager Express or through DBMS_ADVISOR. The Undo Advisor uses AWR data to create its analysis, so there must be sufficient workload statistics available for it to make accurate recommendations. When using the Undo Advisor, two values must be estimated:

- The length of the expected longest running query.
- The longest interval required for Oracle Flashback operations

The larger of these two values is used as input to the Undo Advisor. The Undo Advisor does not alter the size of the undo tablespace, it only offers a recommended size. You must use ALTER DATABASE statements to change the tablespace data file size. The following example changes an undo tablespace with a file called undotbs.dbf to a fixed size of 400MB.

```
ALTER DATABASE DATAFILE '/u01/oracle/dbs/undotbs.dbf' RESIZE 400M;
ALTER DATABASE DATAFILE '/u01/oracle/dbs/undotbs.dbf' AUTOEXTEND OFF;
```

The RETENTION_GUARANTEE clause is used to guarantee the success of long-running queries or Oracle Flashback operations. When enabled, the specified minimum undo retention is guaranteed. Oracle will never overwrite unexpired undo data even when doing so means that transactions fail from lack of space in the undo tablespace. When retention guarantee is disabled (the default), the database can overwrite unexpired undo when space is low. The RETENTION GUARANTEE clause can be specified for an undo tablespace at create time with either the CREATE DATABASE or CREATE UNDO TABLESPACE statement. The clause can be used to modify an existing tablespace using the ALTER TABLESPACE statement. Retention guarantee is disabled with the RETENTION NOGUARANTEE clause.

Temporary Undo

Any time a transaction is performed in the Oracle database, it is necessary for Oracle to create undo information about the transaction in order to maintain transaction consistency. This is true event for data written to temporary tables. While the data written to the temporary tables generates no redo (because there is no need to recover them). However, the undo data generated by operations on temporary tables is written to the undo tablespace. Because the undo tablespace require recovery in the event of an instance or media failure, the undo from operations generates redo.

The parameter TEMP_UNDO_ENABLED has been introduced in Oracle 12c. When set to TRUE (the default), the undo information for operations against temporary tables is stored in the temporary tablespace rather than the undo tablespace. This reduces the amount of data written to the undo tablespace and eliminates the associated redo writes from the operation. The result is improved performance when using temporary tables in Oracle 12c.

Implement partitioning methods

Partitioning improves Oracle's ability to support very large tables by breaking them into smaller and more manageable pieces called partitions. Partitioned tables facilitate SQL tuning by allowing SQL statements to avoid scanning partitions that can be determined not to hold the required data using partition pruning. Partitioning can also facilitate SQL tuning by breaking down large joins of similarly-partitioned objects by using partition-wise joins. Partitioning of tables and indexes works hand-in-hand with parallel queries to improve performance in data warehouses. When an object in the database is partitioned, it is possible for parallel server processes to scan individual table partitions or index partitions when doing so makes sense.

There are three fundamental methods used to control how data is distributed into partitions: Range, Hash, and List. When partitioning data using these methods, it is possible to partition a table at a single-level, or to partition it at two levels for composite partitioning. There are advantages and design considerations for both methods. The specific needs of a given table determine which strategy is more appropriate.

Single-Level Partitioning

In single-level partitioning, a table is defined by specifying one of the following three methodologies, where one or more columns in the table act as the partitioning key:

- **Range Partitioning** -- This method maps data to partitions based on ranges of values of the partitioning key. Each of the partitions is defined with a range of values that determines which records should be placed in it. This is the most common type of partitioning and is often used with dates. Partitions are created with a VALUES LESS THAN clause, which specifies a non-inclusive upper bound for the partitions. Rows that have partitioning key values equal to or higher than this literal are added to the next higher partition. The lower bound is implied by the VALUES LESS THAN clause of the previous partition. The first partition has no lower bound. The highest partition can use a MAXVALUE literal. This represents a virtual infinite value that sorts higher than any other possible value for the partitioning key, including NULL.
- **Hash Partitioning** -- This method uses a hashing algorithm to map data to partitions using the partitioning key that you identify. The hashing algorithm is designed to evenly distribute rows among each of the partitions. This is an ideal method to distribute data evenly across devices. It is easier to implement than range partitioning. Hash partitioning is especially useful when the data to be partitioned is not historical or has no obvious partitioning key.
- **List Partitioning** -- This method allows you to specify a list of discrete values for the partitioning key in the description for each partition. In this fashion, you can control exactly how rows map to partitions. List partitioning provides the ability to group unordered and unrelated sets of data. In list partitioning, the

DEFAULT partition provides a partition to store all values that are not explicitly mapped to any other partition.

Composite Partitioning

This strategy combines the basic data distribution methods. In composite partitioning, a table is partitioned by one data distribution method and then each partition is further subdivided into subpartitions using a second data distribution method. It is possible for the partitioning methods at the two levels to be the same, or different. Composite partitioning provides higher degrees of potential partition pruning and finer granularity of data placement. The possible composite partitioning methods are:

- Range-Range Partitioning
- Range-Hash Partitioning
- Range-List Partitioning
- List-Range Partitioning
- List-Hash Partitioning
- List-List Partitioning

Security

Configure the password file to use case-sensitive passwords

The account passwords in the Oracle password file are case-sensitive by default. It is possible to control the case-sensitivity of the password file by using the IGNORECASE parameter when creating the password file with orapwd. By default, IGNORECASE is set to N, which means that passwords are treated as case-sensitive. The following statement creates a password file that is not case sensitive:

```
orapwd file=orapw entries=100 ignorecase=y
```

By contrast, either of the following statements creates a case-sensitive password file:

```
orapwd file=orapw entries=100 ignorecase=n
orapwd file=orapw entries=100
```

Encrypt a tablespace

Tablespace encryption makes use of Oracle's Transparent Data Encryption (TDE) functionality. Before making use of TDE, it is necessary to create a software keystore, which is a container that stores the TDE master encryption key. There is one keystore per database, and the database locates this keystore by checking the location defined in the sqlnet.ora file. For information on configuring a software keystore, refer to the Oracle 12c Advanced Security Guide. This chapter will assume that a keystore has been configured.

In previous releases, the Oracle software keystore was referred to as the Oracle Wallet. The Software keystore must be open before you can create an encrypted column or tablespace and before you can store or retrieve encrypted data. When you open the keystore, it is available to all sessions. It remains open until you explicitly close it or until the database is shut down.

Transparent Data Encryption is designed to protect data stored on a disk or other media. It does not offer any protection for data in transit. It protects data from unauthorized access by means other than through the database. This would include events such as someone getting hold of backup tapes of a database. TDE encryption also protects data from users who try to access database files directly through the operating system.

Oracle's TDE functionality supports industry-standard encryption algorithms, including the following: 3DES168, AES128, AES192, AES256. The encryption key length is implied by the algorithm name. For example, the AES128 algorithm uses 128-bit keys. You specify the algorithm to use when you create the encrypted column or tablespace. You can pick the algorithm to use for each tablespace or column encrypted -- they do not all have to be the same. While longer key lengths theoretically provide greater security, there is a trade-off in CPU overhead. By default, TDE uses the AES encryption algorithm with a 192-bit key length (AES192). TDE adds salt to plaintext before encrypting it in order to make it harder for attackers to steal data through a brute force attack. TDE also adds a Message Authentication Code (MAC) to the data for integrity checking. The SHA-1 integrity algorithm is used by default.

It is possible to encrypt any permanent tablespace to protect sensitive data. Tablespace encryption is transparent to database users and your applications. When a tablespace is encrypted, all tablespace blocks are encrypted. All segment types are supported for encryption, including tables, clusters, indexes, LOBs, table and index partitions, and so on. To maximize security, data from an encrypted tablespace is automatically encrypted when written to the undo tablespace, to the redo logs, and to any temporary tablespace. There is no disk space overhead for encrypting a tablespace. There are some restrictions involving encrypted tablespaces:

- You cannot encrypt an existing tablespace with an ALTER TABLESPACE statement.
- Encrypted tablespaces are subject to restrictions when transporting to another database.
- When recovering a database with encrypted tablespaces you must open the keystore that contains the encryption key after database mount and before database open, so the recovery process can decrypt data blocks and redo.

The following statement creates an encrypted tablespace with the default encryption algorithm:

```
CREATE TABLESPACE secure_ts
DATAFILE '/u02/app/oracle/oradata/orcl12c/secure01.dbf' SIZE 200M
ENCRYPTION
DEFAULT STORAGE(ENCRYPT);
```

Use Secure File LOBS to store documents with compression, encryption, de-duplication

In Oracle 11g, a new type of Large-Object storage was introduced, SecureFile LOBs and the legacy LOB format renamed to BasicFile LOBs. With Oracle 12c, SecureFiles have become the default for LOB storage when the COMPATIBLE parameter is set to 12.1 or higher. SecureFiles feature provides improved performance over BasicFiles for storing unstructured data. SecureFile LOBs add several new capabilities to LOB data storage:

- Intelligent LOB compression enables users to explicitly compress data to save disk space.
- Intelligent LOB encryption allows encrypted data to be stored in-place and is available for random reads and writes.
- The deduplication option allows Oracle to automatically detect duplicate LOB data and conserve space by only storing a single copy of the data.

- LOB data path optimization includes logical cache above storage layer, read prefetching, new caching modes, vectored IO, and more.

db_securefile parameter

The init.ora parameter, db_securefile, is used to determine the behavior of the Oracle database in reference to using or not using SecureFile LOBs or BasicFile LOBs. The possible values of this parameter are: ALWAYS, FORCE, PERMITTED, NEVER, and IGNORE. The meaning of each of the values is:

- **ALWAYS** -- Attempt to create SecureFile LOBs but fall back to BasicFile LOBs if the tablespace is not using ASSM. *Automatic Segment Space Mgmt*
- **PERMITTED** -- Allow SecureFile LOBs to be created
- **PREFERRED** -- All LOBs are created as SecureFiles unless BASICFILE is explicitly specified in the LOB storage clause or the tablespace is a Manual Segment Space Management tablespace. When PREFERRED is set, cases where BASICFILE would otherwise be inherited from the partition or column level LOB storage are ignored; the LOBs will be created as SecureFiles instead.
- **NEVER** -- Disallow SecureFile LOBs from being created. If a DML statement tries to create a column as a SecureFile LOB, it will instead be created as a BasicFile LOB. If any SecureFile specific storage options or features are in the DML, an exception is created.
- **IGNORE** -- The SECUREFILE keyword and all SecureFiles options are ignored.

The COMPRESS, DEDUPLICATE, and ENCRYPT keywords of the CREATE TABLE statement are used to enable compression, deduplication, and encryption on SecureFile LOBs respectively. Examples of the various options follow. The first statement below creates a SecureFiles LOB column with MEDIUM compression and the second with HIGH:

```
CREATE TABLE sfltab (col1 CLOB)
    LOB(col1) STORE AS SECUREFILE (
        COMPRESS
        CACHE
    );

CREATE TABLE sfltab (col1 CLOB)
    LOB(col1) STORE AS SECUREFILE (
        COMPRESS HIGH
        CACHE
    );
```

The first statement below creates a SecureFiles LOB column with the deduplication option enabled and the second explicitly disables deduplication:

```
CREATE TABLE sfltab (col1 CLOB)
    LOB(col1) STORE AS SECUREFILE (
        DEDUPLICATE
        CACHE
    );

CREATE TABLE sfltab (col1 CLOB)
    LOB(col1) STORE AS SECUREFILE (
        KEEP_DUPLICATES
        CACHE
    );
```

Either of the two statements below will create a SecureFiles LOB column encrypted by a password key:

```
CREATE TABLE sfltab1 (col1 CLOB ENCRYPT IDENTIFIED BY [password_key])
    LOB(a) STORE AS SECUREFILE (
        CACHE
    );

CREATE TABLE sfltab (col1 CLOB)
    LOB(col1) STORE AS SECUREFILE (
        CACHE
        ENCRYPT
        IDENTIFIED BY [password_key]
    );
```

The following statement creates a SecureFiles LOB column with disabled encryption:

```
CREATE TABLE sfltab (col1 CLOB)
    LOB(col1) STORE AS SECUREFILE (
        CACHE DECRYPT
    );
```

DBMS_LOB

SecureFiles inherit the LOB column settings for deduplication, encryption, and compression that were specified at the time the LOB was created. You can use the new procedures added to the DBMS_LOB package to determine or override the inherited values.

- **DBMS_LOB.GETOPTIONS** -- The current settings of a SecureFile LOB can be obtained using this function. An integer corresponding to a pre-defined constant based on the option type is returned. As an example, the value for DEDUPLICATE_OFF is 0. You won't need to know the values for the test. You might need to know the procedure name.
- **DBMS_LOB.SETOPTIONS** -- This procedure sets features of a SecureFile LOB (compression, deduplication, and encryption). It enables the features to be set on a per-LOB basis, overriding the default LOB settings.
- **DBMS_LOB.ISSECUREFILE** -- This function returns TRUE or FALSE depending on whether the LOB locator (BLOB or CLOB) passed to it is for a SecureFile.

DBMS_SPACE.SPACE_USAGE

The existing SPACE_USAGE procedure is overloaded to return information about LOB space usage. It returns the amount of disk space in blocks used by all the LOBs in the LOB segment. This procedure can only be used on tablespaces that are created with auto segment space management.

The following enhancements have been made to SecureFiles in the 12c release:

- **PDML Operations** -- SecureFiles have enhanced support for parallel DML operations. Non-partitioned tables that contain SecureFile LOB columns (and no BasicFile LOB columns) can support parallel DML. Operations that can be parallelized include:
  - INSERT
  - INSERT AS SELECT
  - CREATE TABLE AS SELECT
  - DELETE
  - UPDATE
  - MERGE (conditional UPDATE and INSERT)
  - Multi-table INSERT
  - SQL Loader
  - Import/Export
- **LogMiner** -- LogMiner now fully supports SecureFiles LOBs, including support for deduplication of SecureFiles LOB columns and SecureFiles Database File System (DBFS) operations when database compatibility is set to 11.2 or later. Only SQL_REDO columns can be filled in for SecureFiles LOB columns; SQL_UNDO columns are not filled in.

Configure fined-grained access to network services

The Oracle database contains a set of PL/SQL utility packages, such as UTL_TCP, UTL_SMTP, UTL_MAIL, UTL_HTTP, and UTL_INADDR, which are designed to enable database users to access network services from within the database. In a default database installation, these packages are created with EXECUTE privileges granted to PUBLIC users. Prior to Oracle 11g, this meant that any user with access to an Oracle account also gained access to all of these network services. This release enhances the security of these packages by allowing database administrators the ability to restrict access to these packages.

Creating Access Control Lists

To configure fine-grained access to external network services, you create an access control list (ACL), which is stored in Oracle XML DB. It's possible to create the access control list by using Oracle XML DB itself, or by using the DBMS_NETWORK_ACL_ADMIN and DBMS_NETWORK_ACL_UTILITY PL/SQL packages.

To create the access control list by using the DBMS_NETWORK_ACL_ADMIN package, follow these steps:

First, create the Access Control List and Its Privilege Definitions via the DBMS_NETWORK_ACL_ADMIN.CREATE_ACL procedure.

```
BEGIN
  DBMS_NETWORK_ACL_ADMIN.CREATE_ACL (
    acl          => 'file_name.xml',
    description  => 'file description',
    principal    => 'user_or_role',
    is_grant     => TRUE|FALSE,
    privilege    => 'connect|resolve',
    start_date   => null|timestamp_with_time_zone,
    end_date     => null|timestamp_with_time_zone);
END;
```

- **acl** -- a name for the access control list XML file.
- **description** -- a brief description of the purpose of this file.
- **principal** -- the initial user account or role being granted or denied permissions.
- **is_grant** -- either TRUE or FALSE, to indicate whether the privilege is to be granted or denied
- **privilege** -- either connect or resolve. Connect grants permission to connect to a network service. Resolve grants the user permission to resolve a network host name or an IP address.
- **start_date** -- (Optional) starting date that the entry will be valid.
- **end_date** -- (Optional) ending date that the entry will be valid.

Second, add additional users or roles to the access control list, or grant additional privileges to one user or role, via the DBMS_NETWORK_ACL_ADMIN.ADD_PRIVILEGE procedure.

```
BEGIN
  DBMS_NETWORK_ACL_ADMIN.ADD_PRIVILEGE (
    acl => 'file_name.xml',
    principal => 'user_or_role',
    is_grant => TRUE|FALSE,
    privilege => 'connect|resolve',
    position => null|value,
    start_date => null|timestamp_with_time_zone,
    end_date => null|timestamp_with_time_zone);
END;
```

The matching parameters that exist in ADD_PRIVILEGE and CREATE_ACL have the same meaning. The only new parameter is position, which sets the precedence for multiple users or roles.

Finally, assign the access control list to one or more network host computers using the DBMS_NETWORK_ACL_ADMIN.ASSIGN_ACL procedure. Only one access control list can be assigned to any host computer, domain, or IP subnet, and if specified, the TCP port range. When you assign a new access control list to a network target, Oracle Database unassigns the previous access control list that was assigned to the same target.

```
BEGIN
  DBMS_NETWORK_ACL_ADMIN.ASSIGN_ACL (
    acl => 'file_name.xml',
    host => 'network_host',
    lower_port => null|port_number,
    upper_port => null|port_number);
END;
```

- **acl** --the name of the access control list XML file to assign to the network host.
- **host** -- the network host to which this access control list will be assigned. This setting can be a name or IP address of the network host, or you can enter localhost.

- **lower_port** -- (Optional) For TCP connections, enter the lower boundary of the port range. Use this setting for the connect privilege only; omit it for the resolve privilege. The default is null, which means that there is no port restriction (that is, the ACL applies to all ports).
- **upper_port** -- (Optional) For TCP connections, enter the upper boundary of the port range. Use this setting for connect privileges only; omit it for resolve privileges. The default is null, which means that there is no port restriction (that is, the ACL applies to all ports).

Use and manage Oracle Data Redaction policies

Data Redaction provides runtime redaction of sensitive data being returned by SQL queries prior to being displayed by applications. This ensures that unauthorized users cannot view sensitive data. Oracle Data Redaction provides consistent redaction of database columns across application modules accessing the same database information. It allows you to redact column data by any of the following methods:

- **Full redaction** -- The entire contents of the column data is redacted. The redacted value returned to the querying application user depends on the data type of the column. Columns of the NUMBER data type are redacted with a zero (0), and character data types are redacted with a single space.
- **Partial redaction** -- Only a portion of the column data is redacted. For example, you can redact most of a credit card number with pound signs (#), except for the last 4 digits.
- **Regular expressions** -- Regular expressions can be used to look for patterns of data to redact. Designed for use with character data only, it is most applicable for data with varying character lengths.
- **Random redaction** -- The redacted data presented to the querying application user appears as randomly generated values each time it is displayed, depending on the data type of the column.

- **No redaction** -- The 'None' redaction type option enables you to test the internal operation of your redaction policies, with no effect on the results of queries against tables with policies defined on them.

Data Redaction policies define the way in which the data will be masked, including:

- What kind of redaction to perform (Full, Partial, Random, etc.)
- How the redaction should occur (e.g. for partial redaction, which portion of the data is redacted).
- When the redaction should take place (which users should see redacted vs. actual data).

EXECUTE privileges on the DBMS_REDACT PL/SQL package are required in order to create and manage an Oracle Data Redaction policy. The procedures in that package include the following:

- **DBMS_REDACT.ADD_POLICY** -- Adds a Data Redaction policy to a table or view
- **DBMS_REDACT.ALTER_POLICY** -- Modifies a Data Redaction policy
- **DBMS_REDACT.UPDATE_FULL_REDACTION_VALUES** -- Globally updates the full redaction value for a given data type. You must restart the database instance before the updated values can be used.
- **DBMS_REDACT.ENABLE_POLICY** -- Enables a Data Redaction policy
- **DBMS_REDACT.DISABLE_POLICY** -- Disables a Data Redaction policy
- **DBMS_REDACT.DROP_POLICY** -- Drops a Data Redaction policy

A full data redaction policy redacts the entire contents of a data column. By default, NUMBER data type columns are replaced with zero (0) and character data type columns are replaced with a single space. The UPDATE_FULL_REDACTION_VALUES procedure of the DBMS_REDACT package can be used to modify one or both of these defaults. The following example shows how to use full redaction for all the values in the TRGT.CUST_DATA table CC_NUM column. The expression parameter applies the policy to any user querying the table, except for users who have been granted the EXEMPT REDACTION POLICY system privilege. SYS and SYSTEM automatically have the EXEMPT REDACTION POLICY system privilege. This means that both accounts can always bypass any existing Oracle Data Redaction policies and be able to view data from tables or views with Data Redaction policies.

Redaction policies created on table or view will apply to any views that are created on this target, including materialized views. The redaction policy will continue to be in effect throughout the length of a view chain (a view based on another view) created on the target. However, if another redaction policy is created for one of the dependent views, then for any columns in that view and its dependant views, the new policy will take precedence.

```
BEGIN
  DBMS_REDACT.ADD_POLICY(
    object_schema => 'trgt',
    object_name   => 'cust_data',
    column_name   => 'cc_num',
    policy_name   => 'redact_cc_num',
    function_type => DBMS_REDACT.FULL,
    expression    => '1=1');
END;
```

When you create any Oracle Data Redaction policy, the expression parameter in the DBMS_REDACT.ADD_POLICY procedure specifies the conditions in which the policy applies. It defines a Boolean expression that must evaluate to TRUE for the policy to be applied. It must be based on one of the following functions:

- **SYS_CONTEXT** -- This must be specified with a valid namespace. The default namespace for SYS_CONTEXT is USERENV. This includes values such as SESSION_USER and CLIENT_IDENTIFIER.

- **Application Express function** -- It is possible to use either the V or NV wrappers (for the APEX_UTIL.GET_SESSION_STATE and APEX_UTIL.GET_NUMERIC_SESSION_STATE functions respectively) as part of the expression.

The expression must follow these guidelines:

- Use only the following operators: =, !=, >, <, >=, <=
- Comparisons with NULL must be used with care. The expression must evaluate to TRUE and most comparisons with NULL tend to return FALSE.
- User-created functions in the expression parameter are not permitted.

Some examples of applying a redaction policy using the expression parameter include:

- **User Environment** -- The following example applies a Data Redaction policy based on the session user name:

```
expression => 'SYS_CONTEXT(''USERENV'',''SESSION_USER'') =
''OCPREP'''
```

- **Role** -- It is possible to enable or disable a policy using the SYS_SESSION_ROLES namespace based on a role. The value of the attribute is TRUE if the specified role is enabled for the querying application user and FALSE if the role is not enabled. The following example sets the policy to show the actual data to any application user who has the OCP_ADMIN role enabled, but redact the data for all of the other application users.

```
expression =>
'SYS_CONTEXT(''SYS_SESSION_ROLES'',''OCP_ADMIN'') =
''FALSE'''
```

- **No Filtering** -- The policy can be applied irrespective of the context to any user, with no filtering (minus SYS and users who have the EXEMPT REDACTION POLICY privilege). The following example applies the policy to any user (with the aforementioned exception)

```
expression => '1=1'
```

Granting trusted users the EXEMPT REDACTION POLICY system privilege exempts them from all Data Redaction policies. The person who creates a Data Redaction policy is not exempt from it unless the person is user SYS or has EXEMPT REDACTION POLICY privilege. The EXEMPT REDACTION POLICY system privilege is included in the DBA role. However, the privilege must be granted explicitly to users because it is not included in the WITH ADMIN OPTION for DBA role grants.

When using partial data redaction, only a portion of the column data is redacted. A social security number might have all but the last four digits replaced with an asterisk for example (***-**-1234). It is possible to create policies for columns that use character, number, or date-time data types. For policies that redact character data types, there are a number of pre-defined character redaction shortcuts available. Some of the available shortcuts include:

- **DBMS_REDACT.REDACT_US_SSN_F5** -- Redacts the first 5 numbers of Social Security numbers when the column is a VARCHAR2 data type. For example, the number 987-65-4320 becomes XXX-XX-4320.
- **DBMS_REDACT.REDACT_US_SSN_L4** -- Redacts the last 4 numbers of Social Security numbers when the column is a VARCHAR2 data type. For example, the number 987-65-4320 becomes 987-65-XXXX.
- **DBMS_REDACT.REDACT_US_SSN_ENTIRE** -- Redacts the entire Social Security number when the column is a VARCHAR2 data type. For example, the number 987-65-4320 becomes XXX-XX-XXXX.

- **DBMS_REDACT.REDACT_ZIP_CODE** -- Redacts a 5-digit postal code when the column is a VARCHAR2 data type. For example, 95476 becomes XXXXX.
- **DBMS_REDACT.REDACT_DATE_MILLENNIUM** -- Redacts dates that are in the DD-MON-YY format to 01-JAN-00 (January 1, 2000).
- **DBMS_REDACT.REDACT_DATE_EPOCH** -- Redacts all dates to 01-JAN-70.

The following example shows how Social Security numbers in a VARCHAR2 data type column and can be redacted using the REDACT_US_SSN_L4 shortcut.

```
BEGIN
  DBMS_REDACT.ADD_POLICY(
    object_schema      => 'trgt',
    object_name        => 'cust_data',
    column_name        => 'ssn',
    policy_name        => 'redact_cust_ssns',
    function_type      => DBMS_REDACT.PARTIAL,
    function_parameters => DBMS_REDACT.REDACT_US_SSN_L4,
    expression         => '1=1',
    policy_description => 'Partially redacts last 4 numbers in SS
numbers');
END;
```

Auditing

Enable and configure standard and Unified Audit Data Trail

Prior to Oracle 12c, audit trails were recorded in multiple locations, making it difficult for auditors to use the information. The new unified audit trail consolidates audit information from multiple sources and makes this information available in a standard format in the UNIFIED_AUDIT_TRAIL data dictionary view. The unified audit trail is maintained in a read-only table in the AUDSYS schema in the SYSAUX tablespace. The data is available to SYS and to users who have been granted the AUDIT_ADMIN or AUDIT_VIEWER roles. The AUDIT_ADMIN role can view the data and create audit policies. The AUDIT_VIEWER role can query the views but not create or alter policies. In unified auditing, the audit trail combines the audit records from the following sources:

- Unified audit policies and AUDIT settings
- Fine-grained audit records from DBMS_FGA
- Oracle Database Real Application Security
- Oracle Recovery Manager
- Oracle Database Vault
- Oracle Label Security
- Oracle Data Mining
- Oracle Data Pump
- Oracle SQL*Loader Direct Load

Once configured, unified auditing is always enabled and does not depend on the initialization parameters used in previous releases. If the database is opened in READ-ONLY mode, audit records are written to new operating system files in the $ORACLE_BASE/audit/$ORACLE_SID directory. The V$OPTION view can be queried to determine whether a database has been migrated to use unified auditing:

```
SELECT value
FROM   v$option
WHERE  parameter = 'Unified Auditing';

PARAMETER          VALUE
----------------   ----------
Unified Auditing   TRUE
```

This output shows that unified auditing is enabled. If it were disabled, the query would return FALSE. For newly created 12c databases, mixed mode auditing is enabled by default through the predefined policy ORA_SECURECONFIG. Mixed-mode auditing enables both traditional (pre-12c auditing) and unified auditing. The traditional auditing capabilities are controlled by the AUDIT_TRAIL initialization parameter. When set to a value other than 'none' in 12c, the traditional audit trail will be populated with audit records and the unified audit trail will also be populated. Audit settings can be applied to individual PDBs or to the CDB as a whole, depending on the type of policy. In a Multitenant environment, each PDB, including the root, has own unified audit trail.

When a database from an older release is upgraded to 12c, it is necessary to manually migrate to unified auditing if you want to use this capability. Once unified auditing is enabled, traditional auditing is disabled. To start using unified auditing, at least one unified audit policy must be enabled. To stop using it, disable all unified audit policies. The predefined policy ORA_SECURECONFIG is initially enabled on new 12c databases. The settings for this policy are:

```
CREATE AUDIT POLICY ORA_SECURECONFIG
PRIVILEGES ALTER ANY TABLE, CREATE ANY TABLE, DROP ANY TABLE,
CREATE ANY PROCEDURE, DROP ANY PROCEDURE, ALTER ANY PROCEDURE,
GRANT ANY PRIVILEGE, GRANT ANY OBJECT PRIVILEGE, GRANT ANY ROLE,
AUDIT SYSTEM, CREATE EXTERNAL JOB, CREATE ANY JOB,
CREATE ANY LIBRARY,
EXEMPT ACCESS POLICY,
CREATE USER, DROP USER,
ALTER DATABASE, ALTER SYSTEM,
CREATE PUBLIC SYNONYM, DROP PUBLIC SYNONYM,
CREATE SQL TRANSLATION PROFILE, CREATE ANY SQL TRANSLATION PROFILE,
DROP ANY SQL TRANSLATION PROFILE, ALTER ANY SQL TRANSLATION PROFILE,
CREATE ANY SQL TRANSLATION PROFILE, DROP ANY SQL TRANSLATION PROFILE,
```

```
ALTER ANY SQL TRANSLATION PROFILE, TRANSLATE ANY SQL,
EXEMPT REDACTION POLICY,
PURGE DBA_RECYCLEBIN, LOGMINING,
ADMINISTER KEY MANAGEMENT
ACTIONS ALTER USER, CREATE ROLE, ALTER ROLE, DROP ROLE, SET ROLE,
CREATE PROFILE, ALTER PROFILE, DROP PROFILE,
CREATE DATABASE LINK, ALTER DATABASE LINK, DROP DATABASE LINK,
LOGON, LOGOFF, CREATE DIRECTORY, DROP DIRECTORY;
```

Disabling Unified Auditing

When disabling unified auditing, you should first disable any unified audit policies that are currently enabled. This will prevent the database from going into mixed mode auditing once unified auditing is disabled.

- Log into the database instance as a user with the AUDIT_ADMIN role and query the POLICY_NAME and ENABLED_OPT columns of the AUDIT_UNIFIED_ENABLED_POLICIES data dictionary view. Execute the NOAUDIT POLICY statement to disable any policies that are enabled.
- Connect as user SYS with the SYSOPER privilege.
- Shut down the database.

  ```
  SHUTDOWN IMMEDIATE
  ```

- From the command prompt, run the following commands:

  ```
  cd $ORACLE_HOME/rdbms/lib
  make -f ins_rdbms.mk uniaud_off ioracle
  ```

- From SQL*Plus, restart the database.

  ```
  STARTUP
  ```

By default, audit records are written to system global area (SGA) queues and then periodically written to the AUDSYS schema audit table in the SYSAUX tablespace. Queueing the records rather than immediately writing them to disk significantly improves the performance of the audit trail processes. However, if there is an instance crash or a SHUTDOWN ABORT, the queued writes mean there is a chance that some audit records may be lost. If this is not acceptable, the audit trail can be set to immediately write audit records to the AUDSYS schema audit table. Be aware that on an active database that this setting may affect performance. In a multitenant database, this option can be set for individual PDBs. To set the write mode for unified audit trail records:

- Log in to SQL*Plus as a user who has been granted the AUDIT_ADMIN role.
- Set the AUDIT_TRAIL_MODE property of the DBMS_AUDIT_MGMT package, as follows:
  To use immediate-write mode, run the following procedure:

```
BEGIN
 DBMS_AUDIT_MGMT.SET_AUDIT_TRAIL_PROPERTY(
  DBMS_AUDIT_MGMT.AUDIT_TRAIL_UNIFIED,
  DBMS_AUDIT_MGMT.AUDIT_TRAIL_WRITE_MODE,
  DBMS_AUDIT_MGMT.AUDIT_TRAIL_IMMEDIATE_WRITE);
END;
```

To use queued-write mode, run the following procedure:

```
BEGIN
 DBMS_AUDIT_MGMT.SET_AUDIT_TRAIL_PROPERTY(
  DBMS_AUDIT_MGMT.AUDIT_TRAIL_UNIFIED,
  DBMS_AUDIT_MGMT.AUDIT_TRAIL_WRITE_MODE,
  DBMS_AUDIT_MGMT.AUDIT_TRAIL_QUEUED_WRITE);
END;
```

Any time that the database is not writable, including when the instance is started but the database is closed or when the database is open in read-only mode, audit records are written to external files in the $ORACLE_BASE/audit/$ORACLE_SID directory. The contents of these files can be loaded into the database by running the DBMS_AUDIT_MGMT.LOAD_UNIFIED_AUDIT_FILES procedure. The process to do this is:

- Log into the database instance as a user who has been granted the AUDIT_ADMIN role.
- Ensure that the database is open and writable.

- Run the DBMS_AUDIT_MGMT.LOAD_UNIFIED_AUDIT_FILES procedure.

```
EXEC DBMS_AUDIT_MGMT.LOAD_UNIFIED_AUDIT_FILES;
```

The audit records are loaded into the AUDSYS schema audit table immediately, and then deleted from the $ORACLE_BASE/audit/$ORACLE_SID directory.

Create and enable audit policies

A unified audit policy is a named group of audit settings that track a particular aspect of user behavior in the database. The CREATE AUDIT POLICY statement is used to create a unified audit policy. More than one audit policy can be in effect concurrently in a database. They can contain both system-wide and object-specific audit options. The AUDIT and NOAUDIT SQL statements enable and disable an audit policy respectively. The AUDIT statement can also be used to include or exclude specific users for the given policy. The AUDIT and NOAUDIT statements also enable you to audit application context values. The following types of activities can be audited:

- User accounts (including administrative users who log in with the SYSDBA administrative privilege), roles, and privileges.
- Object actions, such as dropping a table or a running a procedure
- Application context values
- Activities from Oracle Database Real Application Security, Oracle Recovery Manager, Oracle Data Mining, Oracle Data Pump, Oracle SQL*Loader direct path events, Oracle Database Vault, and Oracle Label Security

It is possible to have multiple policies enabled concurrently, but ideally the number of enabled policies should be limited. The unified audit policy syntax is flexible enough to allow one policy to cover a number of audit settings. The best practice is to group related options into a single policy rather than creating multiple policies. Having a small number of policies reduces the logon overhead associated with loading audit policy details into the session's UGA memory. The session's UGA memory consumption is also reduced and the internal audit check functionality is more efficient.

When a unified audit policy is generated with the CREATE AUDIT POLICY statement, Oracle Database stores it in a first class object that is owned by the SYS schema, rather than the schema of the user who created the policy. The basic syntax for the CREATE AUDIT POLICY statement is:

```
CREATE AUDIT POLICY policy_name
{ {privilege_audit_clause [action_audit_clause ] [role_audit_clause
]}
| { action_audit_clause [role_audit_clause ] }
| { role_audit_clause }
}
[WHEN audit_condition EVALUATE PER {STATEMENT|SESSION|INSTANCE}]
[CONTAINER = {CURRENT | ALL}];
```

The following statement creates a policy that would generate an audit trail any time a statement requiring the ALTER ANY TABLE or DROP ANY TABLE system privileges granted via the ocp_admin role was executed.

```
CREATE AUDIT POLICY change_table_pol
PRIVILEGES ALTER ANY TABLE, DROP ANY TABLE
ROLES ocp_admin;
```

Once the policy has been created, it must be enabled using the AUDIT statement with the POLICY clause. The policy can be applied to one or more users, or to all users with specified exclusions. It is also possible to designate whether an audit record is written when the audited action succeeds, fails, or regardless of whether the action succeeds.

Newly-created policies will not take effect until after the audited user's next connection to the database instance. If the audited users are logged in when a policy is enabled, the policy cannot collect audit data until the users log out and back in to the database. The AUDIT statement supports the following optional clauses:

- **BY** -- Used to apply the unified audit policy to one or more users.

  ```
  AUDIT POLICY change_table_pol BY ocpuser;
  ```

- **EXCEPT** -- Used to exclude users from the unified audit policy.

  ```
  AUDIT POLICY change_table_pol EXCEPT jtkirk, jlpicard;
  ```

- **WHENEVER SUCCESSFUL** -- Records only successful executions of the audited activity.

  ```
  AUDIT change_table_pol WHENEVER SUCCESSFUL;
  ```

- **WHENEVER NOT SUCCESSFUL** -- Records only failed executions of the audited activity.

  ```
  AUDIT change_table_pol WHENEVER NOT SUCCESSFUL;
  ```

Note the following:

- **WHENEVER** -- If the WHENEVER clause is omitted, the both failed and successful user activities are written to the audit trail.
- **BY/EXCEPT** -- A unified audit policy can be enabled with either the BY clause or the EXCEPT clause, but not both simultaneously.
- **AUDIT...BY** -- If multiple AUDIT statements are executed on the same unified audit policy with different BY users, all of the specified users are audited.
- **AUDIT...EXCEPT** -- If multiple AUDIT statements are executed on the same unified audit policy with different EXCEPT users, only the last exception user list is used.
- **COMMON policies** -- Common unified audit policies can only be enabled from the root and only for common users.
- **LOCAL policies** -- Local audit policies can only be enabled from the PDB to which it applies.

No unified audit policy is required in order to audit Oracle Recovery Manager events. The UNIFIED_AUDIT_TRAIL view has several fields with names that start with RMAN_ which record RMAN-related events automatically. The RMAN-specific columns in UNIFIED_AUDIT_TRAIL include:

- **RMAN_SESSION_RECID** -- Recovery Manager session identifier. Together with the RMAN_SESSION_STAMP column, this column uniquely identifies the Recovery Manager job.
- **RMAN_SESSION_STAMP** -- Timestamp for the session.
- **RMAN_OPERATION** -- The Recovery Manager operation executed by the job.
- **RMAN_OBJECT_TYPE** -- Type of objects involved in a Recovery Manager session.
- **RMAN_DEVICE_TYPE** -- Device associated with a Recovery Manager session.

Privileges

Use administrative privileges

As of Oracle 12c, there are five different administrative privileges. Three new privileges have been created in order to increase the security of the database by providing a better separation of duties. The principle of least privilege should always be used to grant users the minimum level of privileges required for them to perform their duties.

The three new roles for database administrative activities include backup and recovery, high availability, and key management. The new roles eliminate the need to grant the SYSDBA or SYSOPER roles for common day-to-day operations.

- **SYSDBA** -- This administrative privilege allows most database operations, including the ability to view user data. It is the most powerful administrative privilege and should only be granted is all of the privileges are required by the grantee. The operational tasks granted by this privilege include: Performing STARTUP and SHUTDOWN operations; ALTER DATABASE: open, mount, back up, or change character set; CREATE DATABASE; DROP DATABASE; CREATE SPFILE; ALTER DATABASE ARCHIVELOG; ALTER DATABASE RECOVER; includes the RESTRICTED SESSION privilege.
- **SYSOPER** -- This privilege allows a user to perform most of the operational tasks of SYDBA, but not the ability to view user data. The operational tasks granted by this privilege include: Performing STARTUP and SHUTDOWN operations; CREATE SPFILE; ALTER DATABASE: open, mount, or back up; ALTER DATABASE ARCHIVELOG; ALTER DATABASE RECOVER (Complete recovery only); Includes the RESTRICTED SESSION privilege.
- **SYSBACKUP** -- This allows Recovery Manager (RMAN) users to connect to the target database and perform RMAN backup and recovery either from RMAN or SQL*Plus.
- **SYSDG** -- The SYSDG administrative privilege is used to perform Data Guard operations. This privilege can be used with either Data Guard Broker or the DGMGRL command-line interface. In order to

connect to the database as SYSDG using a password, you must create a password file for it.

- **SYSKM** -- The SYSKM administrative privilege enables the SYSKM user to manage Transparent Data Encryption wallet operations. In order to connect to the database as SYSKM using a password, you must create a password file for it.

Create, enable, and use privilege analysis

Privilege analysis is part of the capabilities provided by Oracle Database Vault. It allows for the creation of a profile for a database user that will capture the list of system and object privileges used. The results can be used to analyze used privileges vs. granted privileges. Using that information, the number of granted privileges can be reduced to only those which the user requires to perform their duties. Privilege analysis helps improve database security by identifying unused or excessive privileges. It is possible to perform privilege analysis with or without having Database Vault configured and enabled.

It is possible to administer the privilege analysis functionality from either Enterprise Manager Cloud Control or the DBMS_PRIVILEGE_CAPTURE PL/SQL package. To utilize the functionality, you must be granted the CAPTURE_ADMIN role, which provides the EXECUTE privilege for the DBMS_PRIVILEGE_CAPTURE package and the SELECT privilege on the views containing the results. The DBMS_PRIVILEGE_CAPTURE package enables you to create, enable, disable, and drop privilege analysis policies. It also generates reports that show the privilege usage, accessible via data dictionary views. The general steps that you use to analyze privileges are:

- Define the privilege analysis policy.

```
BEGIN
  DBMS_PRIVILEGE_CAPTURE.CREATE_CAPTURE(
      name        => 'ocprep_dev_role_pol',
      description => 'Captures ocprep_dev role use',
      type        => DBMS_PRIVILEGE_CAPTURE.G_ROLE,
      roles       => role_name_list('ocprep_dev'));
END;
```

- Enable the privilege analysis policy.

```
EXEC DBMS_PRIVILEGE_CAPTURE.ENABLE_CAPTURE
('ocprep_dev_role_pol');
```

- Disable the privilege analysis policy's recording of privilege use.

```
EXEC DBMS_PRIVILEGE_CAPTURE.DISABLE_CAPTURE
('ocprep_dev_role_pol');
```

- Generate privilege analysis results.

```
EXEC DBMS_PRIVILEGE_CAPTURE.GENERATE_RESULT
('ocprep_dev_role_pol');
SELECT username, sys_priv, object_owner, object_name
FROM   dba_used_privs
WHERE  capture = 'ocprep_dev_role_pol';
```

- Optionally, drop the privilege analysis policy.

```
EXEC DBMS_PRIVILEGE_CAPTURE.DROP_CAPTURE
('ocprep_dev_role_pol');
```

Only one privilege analysis policy in the database can be enabled concurrently. The only exception is that a privilege analysis policy of type DBMS_PRIVILEGE_CAPTURE.G_DATABASE can be enabled concurrently with a privilege analysis of a different type. If a privilege analysis policy is enabled before a database shutdown, it will still be enabled when the database is restarted. The privilege analysis policy must be disabled before it is possible to generate a privilege analysis report. Once you have completed analyzing the results, you can drop the analysis policy. A policy must be disabled before it can be dropped. Dropping a privilege analysis policy also drops all the used and unused privilege records associated with this privilege analysis.

Some of the views associated with privilege analysis include the following. Refer to the Oracle Database Vault manual for the complete list:

- **DBA_PRIV_CAPTURES** -- Lists information about existing privilege analysis policies
- **DBA_USED_PRIVS** -- Lists the privileges that have been used for reported privilege analysis policies
- **DBA_UNUSED_PRIVS** -- Lists the privileges that have not been used for reported privilege analysis policies
- **DBA_USED_OBJPRIVS** -- Lists the object privileges that have been used for reported privilege analysis policies. It does not include the object grant paths.
- **DBA_UNUSED_OBJPRIVS** -- Lists the object privileges that have not been used for reported privilege analysis policies. It does not include the object privilege grant paths.
- **DBA_USED_SYSPRIVS** -- Lists the system privileges that have been used for reported privilege analysis policies. It does not include the system privilege grant paths.
- **DBA_UNUSED_SYSPRIVS** -- Lists the system privileges that have not been used for reported privilege analysis policies. It does not include the system privilege grant paths.

Using Globalization Support

Customize language-dependent behavior for the database and individual sessions

National Language Support (NLS) is one of the most commonly used aspects of the Oracle database that nobody ever thinks about. The default language and location are set when an Oracle database is created. For most installations, the values are seldom changed even temporarily after that. NLS parameters can be specified in several ways:

- **Initialization parameters** -- NLS parameters can be set in the PFILE/SPFILE used by the Oracle server. Parameter file settings affect only the server behavior, not that of clients.
- **Environment variables** -- It is possible to set NLS environment variables on client machines. If set, these variables will override the server behavior for that client machine.
- **ALTER SESSION** -- The ALTER SESSION statement can be used to override the NLS behavior for a given client session.
- **SQL functions** -- NLS parameters can be explicitly set via functions in a SQL statement to hardcode NLS behavior for that statement.

The order of precedence when determining the NLS behavior is shown below. Lower numbers take precedence over higher ones (i.e. using SQL functions to explicitly set behavior will override all other methods):

1. Explicitly set in SQL functions
2. Set by an ALTER SESSION statement
3. Set as an environment variable
4. Specified in the initialization parameter file
5. Default

Some of the most commonly used NLS parameters include the following:

- **NLS_CURRENCY** -- Sets the local currency symbol.
- **NLS_DATE_FORMAT** -- Sets the default date format use by the server.
- **NLS_DATE_LANGUAGE** -- Sets the language used for day and month names.
- **NLS_LANG** -- Sets the language, territory, character set used by the database.
- **NLS_LANGUAGE** -- Sets the language used by the database.
- **NLS_SORT** -- Determines the sequence for character-based sorting.
- **NLS_TERRITORY** -- Sets the territory the database is located in.
- **NLS_TIMESTAMP_FORMAT** -- Sets the default format for timestamp data.

The NLS_LANG environment parameter is the easiest way to determine locale behavior for an Oracle Database. A single parameter can be used to set the language, territory, and the client's character set. It is set as an environment variable on UNIX platforms and the registry on Windows platforms. The NLS_LANG parameter is specified in the following format:

```
NLS_LANG = language_territory.charset
```

The default if the Oracle Universal Installer does not populate NLS_LANG is AMERICAN_AMERICA.US7ASCII. The components of the NLS_LANG parameter controls the defaults used for a number of globalization support features:

- **Language** -- This determines aspects of the server such as the language used for Oracle Database messages, character-based sorting, day names, and month names. If the language is not specified, the value defaults to AMERICAN.
- **Territory** -- This value determines behavior such as the default date, monetary, and numeric formats. If territory is not specified, the value is derived from the language value.

- **Charset** -- The charset value specifies the character set used by the client application. If charset is not specified, the value is derived from the language value.

Specify different linguistic sorts for queries

Numeric sorts are extremely simple. The numbers 3, 4, 2, and 1 can only be sorted two ways: 1-2-3-4 or 4-3-2-1. There are no language or other considerations involved in numeric sorting. By contrast character sorts can change based on the language, may or may not be case-sensitive, and can change based on accent marks on letters. There are several other considerations as well. You can reference the Oracle Database Globalization Support Guide for more details.

The Oracle Database supports several types of sorts:

- **Binary sort** -- Binary sorts use the numeric values of the characters in the character encoding scheme. This is the fastest type of sort. Both the ASCII and EBCDIC standards define the letters A to Z in ascending numeric value so a binary sort produces reasonable results for the English alphabet. However, when other languages are present, a binary sort often produces poor results.
- **Monolingual linguistic sort** -- A linguistic sort operates by replacing characters with numeric values that reflect each character's proper linguistic order. For monolingual sorts, Oracle compares character strings in two steps. First it will compare the major value of the entire string from a table of major values. Usually, letters with the same appearance have the same major value. The second step compares the minor value from a table of minor values. Both the major and minor values are defined by the Oracle Database.
- **Multilingual linguistic sort** -- Multilingual sorts are designed for operations where data in more than one language is being sorted at once. The specifics of multilingual sorts are complex. Refer to the Oracle Database Globalization Support Guide for more details. The exam is unlikely to get into the specifics of how multilingual sorts function.

The NLSSORT function can be used to perform specific linguistic sorts in an ORDER BY clause. When used, it replaces the supplied character string with an equivalent sort string. This is then used by the linguistic sort mechanism to produce the desired sorting sequence. The specific linguistic sort used by an ORDER BY clause is determined by the NLS_SORT session parameter by default. It can be explicitly overridden using the NLSSORT function. The default value of NLS_SORT is BINARY. The following statement will perform a binary sort (case-sensitive) of the characters in table ocp_emp:

```
SELECT * FROM ocp_emp ORDER BY name;
```

Query data using non-case-sensitive and accent-insensitive searches

It is possible to change the sorting to perform a case-insensitive binary sort by appending _CI to the sort type. The following example changes the NLS_SORT session value to BINARY_CI. The statement will then perform a binary sort (case-insensitive) of the characters in table ocp_emp:

```
ALTER SESSION SET NLS_SORT=BINARY_CI;
SELECT * FROM ocp_emp ORDER BY name;
```

The following example changes the NLS_SORT session value to GERMAN. The statement will then perform a German-language sort (case-sensitive) of the characters in table ocp_emp:

```
ALTER SESSION SET NLS_SORT=GERMAN;
SELECT * FROM ocp_emp ORDER BY name;
```

Linguistic sorts can also be made case-insensitive. The following example changes the NLS_SORT session value to GERMAN_CI. The statement will then perform a German-language sort (case-insensitive) of the characters in table ocp_emp:

```
ALTER SESSION SET NLS_SORT=GERMAN_CI;
SELECT * FROM ocp_emp ORDER BY name;
```

Another option is for sorts to be accent-insensitive. This is enabled by using a suffix of _AI. The following example changes the NLS_SORT session value to GERMAN_AI. The statement will then perform a German-language sort (accent-insensitive) of the characters in table ocp_emp:

```
ALTER SESSION SET NLS_SORT=GERMAN_AI;
SELECT * FROM ocp_emp ORDER BY name;
```

The session value of NLS_SORT can be overridden by using the NLSSORT function directly in the ORDER_BY clause.

```
SELECT * FROM ocp_emp
ORDER BY NLSSORT(name, 'NLS_SORT=GERMAN_AI');
```

Use datetime data types

The Oracle database has a number of data types that are designed to contain date and time information. Over the years I have seen administrators and developers who have created tables that store date information in VARCHAR2 fields rather than a DATE or TIMESTAMP field. This is certainly possible to do. A VARCHAR2 field can contain the text string '22-JUN-2014'. When that value is pulled up via a SELECT statement, it will appear to be a date to the user. However, there are numerous problems with storing dates in character fields, including:

- Unless the application has a complex parser to verify the information, invalid dates can be stored. '31-FEB-2015' and '22-JNN-2014' are both valid character strings, but invalid dates.

- Sorting the table by the field will produce a character-based sort rather than a date-based sort. For example, '01-DEC-2014' would sort as earlier than '02-JAN-1992'.
- Date arithmetic cannot be performed on character fields. Oracle cannot determine the number of days between the character data '01-SEP-2014' and '14-OCT-2014' without first converting them to a DATE data type.
- Unless the application performs rigid checking, multiple date formats might be stored in the same field (i.e. '01-MAR-2014', '01/03/2014', 'March 1st 2014').

None of these problems are a concern when date values are stored using Oracle date formats. There are four available datetime formats:

- **DATE** -- The DATE data type stores both date and time information. For each DATE value, Oracle stores the following information: century, year, month, date, hour, minute, and second.
- **TIMESTAMP** -- This is an extension of the DATE data type. It stores the year, month, and day of the DATE data type, plus hour, minute, and second values. The TIMESTAMP data type can store time to a much more granular level than the DATE data type and is useful for storing precise time values. The TIMESTAMP data type has an optional fractional seconds precision parameter that specifies the number of digits Oracle stores in the fractional part of the SECOND datetime field. The value defaults to 6, and can be a number in the range of 0 to 9.
- **TIMESTAMP WITH TIME ZONE** -- This is a variant of the TIMESTAMP data type. It includes a time zone region name or a time zone offset in its value. When a time zone offset is used, it is the difference (in hours and minutes) between local time and UTC. This data type is useful for preserving local time zone information.
- **TIMESTAMP WITH LOCAL TIME ZONE** -- This is another variant of TIMESTAMP that includes time zone information. It differs from TIMESTAMP WITH TIME ZONE in that data stored is normalized to the database time zone. Time zone information is not stored as part of the column data. When data from the column is retrieved,

Oracle returns it in the user's local session time zone. This is useful when date information should always to be displayed in the time zone of the client system in a two-tier application.

The character formats that dates and time zones are displayed in are controlled by three NLS parameters. The format defined by these parameters also determines the character data that Oracle will recognize as a date and be able to implicitly convert into the appropriate DATE/TIMESTAMP data type. The three parameters are:

- **NLS_DATE_FORMAT** -- Defines the default date format to use with the TO_CHAR and TO_DATE functions. The value can be any valid date format mask.
- **NLS_TIMESTAMP_FORMAT** -- Defines the default date format for the TIMESTAMP data type.
- **NLS_TIMESTAMP_TZ_FORMAT** -- Defines the default date format for the TIMESTAMP WITH TIME ZONE and TIMESTAMP WITH LOCAL TIME ZONE data types.

The following example shows how altering the NLS_DATE_FORMAT will change the way that Oracle displays date information:

```
SELECT value
FROM   nls_session_parameters
WHERE  parameter = 'NLS_DATE_FORMAT';

VALUE
------------
DD-MON-RR

SELECT SYSDATE FROM dual;

SYSDATE
---------
22-JUN-14

ALTER SESSION SET NLS_DATE_FORMAT='DD/MM/YY';
```

```
SELECT SYSDATE FROM dual;

SYSDATE
--------
22/06/14

ALTER SESSION SET NLS_DATE_FORMAT='Month dd, yyyy';

SELECT SYSDATE FROM dual;

SYSDATE
--------------
June 22, 2014
```

Obtain globalization support configuration information

Because NLS parameters can be set at multiple levels, determining what the values are at each of the levels is important. This information allows administrators to understand how the database will respond when operations with NLS implications are performed. There are three data dictionary views that can provide information about the NLS parameters that may affect a given database session:

- **NLS_DATABASE_PARAMETERS** -- Lists permanent NLS parameters of the database.
- **NLS_INSTANCE_PARAMETERS** -- Lists NLS parameters of the instance.
- **NLS_SESSION_PARAMETERS** -- Lists NLS parameters of the user session.

The following three queries check the value of NLS_DATE_FORMAT at each of the three levels:

```
SELECT *
FROM   nls_database_parameters
WHERE  parameter = 'NLS_DATE_FORMAT';

PARAMETER          VALUE
----------------- --------------
NLS_DATE_FORMAT   DD-MON-RR
```

```
SELECT *
FROM   nls_instance_parameters
WHERE  parameter = 'NLS_DATE_FORMAT';

PARAMETER            VALUE
----------------- --------------
NLS_DATE_FORMAT

SELECT *
FROM   nls_session_parameters
WHERE  parameter = 'NLS_DATE_FORMAT';

PARAMETER            VALUE
----------------- --------------
NLS_DATE_FORMAT    DD-MON-RR
```

The value at the database level is the Oracle default. The fact that the value at the instance level is NULL indicates that NLS_DATE_FORMAT has not been set as an initialization parameter. This can be verified by querying the V$SPPARAMETER dynamic view:

```
SELECT name, value, isspecified
FROM   v$spparameter
WHERE  name = 'nls_date_format';

NAME                VALUE       ISSPECIFIED
------------------ ---------- ------------
nls_date_format                FALSE
```

The session level value has been inherited from the database default. However, it is possible to change the session-level value using the ALTER SESSION command. The following example does this and checks the result:

```
ALTER SESSION SET NLS_DATE_FORMAT = 'DD-MON-YYYY';

SELECT *
FROM   nls_session_parameters
WHERE  parameter = 'NLS_DATE_FORMAT';

PARAMETER            VALUE
----------------- --------------
NLS_DATE_FORMAT    DD-MON-YYYY
```

Another useful view for obtaining NLS-related information is V$NLS_VALID_VALUES. This view contains all of the legal values for the NLS character set, sort, territory, and language. The following query shows a subset of the values available for NLS_SORT:

```
SELECT value
FROM   v$nls_valid_values
WHERE  parameter = 'SORT'

VALUE
---------------
BINARY
WEST_EUROPEAN
XWEST_EUROPEAN
GERMAN
XGERMAN
DANISH
XDANISH
SPANISH
XSPANISH
...
```

Automating Tasks with the Scheduler

Create a job, program, and schedule

The Oracle Scheduler is implemented by the procedures and functions in the DBMS_SCHEDULER package. The Scheduler enables you to control when and where various tasks occur. The Scheduler provides sophisticated, flexible enterprise scheduling functionality, which you can use to:

- **Run database program units** -- You can run PL/SQL anonymous blocks, PL/SQL stored procedures, and Java stored procedures on the local database or on remote Oracle databases.
- **Run external executables** -- You can run applications, shell scripts, and batch files, on the local system or on one or more remote systems.
- **Schedule job execution using multiple methods** -- The scheduled can employ time-based scheduling, event-based scheduling, and dependency scheduling.
- **Prioritize jobs based on business requirements** -- The Scheduler provides control over resource allocation among competing jobs.
- **Manage and monitor jobs** -- You can track information such as the status of the job and the last run time of the job by querying views using Enterprise Manager or SQL.
- **Execute and manage jobs in a clustered environment** -- The Scheduler fully supports execution of jobs in a Real Application Cluster environment.

To use the Scheduler, you create Scheduler objects. Schema objects define the what, when, and where for job scheduling. Scheduler objects enable a modular approach to managing tasks. One advantage of the modular approach is that objects can be reused when creating new tasks that are similar to existing tasks.

The principal Scheduler object is the job. A job defines the action to perform, the schedule for the action, and the location or locations where the action takes place. Most other scheduler objects are created to support jobs.

Some key points about the Oracle Scheduler:

- You may run PL/SQL and Java stored procedure, C functions, regular SQL scripts, and UNIX or Windows scripts.
- You can create time-based or event-based jobs. Events can be application-generated, scheduler-generated, or generated by a file watcher.
- The Scheduler consists of the concepts: Program, Job, Schedule, Job class, Resource group, Window and Window Group.
- The Scheduler architecture consists primarily of the job table, job coordinator, and the job workers (or slaves).

There are multiple elements of the Scheduler architecture. All except jobs are optional.

- **Programs** -- The scheduler allows you to optionally create programs which hold metadata about a task, but no schedule information. A program may relate to a PL/SQL block, a stored procedure or an OS executable file. Programs are created using the CREATE_PROGRAM procedure.
- **Schedules** -- Schedules optionally define the start time, end time and interval related to a job.
- **Jobs** -- Jobs can either be made up of predefined parts (programs and schedules) or completely self contained depending on which overload of the CREATE_JOB procedure is used to create them.
- **Job Classes** -- Job classes allow grouping of jobs with similar characteristics and resource requirements which eases administration.
- **Windows** -- Windows provide the link between the scheduler and the resource manager, allowing different resource plans to be activated at different times.
- **Window Groups** -- A window group is a collection of related windows.

Creating Jobs

```
DBMS_SCHEDULER.CREATE_JOB(
   JOB_NAME         => 'TEST_JOB1',
   JOB_TYPE         => 'PLSQL_BLOCK',
   JOB_ACTION       => 'BEGIN mytestproc; END;',
   START_DATE       => SYSTIMESTAMP,
   REPEAT_INTERVAL  => 'FREQ=DAILY;INTERVAL=2',
   END_DATE         => NULL,
   COMMENTS         => 'TEST JOB')
```

- **JOB_TYPE** -- Possible values are: plsql_block, stored_procedure, executable
- **JOB_ACTION** -- Specifies the exact procedure, command, or script that the job will execute.
- **START_DATE and END_DATE** -- Specify the date that a new job should start and end. (Many jobs may not have an end_date parameter)
- **REPEAT_INTERVAL** -- You can specify a repeat interval using a PL/SQL date/time expression or a database calendaring expression.
- **COMMENTS** -- Allows you to add descriptive text to the job.

Enabling and Disabling Jobs

All jobs are disabled by default when you create them. You must explicitly enable them in order to activate and schedule them. The following examples show how to enable and disable a job.

```
DBMS_SCHEDULER.ENABLE ('TEST_JOB1')
```

```
DBMS_SCHEDULER.DISABLE ('TEST_JOB1')
```

Creating a Program

A program describes what is to be run by the Scheduler and is a separate entity from a job. A job runs at a certain time or because a certain event occurred, and calls a program. Different jobs can use the same program and run the program at different times and with different settings.

```
DBMS_SCHEDULER.CREATE_PROGRAM(
  PROGRAM_NAME   => 'UPDATE_STATS',
  PROGRAM_ACTION => 'OCPUSER.UPDATE_SCHEMA_STATS',
  PROGRAM_TYPE   => 'STORED_PROCEDURE',
  ENABLED        => TRUE)
```

Once a program exists, it a job can be created using the program component as follows:

```
DBMS_SCHEDULER.CREATE_JOB(
JOB_NAME        => 'TEST_JOB1',
PROGRAM_NAME    => 'UPDATE_STATS',
REPEAT_INTERVAL=> 'FREQ=DAILY;BYHOUR=03',
ENABLED         => TRUE)
```

Creating a Schedule

A schedule object specifies when and how many times a job is run. Schedules can be shared by multiple jobs. When you create a schedule, Oracle provides access to PUBLIC. Thus, all users can use your schedule, without any explicit grant of privileges to do so. You specify the start and end times using the TIMESTAMP WITH TIME ZONE data type. The Scheduler also supports all NLS_TIMESTAMP_TZ_FORMAT settings. You must use a calendaring expression to create the repeat interval.

```
DBMS_SCHEDULER.CREATE_SCHEDULE(
  SCHEDULE_NAME   => 'SCHEDULE_12HR',
  START_DATE      => SYSTIMESTAMP,
  END_DATE        => NULL,
  REPEAT_INTERVAL => 'FREQ=HOURLY;INTERVAL= 12',
  COMMENTS        => 'EVERY 12 HOURS')


DBMS_SCHEDULER.CREATE_JOB(
  JOB_NAME        => 'TEST_JOB02',
  PROGRAM_NAME    => 'UPDATE_STATS',
  SCHEDULE_NAME   => 'SCHEDULE_12HR')
```

Use a time-based or event-based schedule for executing Scheduler jobs

Time-Based Schedules

The DBMS_SCHEDULER.CREATE_SCHEDULE procedure allows you to define a repeating time period on which a job should be executed. Named schedules thus created can then be referenced by multiple jobs.

```
BEGIN
  DBMS_SCHEDULER.CREATE_SCHEDULE(
  schedule_name      =>  'bimonthly_15th',
  start_date         =>  SYSTIMESTAMP,
  repeat_interval    =>
'FREQ=MONTHLY;INTERVAL=2;BYMONTHDAY=15;BYHOUR=9,17;);
END;
/

BEGIN
  DBMS_SCHEDULER.CREATE_JOB (
  job_name           =>  'BIMONTHLY_ALL_HANDS',
  program_name       =>  'BIG_TIME_WASTER',
  schedule_name      =>  'BIMONTHLY_15TH'
  enabled            =>  TRUE,
  comments           =>  'my event-based job');
END;
/
```

The Scheduler job BIMONTHLY_ALL_HANDS will be executed every second month, on the 15th, at 9AM and 5PM.

Event-Based Schedules

An event is a message sent by one application or system process to another to indicate that some action or occurrence has been detected. There are three kinds of events consumed by the Scheduler:

- **Events raised by your application** -- An application can raise an event to be consumed by the Scheduler, which reacts by starting a job. For example, when an employee has been terminated, it can raise an event that starts a job to suspend the employee's access to critical systems.

- **File arrival events raised by a file watcher** -- You can create a file watcher to watch for the arrival of a file on a system. You can then configure a job to start when the file watcher detects the presence of the file.
- **Scheduler-generated events** -- The Scheduler can raise an event to indicate state changes that occur within the Scheduler itself. For example, the Scheduler can raise an event when a job starts, when a job completes, when a job stalls, and so on.

You can create a schedule that is based on an event. The schedule can then be used for multiple jobs. To do so, use the CREATE_EVENT_SCHEDULE procedure, or use Enterprise Manager. The following is an example of creating an event schedule:

```
BEGIN
  DBMS_SCHEDULER.CREATE_EVENT_SCHEDULE (
    schedule_name     => 'EMP_TERM_EVENT_SCHEDULE',
    start_date        => SYSTIMESTAMP,
    event_condition   => 'tab.employees.event_type =
''TERMINATION''',
    queue_spec        => 'emp_events_q, emp_agent');
END;
/

BEGIN
  DBMS_SCHEDULER.CREATE_JOB (
    job_name          => 'TERM_JOB',
    program_name      => 'SUSPEND_ACCOUNT_ACCESS',
    schedule_name     => 'EMP_TERM_EVENT_SCHEDULE'
    enabled           => TRUE,
    comments          => 'my event-based job');
END;
/
```

The scheduler job TERM_JOB will now run whenever the TERMINATION event is raised.

Create lightweight jobs

In comparison with traditional DBMS_SCHEDULER jobs, lightweight jobs have lower creation overhead and generate less redo. Lightweight jobs are ideal when there is a need for a large number of short-duration jobs that run frequently. Lightweight jobs have the following characteristics:

- Unlike regular jobs, they are not schema objects.
- They have a significant improvement in create and drop time over regular jobs because they do not have the overhead of creating a schema object.
- They have lower average session creation time than regular jobs.
- They have a small footprint on disk for job metadata and runtime data.

Lightweight jobs can only be generated via a job template. You create a lightweight job by using the job_style attribute 'LIGHTWEIGHT' while creating the template. The alternative job_style is 'REGULAR', which is the default. Like programs and schedules, regular jobs are schema objects. A regular job offers more flexibility but entails more overhead when it is created or dropped. A lightweight job must reference a program object to specify a job action. The program must be enabled when the lightweight job is created, and the program type must be either 'PLSQL_BLOCK' or 'STORED_PROCEDURE'. You cannot grant privileges on lightweight jobs. They inherit privileges from the specified program. A user with privileges on the program being called has corresponding privileges on the lightweight job.

```
BEGIN
  DBMS_SCHEDULER.create_program(
    program_name    => 'lw_test',
    program_action  => 'BEGIN
                        DBMS_OUTPUT.PUT_LINE(''Hello Lightweight
World'');
                        END;',
    program_type    => 'plsql_block',
    enabled         => true);
END;
/
```

```
BEGIN
 DBMS_SCHEDULER.create_job (
    job_name            => 'LW_JOB_TEST',
    program_name        => 'LW_TEST',
    repeat_interval     => 'FREQ=DAILY;BYHOUR=10',
    end_date            =>  sysdate+7,
    job_style           => 'LIGHTWEIGHT',
    enabled             => TRUE,
    comments            => 'Lightweight job example');
END;
/
```

Use job chains to perform a series of related tasks

A DBMS_SCHEDULER chain is a named series of tasks that are linked
together to achieve a combined objective. Chains allow you to implement
dependency based scheduling. Jobs in a chain will be started depending
on the outcomes of one or more previous jobs. The basic steps to create
and use a chain are:

1. Create a chain object
2. Define the steps in the chain
3. Add rules
4. Enable the chain
5. Create a job that points to the chain

Creating the Chain

You create a chain by using the CREATE_CHAIN procedure.

```
BEGIN
  DBMS_SCHEDULER.CREATE_CHAIN (
     chain_name           => 'ocp_chain',
     rule_set_name        => NULL,
     evaluation_interval  => NULL,
     comments             => 'Working on the chain gang');
END;
/
```

Adding Chain Steps

Once a chain object has been created, you must define one or more chain steps. Each step can point to one of the following:

- A Scheduler program object (program)
- Another chain (a nested chain)
- An event schedule or inline event

```
BEGIN
  DBMS_SCHEDULER.DEFINE_CHAIN_STEP (
      chain_name       =>  'ocp_chain1',
      step_name        =>  'ocp_step1',
      program_name     =>  'ocp_program1');
  DBMS_SCHEDULER.DEFINE_CHAIN_STEP (
      chain_name       =>  'ocp_chain1',
      step_name        =>  'ocp_step2',
      program_name     =>  'ocp_chain2');
END;
/
```

The program or chain used in the step does not have to exist during definition. It must exist and be enabled when the chain runs, or an error will be generated.

The DEFINE_CHAIN_EVENT_STEP procedure allows you to create steps that wait on events. Procedure arguments can point to an event schedule or can include an inline queue specification and event condition.

```
BEGIN
DBMS_SCHEDULER.DEFINE_CHAIN_EVENT_STEP (
    chain_name           =>  'ocp_chain1',
    step_name            =>  'ocp_step3',
    event_schedule_name  =>  'ocp_event_schedule');
END;
/
```

Adding Rules to a Chain

The DEFINE_CHAIN_RULE procedure enables you to add a rule to a chain. Chain rules define when steps are run and define dependencies between steps. Each rule has a condition and an action. If a rule's condition evaluates to TRUE, its action is performed. Conditions are usually based on the outcome of one or more previous steps. Scheduler chain condition syntax takes one of the following two forms:

```
stepname [NOT] {SUCCEEDED|FAILED|STOPPED|COMPLETED}
stepname ERROR_CODE {comparision_operator|[NOT] IN}
{integer|list_of_integers}
```

Starting and Ending the Chain

At least one rule must have a condition that always evaluates to TRUE so that the chain can start when the chain job starts. At least one chain rule must contain an action of 'END'. The following example defines a rule that starts the chain at step **step1** and a rule that starts step **step2** when **step1** completes.

```
BEGIN
DBMS_SCHEDULER.DEFINE_CHAIN_RULE (
    chain_name    =>   'ocp_chain1',
    condition     =>   'TRUE',
    action        =>   'START step1',
    rule_name     =>   'ocp_rule1',
    comments      =>   'start the chain');
DBMS_SCHEDULER.DEFINE_CHAIN_RULE (
    chain_name    =>   'ocp_chain1',
    condition     =>   'step1 completed',
    action        =>   'START step2',
    rule_name     =>   'ocp_rule2');
END;
/
```

Setting an Evaluation Interval for Chain Rules

Chain rules are evaluated at the start of the chain job and at the end of each chain step. It is also possible to configure a chain to have its rules evaluated at a repeating time interval, such as once per hour.

```
BEGIN
DBMS_SCHEDULER.CREATE_CHAIN (
    chain_name          => 'ocp_chain1',
    rule_set_name       => NULL,
    evaluation_interval => INTERVAL '30' MINUTE,
    comments            => 'Chain with 30 minute evaluation
interval');
END;
/
```

Enabling Chains

A chain must be enabled before it can be run by a job.

```
BEGIN
DBMS_SCHEDULER.ENABLE ('ocp_chain1');
END;
/
```

Creating Jobs for Chains

A chain can be initiated by the RUN_CHAIN procedure or by creating and scheduling a job of type 'CHAIN'.

```
BEGIN
DBMS_SCHEDULER.CREATE_JOB (
    job_name        => 'chain_job_1',
    job_type        => 'CHAIN',
    job_action      => 'ocp_chain1',
    repeat_interval => 'freq=daily;byhour=4;byminute=0;bysecond=0',
    enabled         => TRUE);
END;
/
```

Running Chains

You can use the RUN_CHAIN procedure to run a chain without having to first create a chain job for the chain.

```
BEGIN
DBMS_SCHEDULER.RUN_CHAIN (
    chain_name  => 'ocp_chain1',
    job_name    => 'ocp_chain_job');
END;
```

Create Windows and Job Classes

DBMS_SCHEDULER job windows link the scheduler to the Data Resource Manager. This allows different resource plans to be activated at different times. When used in conjunction with job classes (that point to resource consumer groups), windows provides control over the resources allocated to job classes during specific time periods. Only one window can be active (open) at any time, with one resource plan assigned to the window. The affect of resource plan switches is instantly visible to running jobs which are assigned to job classes. The following statement creates a window called finance_window in SYS:

```
BEGIN
  DBMS_SCHEDULER.CREATE_WINDOW (
    window_name       => 'finance_window',
    schedule_name     => 'fin_schedule',
    resource_plan     => 'fin_resourceplan',
    duration          => interval '60' minute,
    comments          => 'Finance window');
END;
/
```

Job classes allow jobs with similar characteristics to be grouped together in order to simplify administration of resource requirements. When the JOB_CLASS parameter of the CREATE_JOB procedure is left undefined, the job is assigned to the DEFAULT_JOB_CLASS. To create a job class, you use the CREATE_JOB_CLASS procedure. The following statement creates a job class called finance_jobs in SYS that uses a service called accounting and is assigned to the resource consumer group finance_group.

```
BEGIN
  DBMS_SCHEDULER.CREATE_JOB_CLASS (
    job_class_name            => 'finance_jobs',
    resource_consumer_group   => 'finance_group',
    service                   => 'accounting',
    comments                  => 'All finance jobs');
END;
/
```

Use advanced Scheduler concepts to prioritize jobs

Advanced scheduler features, such as windows, window groups, and job classes in conjunction with the Data Resource Manager, allow you to create a robust system of job schedules that will automatically adjust resource usage to fit your needs. Jobs that consume significant resources can be made to run when database usage is low. High priority jobs can be made to kick off earlier or be allocated additional resources.

The priority of any given job is not static and can change depending on when it is run. During business hours, jobs supporting application processes would have a high priority, while evenings might allocate more resources to data loads, backup operations and database maintenance processes such as refreshing materialized views. The mechanism to support resource allocation of this type is Scheduler Windows. Every window can be assigned a priority. If windows overlap, the one with the highest priority is chosen over the others because only one can be active at any given time.

Scheduler windows work in tandem with job classes to control database resource allocation. A given window specifies the resource plan that should be activated when the window opens. Job classes in turn map to a resource consumer group or to a database service, which can map to a consumer group. Any job running during a window will be granted resources based on the consumer group of its job class and the resource plan of the window. Windows have three key attributes:

- **Schedule** -- When the window is in effect.
- **Duration** -- How long the window is open.
- **Resource plan** -- The resource plan that activates when the window opens.

The following statement creates a window with low priority for jobs that should be run in the early morning hours (1AM to 5AM) on weekdays.

x

The following statement creates a window with low priority for jobs that should be run in the early morning hours (1AM to 5AM) on weekdays.

```
BEGIN
    DBMS_SCHEDULER.CREATE_WINDOW (
        window_name       => 'wee_hours',
        resource_plan     => 'maintenance_workload_plan',
        start_date        => '28-JAN-13 01.00.00 AM',
        repeat_interval   => 'freq=daily; byday=mon,tue,wed,thu,fri',
        duration          => interval '4' hour,
        window_priority   => 'low');
END;
/
```

Prioritizing Jobs Within a Window

When a database has a significant number of jobs -- some will be more critical than others. Assigning a priority level to jobs helps to ensure that the automatic execution of jobs fulfils your business requirements. When several jobs are to be run in a given window, each will have a set priority (which may be the default). Jobs can be given a priority at either the job or the job class level.

- Class-level prioritization is performed using resource plans.
- Job-level prioritization via the job priority attribute determines start times.

The overall priority of a given job is determined first by the resource consumer group that the job's job class is assigned to and the current resource plan. Within the job class, you can assign priority values of 1-5 to individual jobs. If two jobs in the same job class are scheduled to start at the same time, the higher priority job will take precedence. If two jobs have the same assigned priority value, the job with the earlier start date takes precedence. When no priority is assigned to a job, it defaults to 3. The following statement changes the job priority for ocp_job to a setting of 2:

```
BEGIN
  DBMS_SCHEDULER.SET_ATTRIBUTE (
    name            =>   'ocp_job',
    attribute       =>   'job_priority',
    value           =>   2);
END;
/
```

The priority of individual jobs does not transfer across job classes. If two jobs running in a given window are in different job classes, prioritization is not guaranteed. A high-priority job in one class might be started after a lower-priority job in another.

Loading and Unloading Data

Explain Data Pump architecture

Oracle Data Pump is designed to provide high-speed movement of data and metadata from one database to another. It replaces the export/import functionality that existed in earlier releases of Oracle. Data Pump is made up of three distinct parts:

- **expdp and impdp** – These are command-line clients that use the procedures provided in the DBMS_DATAPUMP package to execute export and import commands. They accept parameters entered at the command line that enable the exporting and importing of data and metadata for a complete database or for subsets of a database.
- **DBMS_DATAPUMP** – Also known as the Data Pump API, this package provides a high-speed mechanism to move all or part of the data and metadata for a site from one database to another. DBMS_DATAPUMP can be used independently of the impdp and expdp clients.
- **DBMS_METADATA** – Also known as the Metadata API, this package provides a centralized facility for the extraction, manipulation, and re-creation of dictionary metadata. DBMS_METADATA can be used independently of the impdp and expdp clients.

Data Pump jobs use a master table, a master process, and worker processes to perform the work and keep track of progress:

- **Master Table** – A master table is used to track the progress within a job while the data and metadata are being transferred. It is implemented as a user table within the database. A user performing an impdp or expdp must have the CREATE TABLE system privilege for the master table to be created plus sufficient tablespace quota. The master table will have the same name as the job that created it. A Data Pump job cannot have the same name as an existing table or view in that schema. The information in the master table is used to restart a job.

- **Master process** – A master process is created for every Data Pump Export job and Data Pump Import job. It controls the entire job, including communicating with the clients, creating and controlling a pool of worker processes, and performing logging operations.
- **Worker Process** – The master process allocates work to be executed to worker processes that perform the data and metadata processing within an operation. Data Pump can employ multiple worker processes, running in parallel, to increase job performance.

Monitor a Data Pump job

It's possible to use the Data Pump Export and Import utilities to attach to a running job. When attached in logging mode, status about the job is automatically displayed during execution in real-time. When attached using interactive-command mode, it's possible to request the job status.

Optionally, a log file can be written during the execution of a job. It summarizes the progress of the job, lists any errors, and records the completion status. You can also determine job status or to get other information about Data Pump jobs, through the Data Pump views:

- **DBA_DATAPUMP_JOBS** – Identifies all active Data Pump jobs in the database, regardless of their state, on an instance (or on all instances for RAC). It also shows all Data Pump master tables not currently associated with an active job.
- **DBA_DATAPUMP_SESSIONS** – Identifies the user sessions that are attached to a Data Pump job. The information in this view is useful for determining why a stopped Data Pump operation has not gone away.
- **V$SESSION_LONGOPS** – Data Pump operations that transfer table data (export and import) maintain an entry indicating the job progress. The entry contains the estimated transfer size and is periodically updated to reflect the actual amount of data transferred.

The V$SESSION_LONGOPS columns that are relevant to a Data Pump job are as follows:

- **USERNAME** - job owner
- **OPNAME** - job name
- **TARGET_DESC** - job operation
- **SOFAR** - megabytes transferred thus far during the job
- **TOTALWORK** - estimated number of megabytes in the job
- **UNITS** - megabytes (MB)
- **MESSAGE** - a formatted status message of the form: 'job_name: operation_name : nnn out of mmm MB done'

Use Data Pump export and import

The Data Pump Export utility is invoked using the expdp command. The actions performed by the export operation are defined by the parameters you specify. They can be supplied either on the command line or in a parameter file. Data Pump Export can be controlled using a command line, a parameter file, or an interactive-command mode.

- **Command-Line** – Enables you to specify most of the export parameters from the command line.
- **Parameter File** – Allows you to specify command-line parameters in a parameter file. The PARFILE parameter cannot be used in a parameter file, because parameter files cannot be nested.
- **Interactive-Command** – Displays an export prompt from which you can enter various commands. Some commands are specific to interactive-command mode.

Data Pump jobs manage the following types of files:

- **Dump files** – Contain the data and metadata being moved.
- **Log files** – Record the messages associated with an operation.
- **SQL files** – Record the output of a SQLFILE operation.
- **Data Files** – Files specified by the DATA_FILES parameter during a transportable import.

There are different expdp modes for unloading different portions of the database. The mode is specified using the appropriate parameter. The available modes are:

- **Full** – In a full database export, the entire database is unloaded. This mode requires the user performing the export to have the DATAPUMP_EXP_FULL_DATABASE role. Specified using the FULL parameter.
- **Schema** – This is the default export mode. If you have the DATAPUMP_EXP_FULL_DATABASE role, then you can provide a list of schemas to export. Otherwise you can export only your own schema. Specified using the SCHEMAS parameter.
- **Table** – In table mode, only a specified set of tables, partitions, and their dependent objects are unloaded. You must have the DATAPUMP_EXP_FULL_DATABASE role to export tables that are not in your own schema. Specified using the TABLES parameter.
- **Tablespace** – In tablespace mode, only the tables contained in a specified set of tablespaces are unloaded. If a table is unloaded, then its dependent objects are also unloaded. Privileged users get all tables. Unprivileged users get only the tables in their own schemas. Specified using the TABLESPACES parameter.
- **Transportable Tablespace** – In transportable tablespace mode, only the metadata for the tables (and their dependent objects) within a specified set of tablespaces is exported. The tablespace data files are copied in a separate operation. Specified using the TRANSPORT_TABLESPACES parameter.

expdp Parameters

The following parameters are applicable to expdp:

- **ATTACH** – Attaches the client session to an existing export job and automatically places you in the interactive-command interface.
- **CONTENT** – Enables you to filter what Export unloads: data only, metadata only, or both.
- **DIRECTORY** – Specifies the default location to which Export can write the dump file set and the log file.

- **DUMPFILE** – Specifies the names, and optionally, the directory objects of dump files for an export job.
- **ESTIMATE** – Specifies the method that Export will use to estimate how much disk space each table in the export job will consume (in bytes).
- **ESTIMATE_ONLY** – Instructs Export to estimate the space that a job would consume, without actually performing the export operation.
- **EXCLUDE** – Enables you to filter the metadata that is exported by specifying objects and object types to be excluded from the export operation.
- **FILESIZE** – Specifies the maximum size of each dump file.
- **FULL** – Specifies that you want to perform a full database mode export.
- **INCLUDE** – Enables you to filter the metadata that is exported by specifying objects and object types for the current export mode.
- **JOB_NAME** – Used to identify the export job in subsequent actions.
- **LOGFILE** – Specifies the name, and optionally, a directory, for the log file of the export job.
- **PARFILE** – Specifies the name of an export parameter file.
- **QUERY** – Allows you to specify a query clause that is used to filter the data that gets exported.
- **SCHEMAS** – Specifies that you want to perform a schema-mode export.
- **TABLES** – Specifies that you want to perform a table-mode export.
- **TABLESPACES** – Specifies a list of tablespace names to be exported in tablespace mode.

impdp Parameters

Many of the above parameters are also applicable to impdp. In addition, several of the more common impdp parameters are:

- **REUSE_DATAFILES** – Specifies whether the import job should reuse existing data files for tablespace creation.
- **SQLFILE** – Specifies a file into which all of the SQL DDL that Import would have executed, based on other parameters, is written.

- **STATUS** – Specifies the frequency at which the job status display is updated.
- **TABLE_EXISTS_ACTION** – Tells import what to do if the table it is trying to create already exists.
- **REMAP_DATAFILE** – Changes the name of the source data file to the target data file name in all SQL statements where the source data file is referenced.
- **REMAP_SCHEMA** – Loads all objects from the source schema into a target schema.
- **REMAP_TABLE** – Allows you to rename tables during an import operation.
- **REMAP_TABLESPACE** – Remaps all objects selected for import with persistent data in the source tablespace to be created in the target tablespace.

The following commands are applicable when using Interactive mode:

- **ADD_FILE** – Add additional dump files.
- **CONTINUE_CLIENT** – Exit interactive mode and enter logging mode.
- **EXIT_CLIENT** – Stop the import or export client session, but leave the job running.
- **KILL_JOB** – Detach all currently attached client sessions and terminate the current job.
- **PARALLEL** – Increase or decrease the number of active worker processes for the current job.
- **START_JOB** – Restart a stopped job to which you are attached.
- **STATUS** – Display detailed status for the current job and/or set status interval.
- **STOP_JOB** – Stop the current job for later restart.

Create external tables for data population

External tables are defined as tables that do not reside in the database. It's possible to have tables in any format for which an access driver is provided. Inside the Oracle data dictionary is stored metadata describing an external table. With this metadata, Oracle provides SQL access to the external table as if it were a regular database table. It's possible to perform SELECT and JOIN operations, or create views or synonyms against external tables. It is not possible to perform DML operations or create indexes on external tables.

The metadata for external tables is created using the ORGANIZATION EXTERNAL clause of the CREATE TABLE statement. An external table definition acts as a view against the external data. An access driver is mechanism by which the external data is read. Oracle Database provides two access drivers for external tables: ORACLE_LOADER and ORACLE_DATAPUMP. ORACLE_LOADER reads data from external files using the Oracle Loader technology using a subset of the control file syntax of the SQL*Loader utility. ORACLE_DATAPUMP allows you to read data from the database and insert it into an external table, and then reload it into an Oracle Database. Note that while ORACLE_DATAPUMP allows writing to external files, the functionality is not performed via DML statements. The ANALYZE statement is not supported for gathering statistics for external tables, but you can use the DBMS_STATS package. Virtual columns are not supported on external tables. For an external table, the DROP TABLE statement removes only metadata in the database. It has no effect on the actual data outside of the database.

You create external tables using the CREATE TABLE statement with an ORGANIZATION EXTERNAL clause. This statement creates only metadata in the data dictionary. The following example creates an external table using the ORACLE_LOADER access method.

```
CREATE TABLE phone_list_ext (
  employee_id        VARCHAR2(5),
  first_name         VARCHAR2(50),
  last_name          VARCHAR2(50),
  phone              VARCHAR2(20)
)
ORGANIZATION EXTERNAL (
  TYPE ORACLE_LOADER
  DEFAULT DIRECTORY ext_tables
  ACCESS PARAMETERS (
    RECORDS DELIMITED BY NEWLINE
    FIELDS TERMINATED BY ','
    MISSING FIELD VALUES ARE NULL
    (
      employee_id        CHAR(5),
      first_name         CHAR(50),
      last_name          CHAR(50),
      phone              CHAR(20)
    )
  )
  LOCATION ('phone_list.txt')
)
PARALLEL 2
REJECT LIMIT UNLIMITED;
```

The example above uses the ORACLE_LOADER access driver. This driver is used for reading text files. Essentially any file that SQL*Loader can read from can be used as an external table. The parameters in the ACCESS PARAMETERS clause are opaque to the database. These access parameters are specific to the access driver. Oracle provides these parameters to the access driver when the external table is accessed. The PARALLEL clause enables parallel query on the data sources. The REJECT LIMIT clause specifies that there is no limit on the number of errors that can occur during a query of the external data.

Only the following ALTER TABLE Clause options are allowed on external tables:

- **REJECT LIMIT** – Changes the reject limit.
- **PROJECT COLUMN REFERENCED** – The access driver processes only the columns in the select list of the query. This setting may not provide a consistent set of rows when querying a different column list from the same external table but can speed up access.

- **PROJECT COLUMN ALL** – The access driver processes all of the columns defined on the external table. This setting always provides a consistent set of rows when querying an external table. This is the default.
- **DEFAULT DIRECTORY** – Changes the default directory specification.

Managing Resources

Configure the Resource Manager

The Oracle Database Resource Manager (DRM) is designed to optimize resource allocation among concurrent database sessions. It attempts to prevent problems that can happen if the operating system makes resource decisions when presented with high overhead without having awareness of the database needs. DRM helps to overcome these problems by giving the database more control over how hardware resources are allocated. DRM enables you to classify sessions into groups based on session attributes, and then allocate resources to those groups in a way that optimizes hardware utilization for your application environment. The information that performs the functions of classifying sessions and assigning resources is called a resource plan. Oracle 12c comes with three pre-configured resource plans for DRM. There is a mixed-workload plan that provides resource management for a mixed environment consisting of both OLTP and DSS/batch jobs. There is a Data Warehouse plan that provides resource management for a data warehousing environment. Finally there is the maintenance plan that provides resource management for the maintenance window. These plans are shipped with Oracle 12c and provide resource management directives that should provide immediate benefits for the majority of database installations. There are three elements of DRM:

- **Resource consumer group**: A group of sessions that are grouped together based on resource requirements.
- **Resource plan**: A container for directives that specify how resources are allocated to resource consumer groups.
- **Resource plan directive**: Associates a resource consumer group with a particular plan and specifies how resources are to be allocated to that resource consumer group.

Resource Plan Directives

A resource plan directive for a consumer group can specify limits for CPU and I/O resource consumption for sessions in that group. This is done by specifying the action to be taken if a call within a session exceeds one of the specified limits. These actions, called switches, occur only for sessions that are running and consuming resources, not waiting for user input or for CPU cycles. The possible actions are the following:

- The session is switched to a consumer group with lower resource allocations.
- The session is killed (terminated).
- The session's current SQL statement is aborted.

The resource plan directive attribute that determines which of the above three actions will be taken is SWITCH_GROUP. This attribute specifies the consumer group to which a session is switched if the specified criteria are met. If the value of this parameter is a consumer group, the session will be switched to that group. If the group name is 'CANCEL_SQL', the current call for that session is canceled. Finally, if the group name is 'KILL_SESSION', then the session is killed.

Per session I/O or CPU Limits

The resource plan directive attributes that can be used in specifying the criteria to use in making switch determinations follow. If not set, all default to UNLIMITED.

- **SWITCH_TIME**: Specifies the time (in CPU seconds) that a call can execute before an action is taken.
- **SWITCH_IO_MEGABYTES**: Specifies the number of megabytes of I/O that a session can transfer (read and write) before being switched.
- **SWITCH_IO_REQS**: Specifies the number of I/O requests that a session can execute before an action is taken.

Be sure you understand the meaning of and difference between the SWITCH_ESTIMATE and SWITCH_FOR_CALL CONCEPTS. These two resource plan attributes can be used to modify the behavior of resource plan switching:

- **SWITCH_ESTIMATE**: If TRUE, the database estimates the execution time of each call. If the estimated execution time exceeds SWITCH_TIME, the session is moved to the SWITCH_GROUP before beginning the call. The default is FALSE.
- **SWITCH_FOR_CALL**: If TRUE, a session that was automatically switched to another consumer group is returned to its original consumer group when the top level call completes. The default is NULL.

The CREATE_SIMPLE_PLAN procedure of the DBMS_RESOURCE_MANAGER package allows a relatively easy way to create a basic resource management plan. A single call can be used to create up to eight consumer groups and allocate resources to them. The procedure supports only the EMPHASIS CPU application method and consumer groups use the ROUND_ROBIN scheduling policy. Consumer groups specified in the procedure are allocated CPU percentages at Level 2. The procedure implicitly includes the SYS_GROUP in the created plan and allocates 100% of the Level 1 CPU to it. It also includes the OTHER_GROUPS consumer group and allocates 100% of the Level 3 CPU to it.

The CREATE_SIMPLE_PLAN procedure contains the following arguments:

- **SIMPLE_PLAN** -- Name of the plan
- **CONSUMER_GROUP1** -- Consumer group name for first group
- **GROUP1_PERCENT** -- CPU resource allocated to this group
- **CONSUMER_GROUP2** -- Consumer group name for second group
- **GROUP2_PERCENT** -- CPU resource allocated to this group
- **CONSUMER_GROUP3** -- Consumer group name for third group
- **GROUP3_PERCENT** -- CPU resource allocated to this group
- **CONSUMER_GROUP4** -- Consumer group name for fourth group
- **GROUP4_PERCENT** -- CPU resource allocated to this group

- **CONSUMER_GROUP5** -- Consumer group name for fifth group
- **GROUP5_PERCENT** -- CPU resource allocated to this group
- **CONSUMER_GROUP6** -- Consumer group name for sixth group
- **GROUP6_PERCENT** -- CPU resource allocated to this group
- **CONSUMER_GROUP7** -- Consumer group name for seventh group
- **GROUP7_PERCENT** -- CPU resource allocated to this group
- **CONSUMER_GROUP8** -- Consumer group name for eighth group
- **GROUP8_PERCENT** -- CPU resource allocated to this group

The following statement creates a resource plan with three groups and allocates a percentage of the Level2 CPU to each.

```
BEGIN
  DBMS_RESOURCE_MANAGER.CREATE_SIMPLE_PLAN(
      SIMPLE_PLAN      => 'OCPREP_SIMPLE',
      CONSUMER_GROUP1 => 'OCPGROUP1', GROUP1_PERCENT => 50,
      CONSUMER_GROUP2 => 'OCPGROUP2', GROUP2_PERCENT => 30,
      CONSUMER_GROUP2 => 'OCPGROUP3', GROUP3_PERCENT => 20);
END;
```

Create resource plans within groups

Complex resource plans are defined as any plan that is not created using the CREATE_SIMPLE_PLAN procedure. That said, it is possible to create some extremely complex plans using DBMS_RESOURCE_MANAGER. Resource plans can cause a single user session to jump back and forth between multiple consumer groups as its resource usage changes.

The full capabilities of DRM are beyond the scope of the exam (and this guide). The example presented is a plan that is complex enough to familiarize you with a number of the DRM calls. In the example below, only two consumer groups are created, START_HERE and BAD_SQL_NO_BISCUIT. Sessions begin in the START_HERE group. If a query takes more than 10 minutes of CPU time, it is switched to the BAD_SQL_NO_BISCUIT consumer group with a maximum utilization limit

of 15%. This limits the amount of resources that they can consume until a
DBA intervenes.

```
BEGIN
  DBMS_RESOURCE_MANAGER.CREATE_PENDING_AREA();

  DBMS_RESOURCE_MANAGER.CREATE_CONSUMER_GROUP (
      CONSUMER_GROUP => 'START_HERE',
      COMMENT        => 'Sessions start here');

  DBMS_RESOURCE_MANAGER.CREATE_CONSUMER_GROUP (
      CONSUMER_GROUP => 'BAD_SQL_NO_BISCUIT',
      COMMENT        => 'Sessions switched here to punish bad SQL');

  DBMS_RESOURCE_MANAGER.CREATE_PLAN(
    PLAN    => 'No_Biscuit',
    COMMENT => 'Find bad queries. Swat bad queries.');

  DBMS_RESOURCE_MANAGER.CREATE_PLAN_DIRECTIVE(
    PLAN                => 'No_Biscuit',
    GROUP_OR_SUBPLAN    => 'START_HERE',
    COMMENT             => 'Max CPU 10 minutes before switch',
    MGMT_P1             => 75,
    switch_group        => 'BAD_SQL_NO_BISCUIT',
    switch_time         => 600);

  DBMS_RESOURCE_MANAGER.CREATE_PLAN_DIRECTIVE(
    PLAN                => 'No_Biscuit',
    GROUP_OR_SUBPLAN    => 'OTHER_GROUPS',
    COMMENT             => 'Mandatory',
    MGMT_P1             => 25);

  DBMS_RESOURCE_MANAGER.CREATE_PLAN_DIRECTIVE(
    PLAN                    => 'No_Biscuit',
    GROUP_OR_SUBPLAN        => 'BAD_SQL_NO_BISCUIT',
    COMMENT                 => 'Limited CPU',
    MGMT_P2                 => 100,
    MAX_UTILIZATION_LIMIT   => 15);

  DBMS_RESOURCE_MANAGER.VALIDATE_PENDING_AREA();
  DBMS_RESOURCE_MANAGER.SUBMIT_PENDING_AREA();
END;
/
```

Assign users to Resource Manager groups

In order to make effective use of a Resource Manager plan, administrators must define which groups that databases users will belong to. The initial consumer group is the one to which any session created by that user will initially belong to.

If a user has not had an initial consumer group set, their initial consumer group will be the consumer group: DEFAULT_CONSUMER_GROUP. The DEFAULT_CONSUMER_GROUP has switch privileges granted to PUBLIC, so all users have the switch privilege for it. When a consumer group is deleted, any users who had that group as their initial consumer group will have DEFAULT_CONSUMER_GROUP as their initial consumer group. If there are active sessions at the time a consumer group is deleted, they are immediately switched to DEFAULT_CONSUMER_GROUP.

The initial consumer group is set by the SET_INITIAL_CONSUMER_GROUP procedure of the DBMS_RESOURCE_MANAGER package. The syntax for this procedure is:

```
DBMS_RESOURCE_MANAGER.SET_INITIAL_CONSUMER_GROUP (
    user           IN VARCHAR2,
    consumer_group IN VARCHAR2);
```

The following example sets the initial consumer group for GJONES to START_HERE:

```
BEGIN
  DBMS_RESOURCE_MANAGER.SET_INITIAL_CONSUMER_GROUP (
    'GJONES',
    'START_HERE');
END;
```

Specify directives for allocating resources to consumer groups

Plan directives are the heart of resource management. They define the boundaries and behavior that ensure system resources are restricted in a predictable fashion. The CREATE_PLAN_DIRECTIVE procedure of the DBMS_RESOURCE_MANAGER package is used to create directives. This procedure has a huge number of parameters, but generally only a few of the parameters are used for creating a single directive. The procedure is:

```
DBMS_RESOURCE_MANAGER.CREATE_PLAN_DIRECTIVE (
    plan                       IN VARCHAR2,
    group_or_subplan           IN VARCHAR2,
    comment                    IN VARCHAR2,
    cpu_p1                     IN NUMBER DEFAULT NULL, -- deprecated
    cpu_p2                     IN NUMBER DEFAULT NULL, -- deprecated
    cpu_p3                     IN NUMBER DEFAULT NULL, -- deprecated
    cpu_p4                     IN NUMBER DEFAULT NULL, -- deprecated
    cpu_p5                     IN NUMBER DEFAULT NULL, -- deprecated
    cpu_p6                     IN NUMBER DEFAULT NULL, -- deprecated
    cpu_p7                     IN NUMBER DEFAULT NULL, -- deprecated
    cpu_p8                     IN NUMBER DEFAULT NULL, -- deprecated
    active_sess_pool_p1        IN NUMBER DEFAULT NULL,
    queueing_p1                IN NUMBER DEFAULT NULL,
    parallel_degree_limit_p1   IN NUMBER DEFAULT NULL,
    switch_group               IN VARCHAR2 DEFAULT NULL,
    switch_time                IN NUMBER DEFAULT NULL,
    switch_estimate            IN BOOLEAN DEFAULT FALSE,
    max_est_exec_time          IN NUMBER DEFAULT NULL,
    undo_pool                  IN NUMBER DEFAULT NULL,
    max_idle_time              IN NUMBER DEFAULT NULL,
    max_idle_blocker_time      IN NUMBER DEFAULT NULL,
    switch_time_in_call        IN NUMBER DEFAULT NULL, -- deprecated
    mgmt_p1                    IN NUMBER DEFAULT NULL,
    mgmt_p2                    IN NUMBER DEFAULT NULL,
    mgmt_p3                    IN NUMBER DEFAULT NULL,
    mgmt_p4                    IN NUMBER DEFAULT NULL,
    mgmt_p5                    IN NUMBER DEFAULT NULL,
    mgmt_p6                    IN NUMBER DEFAULT NULL,
    mgmt_p7                    IN NUMBER DEFAULT NULL,
    mgmt_p8                    IN NUMBER DEFAULT NULL,
    switch_io_megabytes        IN NUMBER DEFAULT NULL,
    switch_io_reqs             IN NUMBER DEFAULT NULL,
    switch_for_call            IN BOOLEAN DEFAULT NULL,
    max_utilization_limit      IN NUMBER DEFAULT NULL,
    parallel_target_percentage IN NUMBER DEFAULT NULL,
    parallel_queue_timeout     IN NUMBER DEFAULT NULL);
```

The descriptions of the parameters are:

- **plan** -- Name of the resource plan
- **group_or_subplan** -- Name of the consumer group or subplan
- **comment** -- Comment for the plan directive
- **cpu_p1 to p8** -- deprecated: use mgmt_p1 to p8 instead
- **active_sess_pool_p1** -- Specifies maximum number of concurrently active sessions for a consumer group.
- **queueing_p1** -- Specified time (in seconds) after which a job in the inactive session queue (waiting for execution) will time out.
- **parallel_degree_limit_p1** -- Specifies a limit on the degree of parallelism for any operation.
- **switch_group** -- Specifies consumer group to switch to, once a switch condition is met. If the group name is 'CANCEL_SQL', then the current call is canceled when the switch condition is met. If the group name is 'KILL_SESSION', then the session is killed when the switch condition is met. Default is NULL.
- **switch_time** -- Specifies time (in CPU seconds) that a session can execute before an action is taken.
- **switch_estimate** -- If TRUE, tells Oracle to use its execution time estimate to automatically switch the consumer group of an operation before beginning its execution. Default is FALSE.
- **max_est_exec_time** -- Specifies the maximum execution time (in CPU seconds) allowed for a session. If the optimizer estimates that an operation will take longer than MAX_EST_EXEC_TIME, the operation is not started and ORA-07455 is issued. If the optimizer does not provide an estimate, this directive has no effect.
- **undo_pool** -- Limits the size in kilobytes of the undo records corresponding to uncommitted transactions by this consumer group.
- **max_idle_time** -- Indicates the maximum session idle time.
- **max_idle_blocker_time** -- Maximum amount of time in seconds that a session can be idle while blocking another session's acquisition of a resource switch_time_in_call. This parameter is deprecated. When specified, switch_time is set to switch_time_in_call (in seconds) and switch_for_ call is effectively set to TRUE. It is better to use switch_time and switch_for_call.
- **mgmt_p1 to p8** -- Resource allocation value for level 1 to 8 (replaces cpu_p1 to p8).

- **switch_io_megabytes** -- Specifies the amount of I/O (in MB) that a session can issue before an action is taken.
- **switch_io_reqs** -- Specifies the number of I/O requests that a session can issue before an action is taken.
- **switch_for_call** -- Specifies that if an action is taken because of the switch_time, switch_io_megabytes, or switch_io_reqs parameters, the consumer group is restored to its original consumer group at the end of the top call. Default is FALSE, which means that the original consumer group is not restored at the end of the top call.
- **max_utilization_limit** -- Specifies the maximum percentage of CPU that this Consumer Group or Sub-Plan can utilize. Valid values are 0% to 100%. NULL implies that there is no limit, or equivalently 100%.
- **parallel_target_percentage** -- Specifies the maximum percentage of the target number of parallel servers in an Oracle RAC environment that a consumer group can use. Any additional parallel statements
- **parallel_queue_timeout** -- Specifies the time (in seconds) that a query may remain in its Consumer Group's parallel statement queue before it is removed and terminated with an error (ORA-07454).

The sample resource plan from the earlier chapter included three plan directives. The first statement allocates 75% of the level 1 CPU resources to the START_HERE group. If a query for a user in this resource group runs for more than 10 minutes (600 seconds), it will be switched to the BAD_SQL_NO_BISCUIT consumer group.

```
DBMS_RESOURCE_MANAGER.CREATE_PLAN_DIRECTIVE(
    PLAN                 => 'No_Biscuit',
    GROUP_OR_SUBPLAN     => 'START_HERE',
    COMMENT              => 'Max CPU 10 minutes before switch',
    MGMT_P1              => 75,
    switch_group         => 'BAD_SQL_NO_BISCUIT',
    switch_time          => 600);
```

The second statement created a directive that assigned the remaining 25% of the level 1 CPU resources to OTHER_GROUPS. Any session that is *not* in the START_HERE or BAD_SQL_NO_BISCUIT will use this directive. There is no switch_group defined for this directive, so users will not be switched to another group for excessive resource use.

```
DBMS_RESOURCE_MANAGER.CREATE_PLAN_DIRECTIVE(
    PLAN                => 'No_Biscuit',
    GROUP_OR_SUBPLAN    => 'OTHER_GROUPS',
    COMMENT             => 'Mandatory',
    MGMT_P1             => 25);
```

The third directive defines the resources for the BAD_SQL_NO_BISCUIT consumer group. Sessions in this group will be allocated 100% of the Level 2 CPU resources. A single user in this group can utilize a maximum of 15% of the available CPU resources.

```
DBMS_RESOURCE_MANAGER.CREATE_PLAN_DIRECTIVE(
    PLAN                    => 'No_Biscuit',
    GROUP_OR_SUBPLAN        => 'BAD_SQL_NO_BISCUIT',
    COMMENT                 => 'Limited CPU',
    MGMT_P2                 => 100,
    MAX_UTILIZATION_LIMIT   => 15);
```

Managing Database Performance

Use the SQL Tuning Advisor

The SQL Tuning Advisor is the Oracle optimizer working in a different capacity. The optimizer has the ability to run in two different modes as described below:

- **Normal mode** – The optimizer compiles the SQL and generates an execution plan. This mode generates a reasonable plan for the vast majority of SQL statements. When running in normal mode, the output of the optimizer is an execution plan and is generally returned within a fraction of a second.
- **Tuning mode** – In this mode additional analysis is performed in an attempt to improve the plan produced in normal mode. The output from the optimizer is a set of suggested actions for producing a significantly better plan. The results from the optimizer in tuning mode can take several minutes to complete and are therefore not practical to use for routine generation of execution plans.

SQL Tuning Advisor can be invoked manually for tuning one or more SQL statements. A SQL Tuning Set (STS) is required to tune multiple statements. SQL Tuning Advisor can make use of the SQL from several different sources, including:

- **Automatic Database Diagnostic Monitor** -- This is the default source. ADDM analyzes key statistics gathered by the Automatic Workload Repository to identify any performance problems including high-load SQL statements.
- **Automatic Workload Repository** -- AWR snapshots of system activity include high-load SQL statements. These SQL statements are ranked by relevant statistics, such as CPU consumption and wait time. You can tune any high-load SQL that ran within the retention period of AWR using SQL Tuning Advisor.
- **Shared SQL area** -- You can use the shared SQL area to tune recent SQL statements that have yet to be captured in the AWR.

- **SQL tuning set** -- A SQL tuning set (STS) is a database object that stores SQL statements along with their execution context. An STS can include SQL statements that are not yet deployed in production.

You can manage the scope and duration of a SQL Tuning Advisor tuning task. The scope of a tuning task can be either of the following:

- **Limited** -- SQL Tuning Advisor will produce recommendations based on statistical checks, access path analysis, and SQL structure analysis. SQL profile recommendations will not be generated.
- **Comprehensive** -- SQL Tuning Advisor carries out all the analysis from the limited scope plus SQL Profiling. When using the comprehensive option, a time limit can be specified for the tuning task. The default is 30 minutes.

Advisor Output

Once SQL Tuning Advisor has analyzed the SQL statement(s), it will return the following:

- Information on optimizing the execution plan.
- The rationale for the proposed optimization.
- The estimated performance benefit.
- The command to implement the advice.

You make the decision on whether or not to implement the recommendations. Oracle recommends using the Enterprise Manager interface for running SQL Tuning Advisor. If EM is unavailable, then you can run SQL Tuning Advisor using procedures in the DBMS_SQLTUNE package. Using SQL Tuning Advisor via the DBMS_SQLTUNE package is a multi-step process:

1. Create a SQL tuning set (if tuning multiple SQL statements)
2. Create a SQL tuning task
3. Execute a SQL tuning task
4. Display the results of a SQL tuning task
5. Implement recommendations as appropriate

SQL Tuning Tasks

A tuning task can be created using the text of a single SQL statement, a SQL tuning set with multiple statements, a SQL statement selected by SQL identifier from the shared SQL area, or a SQL statement selected by SQL identifier from AWR. The following example uses SQL Tuning Advisor to optimize a specified SQL statement text.

```
DECLARE
    v_task_name    VARCHAR2(30);
    v_sqltext      CLOB;
BEGIN
    v_sqltext := 'SELECT first_name, last_name ' ||
                 'FROM   hr.employees e ' ||
                 '       INNER JOIN hr.departments d ' ||
                 '       ON e.department_id = d.department_id ' ||
                 '       INNER JOIN hr.locations l ' ||
                 '       ON l.location_id = d.location_id ' ||
                 'WHERE  e.employee_id < :bindvar';

    v_task_name := DBMS_SQLTUNE.CREATE_TUNING_TASK(
                 sql_text    => v_sqltext,
                 bind_list   => sql_binds(anydata.ConvertNumber(100)),
                 user_name   => 'HR',
                 scope       => 'COMPREHENSIVE',
                 time_limit  => 45,
                 task_name   => 'oce_tuning_task',
                 description => 'Example Tuning Task');
END;
/
```

Once the tuning task has been created, the task is executed to start the tuning process:

```
BEGIN
    DBMS_SQLTUNE.EXECUTE_TUNING_TASK( task_name => 'oce_tuning_task' );
END;
/
```

The status of a task is available in the USER_ADVISOR_TASKS view:

```
SELECT status
FROM   user_advisor_tasks
WHERE  task_name = 'oce_sql_tuning_task';
```

The execution progress of the task is available in the V$ADVISOR_PROGRESS view:

```
SELECT sofar, totalwork
FROM   v$advisor_progress
WHERE  user_name = 'HR'
AND    task_name = 'oce_sql_tuning_task';
```

Once the task has completed, you display a report of the findings and recommendations. For each proposed recommendation, the rationale and benefit is provided along with the SQL statements needed to implement the recommendation. The report is generated with the REPORT_TUNING_TASK function of DBMS_SQLTUNE:

```
SET LONG 1000
SET LONGCHUNKSIZE 1000
SET LINESIZE 100
SELECT DBMS_SQLTUNE.REPORT_TUNING_TASK(
       'oce_sql_tuning_task')
FROM   DUAL;
```

You can use the following APIs for managing SQL tuning tasks:

- **INTERRUPT_TUNING_TASK** -- This will interrupt a task while executing, causing a normal exit with intermediate results.
- **RESUME_TUNING_TASK** -- This will resume a previously interrupted task.
- **CANCEL_TUNING_TASK** -- This will cancel a task while executing, removing all results from the task.
- **RESET_TUNING_TASK** -- This will reset a task while executing, removing all results from the task and returning the task to its initial state.

- **DROP_TUNING_TASK** -- This will drop a task, removing all results associated with it.

Use the SQL Access Advisor to tune a workload

The SQL Access Advisor is designed to help make sure that an efficient path to the data exists. SQL Access advisor offers recommendations intended to achieve the proper set of materialized views, materialized view logs, and indexes for a given workload. As a general rule, as the number of materialized views and indexes increase, query performance improves. SQL Access Advisor weighs trade-offs between space usage and query performance. SQL Access Advisor makes recommendations, each of which will contain one or more actions. If a recommendation contains multiple actions, all of the individual actions must be implemented to achieve the full benefit. If the advisor decides that one or more base tables should be partitioned, it will collect all individual partition actions into a single recommendation. In that case, note that some or all of the remaining recommendations might be dependent on implementing the partitioning recommendation. It is not possible to view index and materialized view advice in isolation of the underlying table's partitioning.

The SQL Access Advisor API can perform the following functions:

- Recommend materialized views and indexes based on collected, user-supplied, or hypothetical workload information.
- Recommend partitioning of tables, indexes, and materialized views.
- Mark, update, and remove recommendations.
- Perform a quick tune using a single SQL statement.
- Show how to make a materialized view fast refreshable.
- Show how to change a materialized view so that general query rewrite is possible.

The SQL Access Advisor relies on structural statistics about table and index cardinalities of dimension level columns, JOIN KEY columns, and fact table key columns. If these statistics are missing for a given table, queries referencing this table are marked as invalid in the workload. SQL Access Advisor will make no recommendations for those queries. Prior to running SQL Access Advisor, you should also ensure that existing indexes and materialized views have been analyzed.

Modes of Operation

SQL Access Advisor has two modes of operation: problem solving and evaluation. The default mode is problem solving. In this mode, SQL Access Advisor will attempt to solve access method problems by looking for new objects to create. When operating in evaluation mode, SQL Access Advisor will only comment on existing access paths that the given workload will use. A problem solving run might recommend creating a new index whereas an evaluation only scenario will only produce recommendations such as retaining an existing index. The evaluation mode is useful in determining which indexes and materialized views are actually being used by a given workload.

Intermediate Results

SQL Access Advisor allows you to see intermediate results during the analysis operation. Previously, results were unavailable until the processing had completed or was interrupted by the user. With the change, it is possible to access results in the recommendation and action tables while the SQL Access Advisor task is still executing. Intermediate results represent recommendations only for the portion of the workload that has been executed up to that point in time. If the entire workload must be evaluated, then you should allow the task to complete normally. Recommendations made by the advisor early in the evaluation process will not have any base table partitioning recommendations. Partitioning analysis requires most of the workload to be processed before it's clear whether partitioning would be beneficial.

Creating Tasks

You create advisor tasks to define what it is you want to analyze and where the analysis results should be placed. It's possible to create any number of tasks, each with a given specialization. All are based on the same Advisor task model and share the same repository. Tasks are created using the CREATE_TASK procedure:

```
VARIABLE task_id NUMBER;
VARIABLE task_name VARCHAR2(255);
EXECUTE :task_name := 'MYTASK';
EXECUTE DBMS_ADVISOR.CREATE_TASK
        ('SQL Access Advisor', :task_id, :task_name);
```

SQL Tuning Sets

The input workload for the SQL Access Advisor is the SQL Tuning Set. An important benefit of using a SQL Tuning Set is that because SQL Tuning Sets are stored as separate entities, they can be referenced by many Advisor tasks. A workload reference will be removed when a parent Advisor task is deleted or when the workload reference is removed from the Advisor task by the user. A SQL Tuning Set workload is created using DBMS_SQLTUNE. You can pull SQL Workload objects into a SQL Tuning Set using DBMS_ADVISOR:

```
EXECUTE DBMS_ADVISOR.COPY_SQLWKLD_TO_STS('MYWORKLOAD','MYSTS','NEW');
```

Linking Tasks and Workloads

Tasks must be linked to a SQL Tuning Set in order to generate advisor recommendations. You create links with the ADD_STS_REF procedure, using their respective names to link the task to a Tuning Set. Once a connection has been defined, the SQL Tuning Set is protected from removal or update.

```
EXECUTE DBMS_ADVISOR.ADD_STS_REF('MYTASK', null, 'MYWORKLOAD');
```

Removing a Link

Before a task or a SQL Tuning Set workload can be deleted, any existing links between the task and the workload must be removed. Links are removed using the DELETE_STS_REF procedure.

```
EXECUTE DBMS_ADVISOR.DELETE_STS_REF('MYTASK', null, 'MYWORKLOAD');
```

Recommendation Options

Parameters for a given task must be defined using the SET_TASK_PARAMETER procedure before recommendations can be generated. If parameters are not defined, then the defaults are used. You can set task parameters by using the SET_TASK_PARAMETER procedure.

```
DBMS_ADVISOR.SET_TASK_PARAMETER (
        task_name IN VARCHAR2,
        parameter IN VARCHAR2,
        value IN [VARCHAR2 | NUMBER]);
```

Generating Recommendations

You can generate recommendations by using the EXECUTE_TASK procedure. After it completes, the DBA_ADVISOR_LOG table will show execution status and the number of recommendations and actions produced. EXECUTE_TASK is a synchronous operation, so control will not be returned to the user until the operation has completed, or is interrupted. Upon completion, you can check the DBA_ADVISOR_LOG table for the execution status. The recommendations can be queried by task name in DBA_ADVISOR_RECOMMENDATIONS and the actions in DBA_ADVISOR_ACTIONS.

```
EXECUTE DBMS_ADVISOR.EXECUTE_TASK('MYTASK');
```

Use Database Replay

Oracle Database Replay captures all external database calls made to the system during the workload capture period. The capture includes all relevant information about the client request, such as SQL text, bind values, and transaction information. Background activities of the database and scheduler jobs are not captured. In addition, the following types of client requests are not captured in a workload:

- Direct path load of data from external files using utilities such as SQL*Loader
- Shared server requests (Oracle MTS)
- Oracle Streams
- Advanced replication streams
- Non-PL/SQL based Advanced Queuing (AQ)
- Flashback queries
- Oracle Call Interface (OCI) based object navigations
- Non SQL-based object access
- Distributed transactions

It is a best practice to restart the database before capturing the production workload. This ensures that ongoing and dependent transactions are allowed to be completed or rolled back before the capture begins. If the database is not restarted before the capture, transactions that are in progress or have yet to be committed will be only partially captured in the workload.

By default, all activities from all user sessions are recorded during workload capture. Workload filters can be used to include or exclude specific user sessions during the workload capture. You can use either inclusion filters or exclusion filters in a workload capture, but not both simultaneously. Inclusion filters specify user sessions that will be captured in the workload. Exclusion filters enable you to specify user sessions that will not be captured in the workload. To add filters to a workload capture, you use the DBMS_WORKLOAD_CAPTURE.ADD_FILTER procedure. To

remove an existing filter, you use the
DBMS_WORKLOAD_CAPTURE.DELETE_FILTER procedure.

You should have a well-defined starting point for the workload so that the database being used to replay the workload can be restored to the same point before starting the captured workload. It is best not to have any active user sessions when starting a workload capture. Active sessions may have ongoing transactions which will not be replayed completely. Consider restarting the database in RESTRICTED mode prior to starting the workload capture. When the workload capture begins, the database will automatically switch to UNRESTRICTED mode and normal operations can continue while the workload is being captured. You begin a workload capture using the procedure DBMS_WORKLOAD_CAPTURE.START_CAPTURE. To stop a workload capture in progress, you use the DBMS_WORKLOAD_CAPTURE.FINISH_CAPTURE procedure.

You can export AWR data from the production machine in order to enable detailed analysis of the workload on both systems. This data is required if you plan to run the AWR Compare Period report on a pair of workload captures or replays. To export AWR data, you use the DBMS_WORKLOAD_CAPTURE.EXPORT_AWR procedure.

The following views allow you to monitor a workload capture. You can also use Oracle Enterprise Manager to monitor a workload capture:

- **DBA_WORKLOAD_CAPTURES** -- Lists all the workload captures that have been created in the current database.
- **DBA_WORKLOAD_FILTERS** -- Lists all workload filters used for workload captures defined in the current database.

After the workload has been captured, it's necessary to preprocess the capture files prior to using them in a replay. Preprocessing converts the captured data into replay files and creates the required metadata needed to replay the workload. After preprocessing the captured workload, it can be replayed multiple times on any replay system running the same version of Oracle. As a general rule, it's recommended to move the capture files to another system for preprocessing. While the capture itself has a minimal overhead, workload preprocessing can be time consuming and resource intensive. It is better that this step be performed on the test system where the workload will be replayed rather than on the production database. Capture files are processed using the DBMS_WORKLOAD_REPLAY.PROCESS_CAPTURE procedure.

After you have preprocessed a captured workload, it can be replayed on the test system. In the workload replay, Oracle will perform the actions recorded during the workload capture. It will re-create all captured external client requests with the same timing, concurrency, and transaction dependencies that occurred on the production system. Database Replay uses a program called the replay client to re-create the external client requests. You may need to use multiple replay clients depending on the scope of the captured workload. The replay client has an imbedded calibration tool to help determine the number of replay clients required for a given workload. The entire workload from the production database is replayed. This includes DML and SQL queries, so the data in the replay system must be as logically similar to the data in the capture system as possible.

Implement real-time database operation monitoring

A database operation can be any group of related database tasks as defined by end users or an application. Examples of operations include ETL processing, a batch jobs, or a multiple SQL-statement transaction. Database operations are either simple or composite.

- **Simple** -- A single SQL statement or PL/SQL procedure or function.
- **Composite** -- Activity between two points in time in a database session, with each session defining its own beginning and end points. A session can participate in at most one composite database operation at a time.

When Real-Time SQL Monitoring was introduced in Oracle Database 11g, it supported only simple operations. With 12c, Real-Time Database Operations provides the ability to monitor composite operations. Oracle automatically monitors parallel queries, DML, and DDL statements as soon as execution begins. By default, Real-Time SQL Monitoring automatically starts when a SQL statement runs in parallel, or when it has consumed at least 5 seconds of CPU or I/O time in a single execution.

The data from Real-Time SQL Monitoring can be accessed from the Enterprise Manager Cloud Control Monitored SQL Executions page, via data dictionary views, or through the DBMS_MONITOR package. The Monitored SQL Executions page in EM Cloud Control is available from the Performance menu. This page summarizes the activity for monitored statements and is the recommended method for using Real-Time SQL Monitoring. You can use it to drill down and obtain additional details about particular statements.

The data dictionary views for Real-Time SQL monitoring include:

- **V$SQL_MONITOR** -- This view contains global, high-level information about the top SQL statements in a database operation. Each monitored SQL statement has an entry in this view. Each row contains a SQL statement whose statistics are accumulated from multiple sessions and all of its executions in the operation. The primary key is the combination of the columns DBOP_NAME, DBOP_EXEC_ID, and SQL_ID.

- **V$SQL_MONITOR_SESSTAT** -- This view contains the statistics for all sessions involved in the database operation. Most of the statistics are cumulative. The database stores the statistics in XML format instead of using each column for each statistic. This view is primarily intended for the report generator.

- **V$SQL_PLAN_MONITOR** -- This view contains monitoring statistics for each step in the execution plan of the monitored SQL statement. The database updates statistics in

V$SQL_PLAN_MONITOR every second while the SQL statement is executing. Multiple entries exist in V$SQL_PLAN_MONITOR for every monitored SQL statement. Each entry corresponds to a step in the execution plan of the statement.

The DBMS_SQL_MONITOR package allows you to define the beginning and ending of a database operation, and generate a report of the database operations. The functions in this package include:

- **REPORT_SQL_MONITOR** -- This function accepts several input parameters to specify the execution, the level of detail in the report, and the report type. If no parameters are specified, then the function generates a text report for the last execution that was monitored.
- **BEGIN_OPERATION** -- This function associates a session with a database operation.
- **END_OPERATION** -- This procedure disassociates a session from the specified database operation execution.

```
DBMS_MONITOR.BEGIN_OPERATION(
    dbop_name IN VARCHAR2,
    dbop_eid IN NUMBER := NULL,
    force_tracking IN VARCHAR2 := NO_FORCE_TRACKING,
    attribute_list IN VARCHAR2 := NULL)
RETURN NUMBER;
```

The BEGIN_OPERATION function is used to begin a composite data operation. It accepts the following parameters:

- **dbop_name** -- Name of operation
- **dbpop_eid** -- Unique number to distinguish the execution provided by the user
- **force_tracking** -- FORCE_TRACKING forces the composite database operation to be tracked when the operation starts. By default, NO_FORCE_TRACKING is in effect, which means that the operation is tracked only when it is sufficiently expensive.

- **attribute_list** -- List of the user input attributes in the form of a comma separated name-value pair (for example, table_name=emp, operation=load)

SQL monitoring is enabled by default when the initialization parameter STATISTICS_LEVEL is set to either TYPICAL or ALL. Oracle will begin monitoring long running queries automatically. The initialization parameter CONTROL_MANAGEMENT_PACK_ACCESS must also be set to DIAGNOSTIC+TUNING (the default) for SQL monitoring to be used.

It is possible to use hints to enable or disable monitoring of specific SQL statements. The MONITOR hint enables monitoring, whereas the NO_MONITOR hint disables monitoring. The first statement below enables SQL Monitoring explicitly and the second disables it:

```
SELECT /*+ MONITOR */ first_name, last_name, email
FROM    employees;


SELECT /*+ NO_MONITOR */ first_name, last_name, email
FROM    employees;
```

You can create a database operation by explicitly defining its beginning and end points using the DBMS_SQL_ONITOR package. A database operation is started with the BEGIN_OPERATION function and ended with the END_OPERATION procedure.

To create a database operation:

- Start SQL*Plus and connect as a user with the appropriate privileges.
- Define a variable to hold the execution ID.

```
var    opid  NUMBER
```

- Begin the database operation.

```
EXEC :opid := DBMS_SQL_MONITOR.BEGIN_OPERATION('rtsm_op');
```

- Run the queries in the operation.

```
SELECT count(*) FROM hr.employees;

SELECT COUNT(*) FROM hr.departments;
```

- End the database operation.

```
EXEC DBMS_SQL_MONITOR.END_OPERATION('rtsm_op', :opid);
```

- Confirm that the database operation completed.

```
SELECT dbop_name, status
FROM   v$sql_monitor
WHERE  dbop_name = 'rtsm_op';
DBOP_NAME   STATUS
---------- ---------
rtsm_op     DONE
```

Use Adaptive Execution Plans

The new Adaptive Query Optimization in 12c enables the optimizer to alter execution plans at run-time and also to discover additional information that can generate better statistics. There are two distinct aspects in Adaptive Query Optimization

- **Adaptive plans** -- This capability focuses on improving the initial execution of a query at run-time.
- **Adaptive statistics** -- This feature is intended to provide additional statistics in order to improve subsequent executions of a query.

Adaptive Plans

Adaptive plans allow the optimizer to make the final plan decision for a SQL statement while it is being executed. The plan chosen by the optimizer prior to execution is instrumented with statistics collectors. The optimizer can detect at run-time if its cardinality estimates differ significantly from the actual number of rows. If so, the plan or a portion of it can be automatically adapted in mid-execution.

The optimizer can predetermine multiple potential subplans for portions of the plan so that it can decide the method to be used on the fly. During execution of the statement, the statistics collector will monitor and buffer rows coming from a portion of the plan. Based on the data collected, the optimizer will make the final decision about which subplan to use. Once the optimizer has chosen the final plan, the statistics collector stops collecting statistics and buffering rows, and simply passes the rows through. On subsequent executions of the child cursor, the optimizer will disable buffering and choose the same final plan.

When an execution plan is altered by Adaptive Query Optimization, the results of the EXPLAIN PLAN command will be different from that of the DBMS_XPLAN.DISPLAY_CURSOR function. The explain plan command will show only the initial or default plan chosen by the optimizer. The results of the DBMS_XPLAN.DISPLAY_CURSOR function will be the final plan used by the query.

It is possible to see all of the operations in an adaptive plan, including the positions of the statistics collectors using the DBMS_XPLAN functions. Adding the format parameter '+adaptive' will result in an additional notation (-) in the id column of the plan. This indicates operations in the plan that were not used (inactive). The SQL Monitor tool in Oracle Enterprise Manager always shows the full adaptive plan but does not indicate which operations in the plan are inactive.

The V$SQL view has a new column (IS_RESOLVED_ADAPTIVE_PLAN) that indicates if a SQL statement has an adaptive plan and if that plan has been fully resolved or not. If the column value is set to 'Y', the plan adaptive and a final plan has been selected. If the column value is 'N', the plan selected is adaptive but the final plan has not yet been decided on. The column value will be NULL for non-adaptive plans.

If the initialization parameter OPTIMIZER_ADAPTIVE_REPORTING_ONLY is set to TRUE (the default value is FALSE), information needed to enable adaptive join methods will be gathered, but no action is taken to change the plan. When set to TRUE, the default plan will always be used but information is collected on how the plan would have been adapted. This information can be viewed by using DBMS_XPLAN to display the plan using the additional format parameter '+report'.

Adaptive Statistics

The optimizer depends on statistics in order to create good execution plans. However, some query predicates are too complex to rely on base table statistics alone. When a SQL statement is being compiled, the optimizer determines whether or not a good execution plan can be generated with the available statistics. If not, dynamic sampling is used to compensate for missing or insufficient statistics. If one or more of the tables in the query does not have statistics, dynamic sampling will gather basic statistics on them. In Oracle Database 12c dynamic sampling has been enhanced to become dynamic statistics.

Dynamic statistics can determine more accurate cardinality estimates for not only single table accesses but also joins and group-by predicates. A new level, 11 has also been introduced for the initialization parameter OPTIMIZER_DYNAMIC_SAMPLING. When the parameter is set to this level, the optimizer can decide to use dynamic statistics for any SQL statement, even where all of the basic table statistics exist. The decision on whether to use dynamic statistics is based on the complexity of the predicates used, the existing base statistics, and the total execution time expected for the SQL statement. At level 11, dynamic sampling will almost certainly occur more often and extend parse times. To minimize the performance impact, the results of the dynamic sampling queries will be persisted in the cache for other SQL statements to share.

Automatic reoptimization is designed to improve execution plans <u>after</u> the initial execution. At the end of the first execution of a SQL statement, the optimizer determines whether the execution information differs significantly from the original estimates. If so, the optimizer looks for a replacement plan for the next execution. Automatic reoptimization is iterative, the optimizer can reoptimize a query multiple times, each time learning more and further improving the plan. Oracle Database 12c supports multiple forms of reoptimization.

- **Statistics feedback** -- Formally known as cardinality feedback, this is designed to improve plans for queries that have cardinality misestimates. When used, the optimizer compares its original cardinality estimates for a SQL statement to the actual cardinalities observed during execution. If they differ significantly, the correct estimates are stored for subsequent use. It will also create a SQL plan directive so other SQL statements can benefit from the information gathered during this initial execution.
- **Performance Feedback** -- This helps to improve the degree of parallelism used for repeated SQL statements when Automatic Degree of Parallelism (AutoDOP) is enabled in adaptive mode. During the first execution of a SQL statement, the optimizer determines what parallel degree (if any) should be used. At the end of the initial execution, the parallel degree used is compared to the parallel degree computed based on the actual performance statistics gathered during the execution of the statement. If the two vary significantly, the statement is marked for reoptimization and the statistics are stored to help compute a more appropriate DOP on subsequent executions.
- **SQL plan directives** -- A SQL plan directive is additional information that the optimizer uses to generate a more optimal execution plan. They are created on query expressions rather than at a statement or object level so that they can be applied to multiple SQL statements. Multiple SQL plan directives can be used for a single SQL statement. SQL plan directives are maintained automatically and stored in the SYSAUX tablespace. Any SQL plan directive that is not used after 53 weeks will be automatically purged. They can be monitored using the views DBA_SQL_PLAN_DIRECTIVES and DBA_SQL_PLAN_DIR_OBJECTS.

Use enhanced features of statistics gathering

Starting with 11g, it has been possible to automatically publish the statistics at the end of the gather operation (the default behavior), or to have the new statistics be saved as pending. When saved as pending, you can validate the new statistics and publish them only if they generate acceptable optimizer plans. The following command will return 'TRUE' if statistics will be published when they are gathered, or FALSE if the statistics will be kept pending.

```
SELECT DBMS_STATS.GET_PREFS('PUBLISH') publish
FROM  dual;
```

The PUBLISH setting at either the schema or the table level. By default, the optimizer uses only published statistics in generating plans. If you want the optimizer to use pending statistics, you may set the initialization parameter **OPTIMIZER_USE_PENDING_STATISTICS** to TRUE (the default value is FALSE). You may publish pending stats for a single table, single schema, or the entire database with the DBMS_STATS.PUBLISH_PENDING_STATS procedure;

- **Database** - DBMS_STATS.PUBLISH_PENDING_STATS (NULL, NULL);
- **Schema** - DBMS_STATS.PUBLISH_PENDING_STATS (schema_name, NULL);
- **Table** - DBMS_STATS.PUBLISH_PENDING_STATS (schema_name, table_name);

GRANULARITY AND INCREMENTAL parameters

For partitioned tables and indexes, DBMS_STATS can gather separate statistics for each partition and global statistics for the entire table or index. The type of partitioning statistics to be gathered is specified in the GRANULARITY argument of the DBMS_STATS gathering procedures. Both types can be important for creating good plans. Oracle recommends setting the GRANULARITY parameter to AUTO to gather both types of partition statistics.

With partitioned tables, new data is often loaded into a new partition. As new partitions are added and data loaded, statistics must be gathered on the new partition, and global statistics must be kept up to date for the entire table. If the INCREMENTAL value for a partition table is set to TRUE, and you gather statistics on that table with the GRANULARITY parameter set to AUTO, Oracle will gather statistics on the new partition and update the global table statistics by scanning only those partitions that have been modified rather than the entire table. If the INCREMENTAL value for the partitioned table is set to FALSE (the default value), then a full table scan is used to maintain the global statistics. This is a highly resource intensive and time consuming operation for large tables. Setting INCREMENTAL to TRUE for a partitioned table requires the SYSAUX tablespace to consume additional space to maintain the global statistics.

New sampling technique

Gathering statistics for a large table can be very time-consuming if the operation reads every row. Sampling a small percentage of the rows provides a much faster operation, albeit with less reliable metrics. The sample size is specified using the ESTIMATE_PERCENT argument of the DBMS_STATS procedures. Prior to 11g, this value has been set to a static value, commonly 5, 10, or 15%. Oracle now recommends setting the parameter to the function DBMS_STATS.AUTO_SAMPLE_SIZE. This function is designed to maximize performance gains while achieving necessary statistical accuracy. AUTO_SAMPLE_SIZE lets Oracle determine the best sample size necessary for good statistics, based on the statistical properties of the particular object.

Multi-Column Statistics

When multiple columns from a single table are used together in the where clause of a query, the relationship between the columns can strongly affect the combined selectivity for the column group. For example, consider a table that has city and state columns. Selecting city and state together produces a much smaller cardinality result than selecting state alone. It is possible to create extended statistics against two or more columns. The resulting metrics can be used by the optimizer to provide better access plans when both columns appear in a query.

```
BEGIN
  cg_name := dbms_stats.create_extended_stats
                (null,'customer_data',
                '(cust_state,cust_city)');
END;
/


SELECT sys.dbms_stats.show_extended_stats_name
            ('sh','customer_data',
            '(cust_state,cust_city)') col_group_name
FROM dual;
```

You will obtain an output similar to the following:

```
COL_GROUP_NAME
----------------
SYS_STU#S#WF25Z#QAHIHE#MOFFMM
```

Expression Statistics

When a function is applied to a column in the where clause of a query (function(col1)=constant), the optimizer has no way of knowing how that function will affect the selectivity of the column. By gathering expression statistics on the expression function(col1), the optimizer will have a more accurate selectivity value. You can also use the **create_extended_statistics** function to accomplish this:

```
SELECT dbms_stats.create_extended_stats
                (null,'customer_data',
                '(lower(cust_city))')
FROM   dual;
```

12c Enhancements

There were two enhancements made to the process of gathering incremental statistics. Incremental statistics are relevant when gathering statistics on partitioned tables. For partitioned tables, Oracle must gather statistics at both the table and partition levels. It is possible for Oracle to derive the global level statistics by aggregating the partition level statistics, and eliminate the need to scan the entire table to produce global statistics.

Prior to 12c, if incremental statistics were enabled on a table and a single row changed in a partition, the statistics for it were considered stale. They could not be used to generate global level statistics until they were re-gathered. A new preference called INCREMENTAL_STALENESS allows the DBA to determine when partition statistics will be marked as stale. It is set to NULL by default, which uses the legacy definition of staleness. Alternately, the parameter can be set to the following values:

- **USE_STALE_PERCENT** -- The partition level statistics will not be considered stale until the percentage of rows changed is greater than the value of the preference STALE_PERCENTAGE (10% by default).
- **USE_LOCKED_STATS** -- If statistics on a partition are locked, they will be used to generate global level statistics regardless of how many rows have changed in that partition since statistics were last gathered.

The second enhancement to incremental statistics involves the exchange partition capability. The exchange partition command allows data from a non-partitioned table to be swapped into a specified partition of a partitioned table. Data is not physically moved by the command -- it simply updates the data dictionary to exchange a pointer from the partition to the table and vice versa. Prior to 12c, it was not possible to generate the statistics on the non-partitioned table required to support incremental statistics. The statistics had to be gathered on the partition after the exchange. In 12c, the statistics (synopsis) can be created on the non-partitioned table prior to the exchange operation. After the exchange, this data can immediately be used to maintain incremental global statistics. The new DBMS_STATS table preference INCREMENTAL_LEVEL can be used to identify a non-partitioned table that will be used in partition exchange. When INCREMENTAL_LEVEL is set to TABLE (the default is PARTITION), Oracle will automatically create a synopsis for the table when statistics are gathered. This synopsis will then become the partition level synopsis after the exchange.

Concurrent Statistics

When the global statistics gathering preference CONCURRENT is set, the Oracle Job Scheduler and Advanced Queuing components create and manage one statistics gathering job per object (tables and/or partitions) concurrently. In 12c, the process of gathering statistics concurrently has been improved to make better use of each scheduler job. For small (or empty) tables, partitions, or sub-partitions, the database can automatically batch the object with other small objects into a single job to reduce overhead. It is also now possible to perform concurrent statistics gathering via the nightly statistics gathering job by setting the preference CONCURRENT to ALL or AUTOMATIC.

Automatic column group detection

When multiple columns from the same table are used in filter predicates, join conditions, or group-by keys, extended statistics on those column groups can improve the accuracy of cardinality estimates by the Optimizer. However, it is often difficult to determine which column groups to create extended statistics for. The Auto Column Group detection can automatically derive this information based on a given workload. Auto Column Group detection is a three step process:

- **Seed column usage** -- Oracle must observe a representative workload, in order to determine the appropriate column groups. The workload can be provided via a SQL Tuning Set or by monitoring a running system. The DBMS_STATS.SEED_COL_USAGE procedure is used to indicate the workload and to tell Oracle how long to observe it.
- **Create the column groups** -- Calling the DBMS_STATS.CREATE_EXTENDED_STATS function for the relevant table(s), will create the necessary column groups based on the usage information captured. Once the extended statistics have been created, they will be automatically maintained whenever statistics are gathered on the table. It is also possible to create column groups manually by specifying the group as the third argument in the DBMS_STATS.CREATE_EXTENDED_STATS function.
- **Regather statistics** -- The final step is to regather statistics on the affected tables.

Use Adaptive SQL Plan Management

The new adaptive SQL plan management feature in 12c means that DBAs no longer have to manually run the verification or evolve process for non-accepted plans. The SPM Evolve Advisor runs a verification process (SYS_AUTO_SPM_EVOLVE_TASK) for all SQL statements that have non-accepted plans during the nightly maintenance window when automatic SQL tuning is in COMPREHENSIVE mode. If the verification process determines that the non-accepted plan performs sufficiently better than the existing accepted plan (or plans) in the SQL plan baseline, the plan will be automatically accepted. The task can accept more than one plan for a given SQL statement. A persistent report is generated that details how the new plan performs in comparison to the existing plans. The evolution task can also be run manually using the DBMS_SPM package.

The Automatic SPM Evolve Advisor task does not have a separate scheduler client. A single client controls both Automatic SQL Tuning Advisor and Automatic SPM Evolve Advisor. The same task enables or disables both advisors. The task can be enabled through Enterprise manager or via the DBMS_AUTO_TASK_ADMIN PL/SQL package. The steps to enable the task using DBMS_AUTO_TASK_ADMIN follow:

- Connect SQL*Plus to the database with administrator privileges and execute the following PL/SQL block:

```
BEGIN
DBMS_AUTO_TASK_ADMIN.ENABLE (
    client_name   => 'sql tuning advisor',
    operation     => NULL,
    window_name   => NULL
    );
END;
```

- Query the data dictionary to confirm the change.

```
SELECT client_name, status
FROM   dba_autotask_client
WHERE  client_name = 'sql tuning advisor';


CLIENT_NAME         STATUS
------------------- --------
sql tuning advisor  ENABLED
```

Executing the DBMS_AUTO_TASK_ADMIN.DISABLE procedure with the same parameters will disable the task. The DBMS_SPM package allows for configuration of automatic plan evolution. Reference the Oracle Database SQL Tuning Guide for details on how to do this.

It is recommended that the SQL Plan Management Evolve task be set to run automatically. However, it is possible use PL/SQL or Cloud Control to manually evolve an unaccepted plan. A manual evolution will allow you to determine is the new plan performs better than any accepted plan currently in the baseline. The following list contains the most relevant DBMS_SPM procedures and functions for managing plan evolution.

- **ACCEPT_SQL_PLAN_BASELINE** -- This function accepts one recommendation to evolve a single plan into a SQL plan baseline.

- **CREATE_EVOLVE_TASK** -- This function creates an advisor task to prepare the plan evolution of one or more plans for a specified SQL statement. The input parameters can be a SQL handle, plan name or a list of plan names, time limit, task name, and description.
- **EXECUTE_EVOLVE_TASK** -- This function executes an evolution task. The input parameters can be the task name, execution name, and execution description. If not specified, the advisor generates the name, which is returned by the function.
- **IMPLEMENT_EVOLVE_TASK** -- This function implements all recommendations for an evolve task.
- **REPORT_EVOLVE_TASK** -- This function displays the results of an evolve task as a CLOB. Input parameters include the task name and section of the report to include.
- **SET_EVOLVE_TASK_PARAMETER** -- This function updates the value of an evolve task parameter. In this release, the only valid parameter is TIME_LIMIT.

Normally, the steps to manually evolve a SQL plan evolution tasks occur in the following sequence:

- Create an evolve task
- Optionally, set evolve task parameters
- Execute the evolve task
- Implement the recommendations in the task
- Report on the task outcome

Perform emergency monitoring and real-time ADDM

The Emergency Monitoring feature of Enterprise Manager Cloud Control allows a DBA to connect to an unresponsive database. The connection is created via a proprietary mechanism and facilitates diagnosis of the performance problem when a normal mode connection is not possible.

On entering the Emergency Monitoring page, the agent will connect directly to the SGA. The agent bypasses the SQL retrieval layer and collects data directly from the SGA to get performance statistics. The page displays collected ASH data and top blocking sessions in the Hang Analysis table refreshed in real-time. The screen enables administrators to identify blocking sessions and kill these blockers with a click of a button. The Emergency Monitoring page is accessed from the Performance Menu in the home page of EM Cloud Control.

Real-Time ADDM

Real-Time ADDM was originally introduced with Oracle Enterprise Manager Cloud Control 12c and much of the functionality is also available in Enterprise manager Express (although EM Express has no equivalent of the diagnostic connection). Real-Time ADDM is designed to assist in the analysis and resolution of problems that cause unresponsive or hung databases. Traditionally performance problems that caused this would require the database to be restarted.

Real-Time ADDM analyzes the current performance of the database via a set of predefined criteria. If any problems are detected, Real-Time ADDM suggests methods for resolving any issues it identifies without restarting the database. Depending on the database state, Real-Time ADDM will use one of two connection modes to the database:

- **Normal connection** -- Real-Time ADDM performs a normal JDBC connection to the database. This mode is intended to perform extensive performance analysis of the database when some connectivity is available.
- **Diagnostic connection** -- This is a latch-less connection to the database that is intended for extreme hang situations when a normal JDBC connection is not possible.

Real-Time ADDM performs a similar type of diagnosis as conventional ADDM to analyze performance, but uses different data. Conventional ADDM makes use of the data from AWR snapshots to perform its diagnosis. Real-Time ADDM makes use of ASH recent activity from SGA data in lieu of AWR snapshots. Real-Time ADDM runs automatically and uses in-memory data to locate performance spikes in the database. If a performance problem is detected, an analysis is triggered automatically. The scans are executed every three seconds by the manageability monitor process (MMON) to obtain performance statistics without lock or latch. MMON will analyze the statistics and trigger a Real-Time ADDM analysis if any of the following issues are detected.

- **High load** -- Average active sessions are greater than 3 times the number of CPU cores
- **I/O bound** -- I/O impact on active sessions based on single block read performance
- **CPU bound** -- Active sessions are greater than 10% of total load and CPU utilization is greater than 50%
- **Over-allocated memory** -- Memory allocations are over 95% of physical memory
- **Interconnect bound** -- Based on single block interconnect transfer time
- **Session limit** -- Session limit is close to 100%
- **Process limit** -- Process limit is close to 100%
- **Hung session** -- Hung sessions are greater than 10% of total sessions
- **Deadlock detected** -- Any deadlock is detected

The MMON slave process will then store the ADDM report that was created in the AWR. The report metadata can be accessed via the DBA_HIST_REPORTS view. Real-Time ADDM employs several controls to ensure that the automatic triggers do not consume too many system resources:

- **Duration between reports** -- If a Real-Time ADDM report was created in the past 5 minutes by the automatic trigger, then no new reports will be generated.
- **Oracle RAC control** -- Automatic triggers are local to the database instance. For Oracle RAC, only one database instance can create a Real-Time ADDM report at a given time because a lock is required

and a query is performed by the MMON slave process before the report is actually generated.

- **Repeated triggers** -- An automatic trigger for any issue must have an impact of 100% or higher than the previous report with the same triggering issue within the past 45 minutes.
- **Newly identified issues** -- If a new issue is found that was not previously detected within the past 45 minutes, a new report is generated regardless of the new active sessions load.

Generate ADDM Compare Period (Use AWR and ADDM)

The Compare Period ADDM feature is used to compare the performance of the database server in two distinct time periods. This is often used to determine why the server is slower (or faster) at different points in time. The ADDM Compare Period functionality is part of Enterprise Manager Cloud Control 12c. It can analyze any Oracle database monitored by Cloud Control that is release 10.2.0.4 or later. The functionality requires exactly two periods to be selected:

- **Comparison Period** -- This is normally the period that exhibits a performance degradation. It is possible, though, to use Compare Period ADDM to determine why performance has improved.
- **Base Period** -- The base period represents a known period in which the database is functioning properly. The base period should be one in which the performance was acceptable, and the workload was as similar to the Comparison period.

The steps to initiate a report from the Compare Period ADDM are:

1. From the Performance menu of EM Cloud Control, select AWR, then Compare Period ADDM.
2. From the Run Compare Period ADDM page, specify the comparison and base periods to be used.
3. Click Run to display the Database Compare Period Report.
4. Examine the Compare Period ADDM report to analyze why the performance changed between the two periods.

The Compare Period ADDM Report contains four sections:

- **Overview** -- This section shows how comparable the two periods were. The value is based on the average resource consumption of the SQL statements common to both periods. When the value is 100%, the workload "signature" in both time periods is identical. If the value is 0%, the time periods have no items in common for the specific workload dimension.
- **Configuration** -- This section displays base period and comparison period values for various parameters categorized by instance, host, and database.
- **Findings** -- This section can display performance improvements or degradations. It can identify the major performance differences caused by system changes. It contains a Change Impact value that represents the scale of a change in performance from one time period to another. If the value is positive, an improvement has occurred, and if the value is negative, a regression has occurred.
- **Resources** -- The information displayed in this section provides a summary of the division of database time for both time periods. It provides the resource usage for CPU, memory, I/O, and interconnect on RAC installations.

Diagnose performance issues using ASH enhancements

Conventional ADDM performs diagnosis from the data in AWR snapshots. When a performance problem is short-lived, ADDM may not report it because it is not considered significant enough in terms of its duration when compared to the interval between AWR snapshots. Snapshot data is not the ideal means for locating and diagnosing transient performance problems. In order to facilitate the identification performance problems that last for short durations, Oracle Database samples active sessions every second and stores the data collected in a circular buffer in the SGA. To keep the amount of data to a manageable level, only sessions that are waiting on an event that does not belong to the Idle wait class are sampled. This collected data is known as Active Session History (ASH). The data can be queried via the **V$ACTIVE_SESSION_HISTORY** view and rolled up in various dimensions into an ASH report, including the following:

- SQL identifier of a SQL statement
- Object number, file number, and block number
- Wait event identifier and parameters
- Session identifier and session serial number
- Module and action name
- Client identifier of the session
- Service hash identifier

It is possible to generate ASH reports using Oracle Enterprise Manager Cloud Control. To run ASH reports from EM Cloud Control:

- Access the Database Home page.
- From the Performance menu, select Performance Home.
- Log in to the database as a user with administrator privileges. The Performance page appears.
- Under Average Active Sessions, click Run ASH Report. The Run ASH Report page appears.
- Enter the date and time for the start and end of the time period when the transient performance problem occurred.
- Click Generate Report.

Once the report has been generated, the ASH report will appear under Report Results on the Run ASH Report page. The report can be used to identify the source of transient performance problems. An ASH report is divided into titled sections:

- **Top Events** -- Details the top wait events of the sampled session activity categorized by user, background, and priority.
- **Load Profile** -- Describes the load analyzed in the sampled session activity. The information in this section can be used to identify the service, client, or SQL command type that may be the cause of the transient performance problem.

- **Top SQL** -- Shows the top SQL statements in the sampled session activity. The high-load SQL statements identified here may be a contributing factor of the transient performance problem.
- **Top Sessions** -- Lists the sessions that were waiting for the wait event that accounted for the highest percentages of sampled session activity. This can help to identify the sessions that may be the cause of the performance problem.
- **Top DB Objects/Files/Latches** -- This section provides additional information about the most commonly-used database resources. The three subsections of this report list the top object, files, and latches that accounted for the highest percentages of sampled session activity.
- **Activity Over Time** -- This section is useful for longer time periods because it provides in-depth details about activities and workload profiles during the analysis period.

EM Cloud Control also contains a new ASH Analytics page that provides a graphical view of the ASH information. This allows for a more interactive method of analyzing the ASH data and provides several capabilities for manipulating the data being analyzed, including:

- Varying the size of the time period to be analyzed.
- Filtering the dimensions to be included
- Drilling down to a load map view that displays the various waits with the importance of each indicated by size.

Explain Multiprocess and Multithreaded Oracle architecture

The Oracle database uses a number of different processes to perform various tasks for the database. The PMON process has one set of jobs while SMON has another set, LGWR a third and so on. This is the multiprocess architecture. If Oracle were a single process database, then there would simply be one gargantuan process that ran everything. The multiprocess architecture makes Oracle more scalable, since only the processes that are needed for any given system are running (and using resources) for that instance.

Prior to Oracle 12c, under the Unix and Linux operating systems, each Oracle process required one operating system process. With this release, it is possible to have Oracle run in a multithreaded mode. When running in the multithreaded model, one operating system process can support multiple Oracle processes running as operating system threads within it.

The multithreaded mode is not enabled when a new 12c database is created. In order to enable this mode, the THREADED_EXECUTION parameter must be set to YES and the database restarted. When running in threaded mode, some background processes on UNIX and Linux will still run as processes (i.e. one Oracle process to one OS process), and other Oracle processes will run as threads within OS processes. For example, PMON and DBW might run as operating system processes, whereas LGWR and SMON might run as threads within a single process. The V$PROCESS view contains one row for each Oracle process connected to a database instance. This view can be queried to determine the operating system process ID and operating system thread ID for each process.

When running in multi-threaded mode, the database must be administered by an account that is authenticated through a password file. Attempting to start an instance that has been set to run in threaded execution mode with an account that has not been authenticated through a password file will result in an ORA-1031 error:

```
SQL> ALTER SYSTEM SET threaded_execution=true SCOPE=SPFILE;

System altered.

SQL> shutdown immediate
Database closed.
Database dismounted.
ORACLE instance shut down.
SQL> startup
ORA-01017: invalid username/password; logon denied
SQL>
```

Use Flash Cache

The Database Smart Flash Cache allows an instance to access multiple flash devices without requiring a volume manager. The feature is supported only for databases running on the Solaris or Oracle Linux operating systems. Enabling the Smart Flash Cache may be beneficial if the following are true:

- The Buffer Pool Advisory section of your Automatic Workload Repository (AWR) report or STATSPACK report indicates that doubling the size of the buffer cache would be beneficial.
- db file sequential read is a top wait event.
- The system has spare CPU cycles.

There are two initialization parameters used to configure Database Smart Flash Cache:

- **DB_FLASH_CACHE_FILE** -- Specifies a list of paths and file names for the files to contain Database Smart Flash Cache. The files can be on the OS file system or an ASM disk group, but they must reside on a flash device. Configuring Database Smart Flash Cache on a disk drive (spindle) can negatively impact performance. If a specified file does not exist, then the database creates it during startup. A maximum of sixteen files is supported.
- **DB_FLASH_CACHE_SIZE** -- Specifies the size of each file in your Database Smart Flash Cache. Each size corresponds (in order) with a file specified in DB_FLASH_CACHE_FILE. If the number of sizes does not match the number of files, an error is generated. The size is expressed as nG, indicating the number of gigabytes (GB).

The V$FLASHFILESTAT view can be used to determine the cumulative latency and read counts of each file and compute the average latency. It is possible to disable a flash device by using the ALTER SYSTEM command to set the DB_FLASH_CACHE_SIZE to zero. Setting the size for any disabled flash device back to the original size will re-enable it. It is not possible to use ALTER SYSTEM to dynamically change the size of Database Smart Flash Cache.

Information Lifecycle Management and Storage Enhancements

Use ILM features

Information Lifecycle Management (ILM) is the act of managing data from creation/acquisition to archival or deletion. Oracle 12c offers two new ILM features that allow the database to intelligently manage space usage: Heat Map and Automatic Data Optimization.

Heat Map

In any given database, not every piece of data is accessed in the same fashion or with the same frequency. Data which is accessed frequently must be on storage media that offers the best possible performance. By contrast, data which is seldom accessed could be kept on storage that has a lower performance without materially affecting the performance of the database. The fastest storage is inevitably the most expensive, so cost factors often make it impractical to be used to store everything in a given database.

Storage tiering is the act of deploying data on multiple types of storage media. When storage tiering is used, the ideal situation is to have the most frequently accessed data stored on the fastest media and the least-frequently accessed data on the slowest. The new Heat Map feature of Oracle is specifically designed for this purpose. It automatically tracks usage information at the row and segment levels. When data is modified, the times are tracked at the row level and aggregated to the block level. Modification times, full table scan times, and index lookup times are all tracked at the segment level. The end result is that using Heat Map, it is possible to obtain a detailed view of how data is being accessed, and how the access patterns change over time.

Automatic Data Optimization

The Automatic Data Optimization (ADO) feature enables database administrators to create policies for data compression and data movement. One of the features of ADO is Smart Compression, which makes use of information from the Heat Map to associate compression policies and compression levels with the way the data is utilized. Periodically the database will evaluate ADO policies and use Heat Map information to determine when to move and/or compress data. Once enabled, ADO works in the background during maintenance windows without user intervention, but can also be executed manually by the DBA. ADO policies can be specified at the segment or row level for tables and table partitions.

Perform tracking and automated data placement

To implement your ILM strategy, you can use Heat Map in Oracle Database to track data access and modification. Enabling the Heat Map in Oracle is one way of implementing an ILM strategy. Heat Map tracking can be enabled and disabled at the system or session level with the ALTER SYSTEM or ALTER SESSION statements using the HEAT_MAP clause. Once enabled, all accesses to objects in all tablespaces except SYSTEM and SYSAUX are tracked by the in-memory activity tracking module. The following SQL statements enable and disable Heat Map tracking for the database instance respectively.

```
ALTER SYSTEM SET HEAT_MAP = ON;

ALTER SYSTEM SET HEAT_MAP = OFF;
```

There are several views that can be used to analyze the data returned by Oracle's Heat Map tracking:

- **V$HEAT_MAP_SEGMENT** -- Displays real-time segment access information.
- **DBA_HEAT_MAP_SEGMENT** -- Displays the latest segment access time for all segments.
- **DBA_HEAT_MAP_SEG_HISTOGRAM** -- Displays segment access information for all segments.
- **DBA_HEATMAP_TOP_OBJECTS** -- Displays heat map information for the top 1000 objects.
- **DBA_HEATMAP_TOP_TABLESPACES** -- Displays heat map information for the top 100 tablespaces.

In order to automatically move data between different storage tiers, you must specify one or more Automatic Data Optimization (ADO) policies. ADO policies can be specified at the row, segment, and tablespace level either at the time of creation or via an ALTER statement for existing objects. ADO policies can be specified with a scope of SEGMENT, ROW, or GROUP. The following statement shows ILM policies for the current user:

```
SELECT policy_name, policy_type, enabled
FROM   user_ilmpolicies;
```

The SQL CREATE and ALTER TABLE statements have an optional ILM clause that allows an ADO policy to be created, deleted, enabled or disabled. The policy clause will determine policy used to compress or alter the storage tiering for that object. ILM ADO policies are given a system-generated name, such P1, P2, ... Pn.

Segment level policies execute only a single time. Once the policy has executed successfully, it will be disabled and is never evaluated again unless it is explicitly re-enabled. Row level policies are not disabled after a successful execution and will execute multiple times.

The default mappings for compression that can be applied to group policies are:

- **COMPRESS ADVANCED** on a heap table maps to standard compression for indexes and LOW for LOB segments.
- **COMPRESS FOR QUERY LOW/QUERY HIGH** on a heap table maps to standard compression for indexes and MEDIUM for LOB segments.
- **COMPRESS FOR ARCHIVE LOW/ARCHIVE HIGH** on a heap table maps to standard compression for indexes and HIGH for LOB segments.

The following examples add ILM policies to a partition of the HR.SALES table:

```
ALTER TABLE hr.sales MODIFY PARTITION sales_q1_2002
  ILM ADD POLICY ROW STORE COMPRESS ADVANCED ROW
  AFTER 45 DAYS OF NO MODIFICATION;

ALTER TABLE hr.sales MODIFY PARTITION sales_q1_2001
  ILM ADD POLICY COMPRESS FOR ARCHIVE HIGH SEGMENT
  AFTER 9 MONTHS OF NO MODIFICATION;

ALTER TABLE hr.sales MODIFY PARTITION sales_q1_2000
    ILM ADD POLICY COMPRESS FOR ARCHIVE HIGH SEGMENT
    AFTER 12 MONTHS OF NO ACCESS;
```

If existing ILM policies conflict with a new policy that you want to add, you will need to disable or delete the legacy policy. You can disable or delete ILM policies for ADO as shown in the following examples:

```
ALTER TABLE sales MODIFY PARTITION sales_q1_2002 ILM DISABLE POLICY
P2;
ALTER TABLE sales MODIFY PARTITION sales_q1_2002 ILM DELETE POLICY
P2;
```

Move a data file online

It is now possible in 12c to use the ALTER DATABASE MOVE DATAFILE SQL statement to rename or relocate a data file while the database is open and users are accessing it. When a data file is renamed or relocated, the pointers in the database control files that reference it are changed. At the same time, the files are also physically renamed or relocated in the operating system.

If there is already a file at the same name and location as the destination specified by the ALTER DATABASE statement, the statement will fail with an error by default. However, if the REUSE keyword is specified in the statement, Oracle will overwrite it with the datafile being renamed or moved.

When a data file is renamed or relocated with the ALTER DATABASE MOVE DATAFILE statement, a copy of the data file is created during the operation. There must be adequate disk space for both the original data file and the copy for the statement to succeed. At the end of the operation, the original file is deleted by default. If the KEEP option is specified, then the original is not deleted at the end of the operation. However, the database will only use the data file in the new location after the operation is completed.

The following examples demonstrate renaming a datafile, moving a datafile, moving a datafile with REUSE, and moving a datafile with KEEP respectively:

```
ALTER DATABASE MOVE DATAFILE '/u01/oracle/ocpdb/user1.dbf'
   TO '/u01/oracle/ocpdb/user_ts1.dbf';

ALTER DATABASE MOVE DATAFILE '/u01/oracle/ocpdb/user_ts1.dbf'
   TO '/u02/oracle/ocpdb/user_ts1.dbf';

ALTER DATABASE MOVE DATAFILE '/u01/oracle/ocpdb/user_ts1.dbf'
   TO '/u02/oracle/ocpdb/user_ts1.dbf' REUSE;

ALTER DATABASE MOVE DATAFILE '/u01/oracle/ocpdb/user_ts1.dbf'
   TO '/u02/oracle/ocpdb/user_ts1.dbf' KEEP;
```

In-Database Archiving and Valid-Time Temporal

Differentiate between ILM and Valid-Time Temporal

Oracle's Information Lifecycle Management (ILM) toolset is designed to optimize the way in which the storage resources of a database are utilized. As a general rule, the faster a given type of storage is, the more expensive it is. The quantity of data stored in enterprise databases using Oracle is often too large to justify purchasing enough top-tier storage to contain the complete contents of the database. ILM is designed to improve the utilization of storage and the performance of a database by making it more feasible to have tiered levels (speeds) of storage options. Using capabilities in ILM, Oracle can automatically move data among the storage tiers based on how frequently it is accessed. Alternately, ILM can improve storage utilization by compressing data that is accessed infrequently. Whether ILM compresses or moves data – the purpose is to optimize storage resource utilization with minimal impact to database performance.

The new Temporal Validity capability of Oracle allows you to create a valid time dimension for each row of a table. The data for this is stored in two hidden columns in the table definition. When querying the table, rows will be displayed whether or not they are "temporally valid" unless the query includes a filter against these columns. Temporal Validity has no effect on storage usage or database performance. It is simply providing a new means for filtering data.

Set and use Valid-Time Temporal

The new Temporal Validity feature of Oracle 12c provides a method of defining a range of time for each row in a table when it has real-world validity. The date range that indicates when a row is valid can be set by users and applications. In terms of ILM, the valid time attributes signify when data is valid and when it is not. Using these attributes, a query can return only rows that are currently valid.

Concepts that are integral to valid time temporal modeling include:

- **Valid time** -- This is a user-defined representation of time. Examples of a valid time include project start and finish dates, and employee hire and termination dates.
- **Tables with valid-time semantics** -- These tables have one or more dimensions of user-defined time, each of which has a start and an end.
- **Valid-time flashback queries** -- This is the ability to do as-of and versions queries using a valid-time dimension.

A valid-time period requires a pair of date-time columns be specified in the table definition. The columns can be explicitly added to the table, or they can be created implicitly. A valid-time period can be added during the create table or alter table process. The following statement creates a skeletal employees table that has valid-time temporal columns to define the specific 90-day probation period for the employee. No date columns are explicitly created, but the PERIOD FOR clause will create the columns implicitly.

```
CREATE TABLE probationary_emps (
emp_id      NUMBER PRIMARY KEY,
first_name  VARCHAR2(20),
last_name   VARCHAR2(25),
PERIOD FOR emp_probation);
```

When the table is described, only the EMP_ID, FIRST_NAME, and LAST_NAME columns appear:

```
DESCRIBE probationary_emps
Name               Null?      Type
---------------    ---------  --------------
EMP_ID             NOT NULL   NUMBER
FIRST_NAME                    VARCHAR2(20)
LAST_NAME                     VARCHAR2(25)
```

Querying the USER_TAB_COLS table shows that three additional hidden columns were created in the table:

```
SELECT column_name, data_type, column_id AS CID,
       internal_column_id AS ICID, hidden_column AS HID
FROM user_tab_cols
WHERE table_name = 'PROBATIONARY_EMPS';

COLUMN_NAME           DATA_TYPE                      CID ICID HID
--------------------  ----------------------------  --- ---- ---
EMP_PROBATION_START   TIMESTAMP(6) WITH TIME ZONE         1  YES
EMP_PROBATION_END     TIMESTAMP(6) WITH TIME ZONE         2  YES
EMP_PROBATION         NUMBER                              3  YES
EMP_ID                NUMBER                         1    4  NO
FIRST_NAME            VARCHAR2                       2    5  NO
LAST_NAME             VARCHAR2                       3    6  NO
```

The following INSERT statements populate the table with two rows, each of which has a probation start and end dates with a 90-day span:

```
INSERT INTO probationary_emps(emp_probation_start, emp_probation_end,
     emp_id, first_name, last_name)
  VALUES ('01-OCT-13 12.00.01 PM CET', '30-DEC-13 12.00.01 PM CET',
     1234, 'John', 'Doe');
INSERT INTO probationary_emps(emp_probation_start, emp_probation_end,
     emp_id, first_name, last_name)
  VALUES ('14-SEP-13 12.00.01 PM CET', '13-DEC-13 12.00.01 PM CET',
     5678, 'Fred', 'Rogers');

SELECT emp_id
FROM   probationary_emps;
    EMP_ID
----------
      1234
      5678
```

Querying the table with a where clause that uses the hidden date field to filter the rows returned works exactly as you would expect:

```
SELECT emp_id
FROM   probationary_emps
WHERE  emp_probation_start < '20-SEP-13 12.00.01 PM CET'
AND    emp_probation_end > '20-SEP-13 12.00.01 PM CET';

    EMP_ID
----------
      5678
```

That functionality does not do anything beyond what could be accomplished by adding normal DATE columns to the table. A somewhat more interesting capability is provided by the DBMS_FLASHBACK_ARCHIVE PL/SQL package. It contains the ENABLE_AT_VALID_TIME procedure. This procedure can be used to set the valid time visibility as of a supplied time.

```
EXECUTE DBMS_FLASHBACK_ARCHIVE.enable_at_valid_time
          ('ASOF', '20-DEC-13 12.00.01 PM');

SELECT emp_id
FROM   probationary_emps;

    EMP_ID
----------
      5678
```

It can be used to set the visibility of temporal data to what is valid data for the current session's time.

```
EXECUTE DBMS_FLASHBACK_ARCHIVE.enable_at_valid_time('CURRENT');
SELECT emp_id
FROM   probationary_emps;

no rows selected
```

The procedure can be used to set the visibility of temporal data to the full table (the default):

```
EXECUTE DBMS_FLASHBACK_ARCHIVE.enable_at_valid_time('ALL');
```

Use in-database archiving

The In-Database Archiving feature allows rows to be kept in a production database, but be kept invisible from applications. The idea is to have this data available in order to meet data compliance requirements but minimize impact to the performance of production applications. The archived data can be compressed to help improve backup performance. To use In-Database Archiving for a table, it must have ROW ARCHIVAL enabled and the value of the hidden column ORA_ARCHIVE_STATE must be set to a non-zero value.

When the ROW ARCHIVAL VISIBILITY session parameter is set to ACTIVE, only those rows with a value of zero in the ORA_ARCHIVE_STATE column will be displayed. When the parameter is set to ALL, queries will return both archived and non-archived rows in the table. The following example demonstrates In-Database Archiving:

```
ALTER SESSION SET ROW ARCHIVAL VISIBILITY = ACTIVE;

CREATE TABLE archival_test
  (col1    NUMBERL,
   col2    VARCHAR2(20)) ROW ARCHIVAL;

INSERT INTO archival_test (col1, col2)
   VALUES (1, 'Record One');

INSERT INTO archival_test (col1, col2)
   VALUES (2, 'Record Two');

INSERT INTO archival_test (col1, col2)
   VALUES (3, 'Record Three');

INSERT INTO archival_test (col1, col2)
   VALUES (4, 'Record Four');

SELECT col1, col2, ora_archive_state
FROM   archival_test;

COL1   COL2            ORA_ARCHIVE_STATE
-----  ------------    ------------------
    1  Record One                       0
    2  Record Two                       0
    3  Record Three                     0
    4  Record Four                      0
```

```
UPDATE archival_test
SET    ora_archive_state = '5'
WHERE  col1 = 3;

SELECT employee_id, ORA_ARCHIVE_STATE FROM employees_indbarch;

SELECT col1, col2, ora_archive_state
FROM   archival_test;

COL1   COL2          ORA_ARCHIVE_STATE
-----  ------------  -----------------
   1   Record One                    0
   2   Record Two                    0
   4   Record Four                   0

ALTER SESSION SET ROW ARCHIVAL VISIBILITY = ALL;

SELECT employee_id, ORA_ARCHIVE_STATE FROM employees_indbarch;

COL1   COL2          ORA_ARCHIVE_STATE
-----  ------------  -----------------
   1   Record One                    0
   2   Record Two                    0
   3   Record Three                  5
   4   Record Four                   0
```

ABOUT THE AUTHOR

Matthew Morris is an Oracle Database Administrator and Developer currently employed as a Database Engineer with Computer Sciences Corporation. Matthew has worked with the Oracle database since 1996 when he worked in the RDBMS support team for Oracle Support Services. Employed with Oracle for over eleven years in support and development positions, Matthew was an early adopter of the Oracle Certified Professional program. He was one of the first one hundred Oracle Certified Database Administrators (version 7.3) and in the first hundred to become an Oracle Certified Forms Developer. In the years since, he has upgraded his Database Administrator certification for releases 8i, 9i, 10g, 11g and 12c, become an Oracle Advanced PL/SQL Developer Certified Professional and added the Expert certifications for Application Express, SQL, and SQL Tuning.

26442726R00254

Made in the USA
Middletown, DE
29 November 2015